SUGONG

SUGONG

THE LIFE OF A SHAOLIN GRANDMASTER

NICK HURST

Published in Great Britain by
SportsBooks Limited
1 Evelyn Court
Malvern Road
Cheltenham
GL50 2JR

© Nick Hurst 2012
First Published April 2012

Cover Art Direction and Design by ODD London
oddlondon.com

A catalogue record for this book is available from
the British Library.

ISBN 9781907524219

Printed and bound in England by TJ International Ltd,
Padstow, Cornwall

For Tai-Sugong, Sugong, and Sifu

CONTENTS

A QUICK NOTE ON...

Martial arts
Although about a martial artist, this is not a martial arts book. Some history and theory is covered to provide context, but this is intended as a start, not an end, to further exploration.

History
Because of the impact times and places had on Sugong, I have provided brief histories. Again, these are overviews, not in-depth analyses.

Chinese language
While aesthetically pleasing, the system of Chinese characters is incomprehensible without dedicated study. There are two main romanised versions. The official one is *Pinyin* and it is almost as baffling as the character system but without its charm. To understand it, one must disassociate the sounds usually attributed to the letters of the alphabet for a new form of pronunciation. Some of the main themes: x is pronounced sh, q is pronounced ch, z is pronounced like a sharp j. Pinyin deposed a more understandable system called Wade–Giles. When a name or place is firmly entrenched with a system's spelling I have adhered to it. But throughout his life, Sugong interacted with speakers of many different Chinese dialects, all

with their own different readings of Chinese characters, most without standard romanisation. Furthermore, many names and places have come courtesy of recollection, rather than written record. The combination of these factors means that some spellings may not be totally accurate to either Pinyin or Wade–Giles. I apologise for any confusion.

Chinese names
Contrary to western practice, Chinese surnames precede given names, which usually consist of two parts. For example, the actor Chow Yun Fat's surname is Chow, his given names Yun Fat. Some ethnic Chinese have Western as well as Chinese names. The Western name most commonly precedes the traditional Chinese naming structure. So in the case of the actor Tony Leung Chiu Wai, his surname is Leung, and his given names Chiu Wai. Pinyin spellings often co-join both given names into one, for example Mao *Zedong*. Wade–Giles spellings sometime include hyphenation between the names, e.g. Chow Yun-Fat. I have written them in two parts.

Lastly
Memoirs can make valuable contributions to social histories, but individually they have their limitations. This book is based mainly on recollection, where time, memory and a preference for one's own side of the story can provide obstacles to definitive historical fact.

There will doubtless be some inaccuracies, and I have changed some names, conversations and circumstances to protect the identity of characters. I hope I have kept errors to a minimum, and those that there are do not offend.

For some it's a form of spiritual development. For others, a route to health and well-being. Sugong started kung fu because he liked to fight. And he wanted to win.

INTRODUCTION

'You want to know about my parents? Go ask them and stop bothering me.'

With Sugong nearing eighty with parents who could reasonably be assumed dead, it wasn't the most auspicious way to start.

After spending six months of a sabbatical training with him, Sugong's adventure story of a life had awakened a desire to write that had long been snoozing and I had decided to take the plunge. It was not a decision easily reached; partly because of the leap into new terrain it required; partly because I knew Sugong's combustible character. I had still not expected him to erupt at the first question, especially as I had thought it one of the less sensitive.

It was a pattern to which I would have to become accustomed. Interviews would start after training and end at whatever point Sugong exploded in rage. Having picked up the odd word or two, I had my suspicions that both my intelligence and the virtues of my female ancestors were at times called into question. But I was shielded from the worst by my translator, CG. Speaking only the barest of Hokkien myself, all questions and answers had to go through him and Sugong showed no reluctance in shooting this messenger, who was regularly peppered with oratory shot.

Questions he took particular offence to could result in all interviews being put on hold. Both question and the subject's mood had to be carefully considered and a fine line trod. A query that on one day might result in a slightly scary look and a gentle rebuke – 'the cheeky rascal' – before an answer was forthcoming, would on others see a torrent of invective and the suspension of further talks. This could last anywhere from two weeks to six months.

At the end of the longest lull, I had to point out that for all my enjoyment of training it was the book that he had agreed to (and was apparently enthusiastic about) that was the reason for my being there. Without the information I needed to write it I would have to return to England and the world would remain *sans* Sugong book.

He grudgingly relented and this is the result.

Prologue

Bashing triads

Quick, follow them,' said Mr Tan. 'They're going to bash up some triads.'

'They're what?' I asked, still under the impression that we were going for tea.

'They're going to bash up some triads. Go on,' he urged. 'I've got to park the car. I'll be there in a minute.'

I should probably explain at this point that this wasn't the Sunday-afternooned environment of Muswell Hill, North London, where I had grown up. I was in Penang, Malaysia. And the people about to 'bash up some triads' were my Shaolin kung fu grandmaster, Sugong, and his senior student, Subec.

I should also say that when I had left my job to go to Malaysia, the intention had been to train with my sugong. No one had mentioned fights with gangsters. However, he was my grandmaster and in the martial arts world that counts for a lot. He was also eighty years old, and while he was still far more capable than me in taking out a gang of triads, I felt duty bound to try to pitch in. So I followed.

There had been no indication that we were about to go for a fight. The day before the four of us had come up to Penang, an ex-colonial island state just off north-west Malaysia. Sugong and Subec wanted to catch up with old buddies, I wanted to see what I could find out for my book, and Mr Tan was just along for the ride.

We were about to start the journey back to Kuala Lumpur when Subec got a call on his mobile. A gunfire burst of Hokkien Chinese had ensued, none of which I understood, and our course had altered.

Penang is famous for good food, and the three of them were obsessed with eating as much of it as possible during our stay. Or at least they wanted to order and sample as much as they could. After a few mouthfuls they would push their plates toward me and order 'chia' – eat. Despite my 12½ stone I was apparently still too skinny.

So when we pulled up at the back of a group of old buildings, their crumbling facades housing menacing dark doorways, I assumed we were just going into a coffee shop by the back way.

The only thing I had found a little strange was when Sugong jogged to catch up with Subec. I had never seen him break out of a slight swagger.

Now I was following the way they had just gone.

I would like to claim I was just a bit rusty at triad-bashing. But if truth be known I had never beaten up any gangsters, be they triads, mafiosi or yardies. I was slightly daunted at the prospect of starting now.

The doorway seemed to grow darker and more ominous as I approached. I started to picture warren-like corridor kitchens, filled with boiling water, choppers and blood-thirsty triads.

My stomach tensed as I prepared myself for the explosion of violence from within.

I hadn't known this was part of the deal.

1

BASICALLY, I LIKED TO FIGHT

Sugong wasn't born into great riches. He wasn't even born into much comfort. But to be born in 1927 China to a peasant family that could see him past starvation meant he was better off than most.

School was a luxury too far. His parents were farmers who worked the fields, tending goats and cattle. Male sons were a valuable commodity not to be wasted on education, and Sugong's working life began at the age of five.

He grew up in Fujian province in the south-east of China, an area famous for Oolong tea and emigrants. At the time China was in turmoil. Struggles between the nationalist Kuomintang (KMT) party, the Communists and regional warlords added to the substantial worries that peasants already had meeting the demands of their landlords.

It was a time when life was ruled by 'the way of the fist'. Sugong's parents' wedding anniversaries were a yearly reminder.

After the British introduced opium in the 19th century to balance their trade deficit, demand for the drug grew rampantly. The peasantry of the country were not slow to see an opportunity, and rather than let the British reap all the rewards they began cultivating it themselves.

But it was a land of vested interests and it would appear the Chai Lien Bu village crop went against someone else's. The point was made when a militia swept in on horseback and hacked the harvest to the ground.

In a poverty-stricken village the destruction of a valuable investment went far beyond an irritation or disappointment. The peasants trod a fine line between subsistence and starvation. Losing a major source of income could mean the difference between having food to eat or not. When the elders met they decided it would not be allowed to happen again.

The fields were re-sown but this time greater attention was paid to whom this might displease. Their vigilance paid off. On the day of Sugong's parents' wedding a warning was received and the villagers took up arms to wait for the unsuspecting intruders.

Justice was as immediate as it was brutal. When the last of the militia had been hacked to death, the bodies were piled up and buried. No more incursions followed.

In this time and atmosphere there was little chance of children becoming poets or philosophers. In the case of Sugong, a mischievous nature coupled with a hot temper meant that this would have been unlikely in any case.

From as young as memory serves he found himself in trouble, his quarrelsome nature requiring flights of foot from well-deserved beatings. There were only two options that would see him through to adulthood. The impossible – avoiding trouble – and the inevitable – learning to fight.

China was not short of fighters. The techniques of martial artists may have been superseded by gleaming weapons in large-scale warfare. But in the every day battleground of village and town, kung fu remained king.

Most peasants knew the rudimentaries of fighting – in fact Sugong's father had often demonstrated the use of the staff in punishment for his son's various misdemeanours. But Sugong's first exposure to real artistry came when he was seven.

Entertainment was limited in peasant villages in 1930s China. What there was tended to be of the more traditional variety, with travelling performers touring the towns. This was how Sugong came across Lao Ping Sun.

As was often the case when the villagers gathered for rare non-working occasions there was something of a festival atmosphere. People gathered from the surrounding villages, food and drink were enthusiastically consumed, and expectancy grew.

When Lao entered the performer's clearing he struck a suitably imposing figure. He was a fearsome man; tall and well-built with intense dark eyes and a long beard and moustache. Excessive facial hair was considered ferocious at the time and Sugong was sold on art and man by the end of the performance. The fight at its conclusion sealed the matter.

Then as now prowess in the martial arts was taken very seriously; people took pride in their heritage and their skills. This made a performer's profession a precarious one, often chosen by those with no other choice. This was because of the regularity with which they were called to prove their skills.

There is a Chinese saying that behind every mountain is a higher one. The idea is that humility should be retained despite apparent ability as there is always someone bigger, faster or stronger.

To be a martial arts performer was to set a path toward the inevitable discovery of who this was. And the injuries picked up in the course of the quest would reduce life expectancy even before the painful encounter.

This was not to be the day Lao found his superior. Instead a villager gained a painful and public lesson in humility.

Sugong was not concerned with the man's self-inflicted misfortune. He had found his get-out-of-jail card. It would prove essential in hauling his troublesome character past an early demise.

Sugong was born Quek Chong Tze, the second eldest of what would be six children. In the hierarchical family structure of China he was born one too late.

To be born male was definitely an advantage over being female, and of limited use until foisted on tottering, bound feet to another family.

But the first son was top of the heap. It was through him that the hopes of the family heritage would be passed. He would carry on the name and reputation. And in anticipation of this he was the one invested in. As a result he had the greatest say in the family, after the all-powerful patriarch.

Sugong got on well with almost all of his siblings. Unfortunately the one that he was on less friendly terms with was his elder brother. Even less fortunately he got on no better with his father.

This did not make for a happy home atmosphere but it did have benefits to Sugong's martial arts. It meant that the small amount of time he had free from work was not spent lounging at home. Instead it was dedicated to staying away from it; and the best way to do this was through training.

As a first master Lao Ping Sun was almost everything a young boy wanting a pugilistic education might have hoped for: a fearsome fighter with the experience to teach the real-life applications of kung fu. More importantly, in an art where many were notoriously jealous of their secrets and skills, he was willing to share.

But it was at a price, for Lao was not a conventional master. He was a drug addict. And payment was to be made in opium.

Like any other seven-year-old, Sugong didn't have a stash of drugs next to his piggy bank. He didn't even have a piggy bank or anything else bar a questionable attitude. But it was at this time that his uncle, Quek Wei Leng, first became of assistance.

Like Sugong's father, Quek Wei Leng was not born with a silver spoon in his mouth. But he had two advantages. The first was his position as the eldest son. The other was his shrewd and wily character. Whereas Sugong's father would live a peasant's life of hardship to his last day, Uncle Wei manoeuvred an escape.

Adept at working social networks, he found himself in a position to vouch for a local official. The man in question was in charge of shipping in the province, and had been accused of abusing his privileges.

In large part due to Uncle Wei's court intervention, he was cleared. Uncle Wei was richly rewarded for his testimony and this allowed him to become a landlord and a fast-rising official in the governing KMT Party. It also meant that Sugong's father worked for him and had to follow his dictates, both as elder brother and as boss.

The first benefit Sugong would get from his uncle's position was the least readily offered; a regular supply of opium.

While the grand, wise masters in kung fu movies search for knowledge and wisdom, Lao Ping Sun was mainly interested in his next pipe. This could make him an unenthusiastic teacher. But after smoking he became much more amenable, and it became Sugong's quest to ensure that he had access to the required supply.

Diligence was needed. While Uncle Wei was fond of his nephew Chong Tze, he would not have been beyond handing out a good thrashing had he found Sugong's sticky hands in his stash.

Sugong needed to sneak regularly into his room to relieve him of some of his vice. It required a careful balancing act. He had to take out enough to satisfy Lao Ping Sun but not so much as to arouse suspicion. It was not a stress-free way to get kung fu tuition. But to Sugong it was worth it.

Unaware of the reason for his under-weight measures of opium, Uncle Wei came to Sugong's assistance more knowingly when he was eleven. It was he who 'encouraged' Sugong's father to finally send him to school.

While responsibility for his late introduction to education can partly be blamed on circumstance, Sugong's preference for trouble-making and his resistance to learning had also played their part. But at the behest of his uncle he started to attend.

It is fair to say that it was not a complete success. There could be little argument with suggestions he was not a model student. Having lived for eleven years under the law of his own trouble-ready hands, his attitude to authority was not quite what the school was hoping for.

It was not the case that he was a bully but he was equally sure he would not be a victim. In situations of conflicting opinions he was happier to administer his own justice than seek that of the teachers.

The school had no plans to overhaul its disciplinary system for replacement with the Quek Chong Tze model and he was frequently hauled in for talks with the headmaster. His expulsion when it came was not a great shock. More surprising was the time it had taken.

Just as his uncle had been instrumental in getting Sugong to start school, he was an unknowing but pivotal figure in the ending of Sugong's education.

As a rare treat for his nephew Uncle Wei gave Sugong a pen. It was nothing special compared to other pens. But this was a small village school and there weren't any other pens. This made it a priceless treasure, one that Sugong intended to guard.

Quite why his teacher decided to confiscate it isn't clear. It could have been punishment for misbehaviour. It may just as easily have been an impoverished teacher in search of subsidy. Whatever the reason, Sugong was not about to give up his prize without a fight.

Rural village schools in 1930s China were not always places for the faint-hearted. Sugong's reluctance to receive an education had been tolerated. His fights with other students had been punished but ultimately forgiven. But the school decided that to sanction thirteen-year-old boys beating their teachers would lead them down a fast-deteriorating path. Sugong's brief flirtation with education was at an end.

2

AN UNLIKELY MONK

The logical option would have been a return to working the fields. But Sugong had different ideas. Any free time outside of school and work was increasingly dedicated to kung fu. But it wasn't enough; he wanted to train more and be distracted less. His mind was set on Kai Wan Temple.

Kai Wan Temple, in the town of Chun Zhou, was famous in the district for its kung fu. Sugong knew of it through an uncle who had been a non-martial monk there.

As circumstance would have it, his cousin, the son of Uncle Wei, was going to high school in the town and Sugong sensed an opportunity. He offered to help his older cousin by cooking for him, doing his chores and generally carrying out the duties of a servant.

His privileged cousin was more than happy with the arrangement and Uncle Wei had no qualms. Sugong's strained relations with his parents meant the removal of a disruptive figure from their household was not an unduly upsetting prospect for them either. So it was that he packed up his meagre belongings and set off.

While Sugong's plan was a good one it had a flaw. In return for taking care of his cousin he would have a place to stay and food to eat but he wouldn't have any money. This would make paying for his kung fu tuition difficult. What he lacked in formal education Sugong compensated with guile. Knowing that martial arts training was available to the apprentice monks of the temple, he signed up.

It is difficult to think of a less likely monk than the troublesome young Sugong but the order at Kai Wan must have seen something in him as they agreed to take him on. For three years, despite a complete lack of interest in progressing to monkhood, he learned the mantras, followed the rituals and did everything that a good apprentice should. But what he really cared about was his training.

Things were far from perfect even here. While Lao Ping Sun may have been an unconventional first master, Sugong had thought highly of him. His new teacher was not a senior instructor within the temple and while his teaching was competent it was far from inspired.

The style itself was also a problem. Called Shaolin Ngo Chor (Shaolin Five Ancestors) he did not enjoy it as much as the Tai Chor (Grand Ancestor) style he had been learning. He was given a solid grounding in the basics – stance work, punching, kicking and tumbling – but it was a far cry from Lao's more unorthodox methods. The focus in these classes led them wherever the master's drug-addled mood took him on that given day.

To make matters worse, Sugong was not held in favour by his new master. While he was to blame for much of his trouble with authority, in this case he was not at fault. The other students were from well-to-do families. They could afford to pay for their tuition, unlike the freeloader Sugong, and they were preferred for it.

Home life offered little respite. For the work that Sugong did he was allowed to eat with his cousin when he cooked. But if his cousin didn't eat Sugong didn't either. As his cousin had his lunch at school this meant Sugong's diet was restricted to two meals a day.

After three years in Chun Zhou, Sugong's cousin finished his schooling and left. Sugong had two options: to become a monk or return home.

Back in the village Sugong put his mind to escaping it again. He found the confines of rural life suffocating and he was eager to experience the adventure he imagined elsewhere. But before he could set off in search of it he had a wedding to attend.

It should have been a day of celebration. Sugong was certainly looking forward to it. He didn't know his cousin Mei Li well and he had no interest in the ceremony itself. But with a large attendance inevitable there would be plenty of opportunities to charm girls, argue with guys, and he might even find a fight. At sixteen years old, and newly returned from Kai Wan Temple, life couldn't get much better.

And it had all been going without fault until he was kidnapped.

Unknown to Sugong, the wedding was taking place in controversial circumstances. Before becoming engaged to her present fiancé, Mei Li had been engaged to Leong Tat Keng from the nearby Leong town. Tat Keng had agreed to the arrangement, despite living in Singapore and hardly knowing Mei Li. At the time marriage was a matter of family requirement rather than romance.

This wouldn't have been a problem, but as Leong Tat Keng repeatedly postponed his return, Mei Li grew older, and as she did she became jittery. Past a certain age a girl's prospects for marriage, and with it her chances of future prosperity, dramatically receded. Dubious of Leong's commitment she became engaged to another man.

The Leongs were furious. This represented a massive loss of face, shaming their family, but despite their anger, Mei Li's new engagement held. And the Leongs plotted their revenge.

Unwittingly Sugong was the perfect kidnap fodder. By now Uncle Wei was a senior official in Fujian. To capture a favoured nephew of his would guarantee the Leongs a good degree of leverage.

It all happened very suddenly. One minute Sugong had been walking along at the tail of the wedding cortège, the next he found himself flung across the back of a horse with a throbbing head.

When he reached the Leong village he was jerked from the horse, dragged roughly up the stairs of a small stone building, and thrown into a dark unfurnished room. He had no idea why he had been abducted but he knew his future wouldn't be bright if his captors failed to get what they wanted.

Not prone to inaction, he looked for a way to take matters into his own hands. While there wasn't much in the room there was a small window. When he managed to force it open, he saw he was on the first floor and would be able to make the drop. He soon regretted it.

The fall itself wasn't a problem. He had just spent three years throwing himself around a temple. The real issues started when someone started firing a gun.

The uneven surface of the fields was a far cry from an Olympic-standard track. But with a hail of bullets following, Sugong flew across them. He didn't know which direction was the right one but the opposite one to the source of the gunfire seemed a good start.

It wasn't. With enough adrenalin pumping to fuel a race-horse, Sugong's senses were more attuned to flight than sight. He had put a good distance between him and his kidnappers when he ran straight into some villagers returning from the coast.

They were rough, hard men who had been labouring since childhood. They weren't sure who the strange boy fleeing from the direction of their village was but they were not going to let him get past before he had answered a few questions. Sugong found himself clamped by large calloused hands.

The pindar stick is the one peasants use to carry baskets of fruit, vegetables and other goods at either end. In this case it was being used to carry bags of salt back from the coast. It can also be used as a weapon. And as a common instrument of everyday rural life it is a good one to be able to use. Sugong's father had threatened, chased and beaten him with one at times, and it was the stick that Lao Ping Sun had taught him when he was younger.

When the gunmen caught up Sugong was reacquainted with its effectiveness.

Pleasantries were deemed surplus to requirements. As soon as the group arrived Sugong was smashed over the head with the butt of a gun. After he fell to the ground he saw very little through his arms, other than glimpses of swinging sticks and the gun, as he tried to protect his head.

He came to in the room from which he had escaped. As he tried to straighten up he found himself restricted on two fronts. The first was the excruciating pain he felt at the slightest of movements. The other was the chains that bound his wrists to his ankles. Despite being in no state to walk, let alone run away, his captors had clearly decided not to leave it to chance.

For two days Sugong remained trussed up, unsure what was going on and what would happen. Unknown to him, meetings were being held between the village elders of the Quek and Leong clans. Some kind of resolution had to be found that would compensate the Leongs for the loss of face the unilateral termination of engagement had caused. It would also have to allow the Queks to regain family pride in light of the disruption to the wedding and the kidnap and beating of one of their own.

Although seemingly as delicate a peace-making operation as a resolution in the Middle East, they managed to come to an agreement. Quite what it was Sugong never learned. He was still seen as a child and it wasn't considered necessary to inform him. He didn't really care. He was just relieved to be alive. This wasn't by a long way though. After a serious beating and two days confinement he was not in a good way. After being carried home he was bed-ridden for two weeks, allowing his injuries to heal and his sense of injustice mount.

The kidnap would prove to be a pivotal moment. At a time when he might have given up martial arts it pushed him the other way. Despite his training with Lao Ping Sun and at Kai Wan he decided he wasn't good enough. He was going to have to train more often and more whole-heartedly. Only then would he be able to track down Leong Tat Keng and have his revenge.

3

THE MASTER OF MY MASTER

I turned the corner and there he was. An eighty-year-old package of armour-plated energy. He radiated charisma, presence, call it what you like. I would have felt a moment of awe even if he hadn't. He was my grandmaster and I had spent the last ten years training under the stern gaze of his picture in London. Now I was alone in Kuala Lumpur and about to come under far more critical examination.

To go back almost to the start; after five years of job peaks and troughs in advertising I was at one of the lowest points. Dropped in a metaphorical hole, I was frantically trying to claw my way out before a crucial meeting that loomed ominously closer. With preparations still in disarray on the day itself my hyper-stress was beginning to give way to a resigned state of doom.

Then news started emerging of problems on the tube. Unsure of what they were, it seemed promising at least, a glimmer of hope. Half an hour later and more details emerged. There'd been explosions and the network was in chaos. My first thoughts shamefully centred on my own predicament.

'Surely Maggie won't be coming?'

Ten minutes later and my desperate wishes were confirmed by a shout from the secretary.

'The tube's been bombed. Maggie's turned around. She's heading back to Birmingham.' Her voice softened. 'You lucky bastard.'

So it was that before I shared London's shock at the 7/7 bombings I was one of the very few to see a silver lining in that very dark cloud.

A new direction was clearly needed.

One week later I was made the best financial offer of a career not hitherto distinguished by reward. I turned it down and began to plan.

Before that, the start – ten years earlier – saw me reclined on a student-house sofa. I had got up just in time for an afternoon smoke. Always quite skinny, a recent fondness for alcohol and late-night kebabs had brought the alarming first signs of a belly that seemed unlikely to revert to washboard proportions. My main university achievement to date had been refining a predisposition to relaxation. The time had come to choose a direction: the Ray Winstone route, manly in its admittedly overweight way and surely the easier option, or a path to fitness before it was too late.

Fate sided unkindly with the more demanding. A kung fu craze was sweeping England. Programmes swamped the TV schedules, rappers sampled lines from classic films, and Michael, one of my best friends, had just re-started the classes he had gone to as a child. Early memories of watching *The Water Margin* series were awakened and a decision was made.

Kung fu was cool, and if there was going to be a mean-ass motherfucker cutting swathes through the crowds it was going to be me.

So I joined Michael for a class and soon had a *sifu*, Master Lai, and a school, *Nam Pai Chuan*. Classes gradually moved from being something I loved to something I couldn't do without. And throughout I was followed by the eyes of my grandmaster looking down from his photo on the wall.

So it was that after ten years of training I quit my job, packed my bags and headed to Malaysia.

Arriving to find out Master Quek was visiting his Chinese hometown wasn't the best start. A week on the paradise island of Pulau Perhentian eased my distress. Maybe this wouldn't be so tough after all. Then back to KL and good news(?). Master Quek was back and he was expecting me at class that evening.

I was picked up from the train station by one of his students, Ji Hang, with plenty of time to spare. Unfortunately this wasn't Ji Hang's regular training ground, and after circling all the surrounding roads and roundabouts we were running late.

Ji Hang had his concerns.

'I hope he's in a good mood. Otherwise I'm going to get such a scolding.'

I later came to realise that Master Quek's 'scoldings' were a quaint way to describe what might otherwise be referred to as a bollocking.

But before I could reply we were round a corner and there he was.

Before I flew out, my unusual trip had elicited a lot of questions. For the most part they weren't particularly insightful.

'Are you going to be really hard when you get back?'
or
'Pa-pa-pow,' accompanied by flailing arms and chopping hands. 'You going to be able to do that?'

The area that interested most people concerned the dojos in which I would be training. Some purpose-built training hall packed with rows of silk-robed, shaven-headed obsessives? A sparse *Kill Bill*-esque mountain retreat where I would break wooden slabs under the unflinching gaze of a silver-bearded master? I'd had no idea of the right answer but I certainly hadn't been expecting the one that confronted me.

A dark school playground with pools of gloomy light, it might generously have been referred to as atmospheric. Ten students were lined up in two rows. These couldn't quite be referred to as neat, as they had to stagger to avoid puddles of rain. It would have taken the Emperor's courtesans to see the collection of over-sized T-shirts and Sunday afternoon tracksuit bottoms as flowing robes. And I don't think the concrete was spring-mounted.

In front of them was Master Quek in mid-'scolding'. Ji Hang did not look reassured. His worries proved baseless when there was a sudden distraction. I tried to follow the sets of eyes before I realised it was me. I squirmed as I tried to appear shorter and narrow my obviously too round eyes. As I was doing my chameleon-best to blend in with Chinese society I was acknowledged by Master Quek.

'Acknowledged' was probably an exaggeration. Unfamiliar with Mandarin or Cantonese, I certainly didn't understand his rural Hokkien dialect. In any case after a very cursory glance he spoke to Ji Hang and the other students.

'He wants you to get changed,' Ji Hang informed me, although I could not help wondering whether further observations had been made. Despite my linguistic failings I had doubts that Hokkien was that inefficient with its words.

I went and got changed.

When I came out I decided the time was as good as any to make an attempt for the good books. Releasing Master

Lai's letter of introduction from my clammy grasp, I waited nervously as it was read out to Master Quek. Gauging a degree of success I followed up quickly with my *ang pao*.

An ang pao is a red envelope of money presented at a myriad of Chinese occasions. These range from weddings to birthdays, and include more random situations – such as foisting yourself on an unsuspecting grandmaster – where an acknowledgement of friendship or respect is due.

A big smile, a laugh, and words and gestures that seemed to suggest 'you shouldn't have' confirmed to my mind that I should. Lateness and bad moods had faded to forgotten memory.

But instead of starting training, one of the students, Mr Lee, told me Master Quek wanted to talk. Accompanied by Ji Hang we went to the canteen. Clearly curious about the strange new foreign recruit, Master Quek interrogated me through our intermediaries. Disconcertingly, while I caught him sneaking the odd glance, he hardly looked in my direction.

The relationship between sifu and student is complex. Hierarchies, rituals and etiquettes forged long ago make the world of martial arts different to most societies or clubs. Most immediately apparent is a delineation by hierarchy. There may be some kind of Confucianist aspect to this, but just as relevant is the skill differential between newcomer and experienced student. Whereas a good painter is just a better painter than you, a good martial artist is someone who can kick your arse. Instinctively a beginner shows an according level of respect.

This is taken to its apex with the sifu. Although the best translation in English is 'master' it is not entirely accurate. Sifu is used as a term of respect for an expert in an art or science with the skills to guide others. A good sifu will inspire with his strength of character and ability.

A really good one may take his students' admiration to the brink of awe.

Having trained with my sifu, Master Lai, for around ten years, I felt ridiculous when occasionally star-struck in his presence. To be in front of the man that likely left him tongue-tied was definitely not a situation to put me at ease.

Despite my letter and ang pao I'd had no idea how Master Quek was going to react when I turned up. A copy of the letter had been sent in advance, but as he had been in China it hadn't been seen.

With waves of Hokkien deflecting uncomprehended from my ears, I satisfied myself watching the conversation. I was still not sure I wouldn't be turned away, although some kind of grudging acceptance seemed more likely. A wide-armed welcome was probably pushing it. Eyes fixed on Master Quek, I got the impression he was also unsure. Undecided, he appeared to go for a temporary measure somewhat closer to grudging than gushing.

As he sneaked quick looks and sized me up, I was trying to get the measure of him as well. I was surprised to see a hint of something I had not expected. Shyness.

The communication factor undoubtedly played a part; I had heard that he was not fearful or retiring. But strange foreigners didn't turn up out of the blue on a regular basis, and his hidden glances suggested a degree of uncertainty at what to expect from an unpredictable *gwei lo* (a white foreigner in Cantonese, or literally translated, ghost man).

'Sugong wants you to follow him home after class,' Ji Hang interrupted my thoughts using the Hokkien for grandmaster. 'He wants to show you where to get off the bus. You can train on five days; Tuesday, Wednesday, Thursday, Saturday and Sunday. You're lucky, Wednesday will be a private class.'

'That's great,' I said, genuinely delighted. 'But how do I follow him?' – now slightly worried – 'I don't have a car.'

'No, you follow him in his car.'

In a reflection of its history and racial mix Malaysia has more than one widely spoken language. Malay is the official one, but English, Mandarin, Cantonese and Tamil are also common. Many Malaysians are bi- or tri-lingual. Sometimes they use the languages all at once; other times they improvise on their foundations. To follow someone was to get a lift.

Barring the odd exception I could understand Ji Hang without problem. He was not having the best of luck with Sugong.

'Did he say anything else?' I asked.

'Yes... but I didn't get most of it,' he said apologetically. 'Hokkien's not my first language and I'm a bit rusty. Plus, he speaks village Hokkien – it's not very easy to understand.'

I felt reassured that someone else was mired in confusion, but a little concerned that the someone was my translator. My musings were cut short by Sugong getting up briskly, waving a cursory goodbye to the rest of the class and nodding for me to follow. My heart accorded the situation a short drum-roll.

Before setting out I had heard about Sugong's continued vitality and I was suitably impressed with what I found. He did not have much hair to admire as his one concession to age was a hairline that had slightly receded. What remained was shaved short but it had not lost its colour, the bristle still resolutely dark. His wispy beard was white though, a satisfying gratification of a grandmaster wish list.

Although not of the personality normally associated with male grooming products, his skin was as free of wrinkles as a pensioner could hope for and would have been a great advertisement for a lifetime of moisturising. His eyes were sharp (I would later find them piercing) and lively, and it was clear that his faculties were more than ship-shape.

He was not too much more than five feet tall but despite this he cut an imposing figure. His plimsolls gave him a boyish quality but the bulging muscles his vest revealed before he pulled over his shirt countered any impression of fallibility. And despite his eighty years his walk was the swagger of a man under half his age, its confidence challenging all who might stand in his way.

For all the inspiration in his vitality as I followed I had a nagging apprehension about what he would be like behind the wheel.

We rounded the corner to face a pristine, gleaming white 1980s Mercedes. I got in and found myself confronted by a dashboard assortment of gold Buddhist statues and a compass. I very much hoped that he was planning to navigate by more conventional means. He climbed into the driver's seat and turned the key.

My head was blasted into the headrest by classical Chinese vocals accompanied by a thumping karaoke beat. I wasn't sure whether I had entered *Pimp My Ride*, a London mini cab or *Karate Kid*. Without prior knowledge of what grandmasters drive it seemed suitably surreal.

Out of the school gates we stalled immediately. From that point on his aggression could not be faulted. Fifty metres down the road and the horn was put to good use – someone had failed to immediately get off their marks at a green light. Then foot to the floor and copious Hokkien cursing as a driver considered overtaking. 'Yeah, fuck you buddy' seemed to be the gist.

Impending death aside I was unsettled by the glove box. It kept falling open to reveal a full complement of neatly stacked Chinese classics. As it fell open I would close it. A 'thtuk', and it would promptly return to its resting state. After a few goes at this Sugong started to make forceful gestures – 'slam it harder'.

I did as told, my worries about whether this might break the latch outweighed by a concern that failure would result in another eyes-off-the-road gesture. Ten seconds' success.

'Aahh', his satisfied sigh was quickly followed by the door falling open again. Eyes nowhere near the road, he leant over me and gave it a solid slam. It bounced closed and then straight back on my knees.

'Mm,' a less satisfied grunt. The remainder of the journey saw the glove-box door in its position of choice.

We made it, but just as I was starting prayers of thanks I felt the car roll back. Sugong, halfway out of the door, managed to hop back in and pull the handbrake before the car ended up in the cross-traffic at the bottom of the road. I got out quickly. Even with the engine off this car was clearly still a menace.

After a brief stop at his home and an introduction to Madame Quek, the three of us were back in. This promised to be a shorter journey; the English-speaking Madame Quek explained they were just showing me where to get off the bus the next morning.

Some steps descending steeply from the edge of the pavement were pointed out as the site for training and then we stopped again. Madame Quek and I both got out, and I found myself in a conundrum. On the one hand I was desperate to hear her explanations and directions. On the other I felt I needed to help Sugong.

Rather than pull over he had stopped in the middle of the road. Another driver had taken exception to this and started shouting at him. Anxious that my grandmaster not be disrespected I was unsure how to deliver a stinging rebuke in a language I didn't speak.

A solution of sorts was presented by the car negotiating Sugong's and speeding off. But my discomfort was not yet over. I was forced into some awkward shuffling as Sugong was given a 'scolding' by his wife; clearly even Shaolin grandmasters have their Achilles heels. Luckily an escape was presented in the form of the bus. I was bundled aboard and could finally relax.

I had arrived but I would not be relaxing for long. Tomorrow would see the start of training.

4

Uncles, aunts and the army

Sugong was a young man on the cusp of adulthood, keen for bright lights and excitement. Chai Lien Bu village wasn't going to provide them. He needed to head to a city and he chose Xiamen. Xiamen is the coastal capital of Fujian. Now linked to the mainland by a bridge and expanded by land reclamation, in the 40s its main centre was an island. It was a much bigger place than Sugong had ever been.

Getting there wasn't a journey of luxury. A bumpy train ride was followed by the promise of the fantastically futuristic *hoi chun* (diesel boat). The reality of travelling on a diesel-powered ferry quickly stripped away the glamorous veneer and by the time he disembarked Sugong and the hundreds of other passengers were coated head-to-toe in grime.

On landing Sugong didn't have time to gawp and wonder at the scale of his new surroundings, the huge buildings, large roads, and the astounding number of cars. Unless he wanted to sleep on the streets he needed to find a job and lodgings fast. After a quick lunch and a scrub-down he scouted the area, and within a couple of hours he had a job; a waiter/odd-job man at a café. In addition to providing employment, the owner also offered a canvas bunk in a small room above the shop. A change of clothes later and his Xiamen working life had begun.

Sugong had gone to Xiamen to find a great master and live a life of excitement. He soon found that it was not going to be easy to do either. His meagre earnings meant that wild extravagances extended no further than the price of a pack of cheap cigarettes and he had no greater success tracking down an eminent master.

But it was still a happy time. Used to poverty, a little hardship was not going to cause him sleepless nights. The money he earned was his own and while there may not have been much of it it was his to spend as he wished. He was young, he had friends, and he was free. But it was just a start.

Fujian's history of trade, travel and piracy resulted in its contributing heavily to Chinese numbers overseas. In the 1940s Xiamen was a prime staging post for emigrants seeking the perceived riches of Singapore. If Xiamen promised excitement and prosperity beyond the dreams of young peasant boys, Singapore offered a whole new world. As Sugong began to hear more about it he became increasingly sure that it was one for him.

Getting there was not so easy. The Japanese had eased restrictions on immigration after they bulldozed their way past the British in 1942 but it was something of a mixed blessing. Massacres and repression had diminished Singapore's allure.

The return of British rule renewed the city state's attraction, but with it the obstacles to entering. Sugong knew that possibilities would only open up to him by hook or by crook. When his chance came it was from a crook.

One day he was in the Seng Seong Hotel catching up with 'relatives'. The hotel was owned by a man called Leong from a nearby 'village' to Sugong's. Despite sharing the same surname this Leong was not a family member of those involved in the kidnap incident. Sugong's 'village' was actually made up of a number of villages with a total population of around seven thousand male Queks.

The Leong village had about ten thousand male Leongs. Intermarriage within the clan was common, and despite often tenuous blood links, they would call themselves relatives. When away from home the clan instinct would kick in more strongly: in Xiamen the Leongs would become relatives; in Singapore anyone from Fujian.

Catching up with his relatives at the hotel, Sugong heard some interesting news. A Leong living in Singapore was looking to take two youngsters from China to work for her. Sugong knew just the youngster and asked Leong to put him in touch. A meeting was arranged and a few days later Sugong returned to the hotel.

Birth had not been kind to Mrs Leong. It did not bless her with aesthetically pleasing features, and compounded its ill-humour with the two large marks it left on either side of her face. One was red, the other dark brown. But for the time being Sugong concurred with the theory of beauty being only skin deep. He was ready to extend his charm to anyone who could offer a passage to Singapore.

Chinese of a younger generation refer to their elders as Auntie or Uncle as a sign of respect, whether there is any relationship or not. Sugong extended the courtesy, but was eager to impress upon her his more literal claim to the term as well. His pitch for her favour then moved on to his work experience but, more importantly, he name-dropped Uncle Wei. As a leading figure in the province his uncle's name carried weight. Whether Red-Faced Auntie was swayed by his deference, his disposition to hard work, or, more probably, access to this valuable contact, wasn't clear. It didn't really matter. The job was Sugong's, as soon as the papers could be arranged.

Getting immigration papers for Singapore was not an easy task. This was not because of failings within the system but rather the lack of them. There were clear entrance criteria for immigrants and Sugong didn't meet them. His papers would need to be less official and arranging this could take months. He decided to return to his village to catch up with and say goodbye to his loved ones.

It wasn't to be a holiday. Once back he went to work for Uncle Wei, collecting rent from the peasants who worked his land. It was not a job Sugong disliked. A sociable person, he was more than happy to visit the villages and catch up on gossip. He wasn't impartial to a bit of gambling either and finding a game of mahjong wasn't hard. Whether a better gambler, or just on a lucky streak, Sugong did well. The villagers ended up owing him a hundred sects of rice – a significant amount. Sugong was delighted. They were not.

In addition to the money they had to pay their landlord, they now found themselves indebted to the nephew. It added insult to injury and, like good gamblers, they began to look for an angle out. They decided their best chance would be through Uncle Wei. A delegation went to visit him, complaining vociferously about his nephew's corrupting influence. Uncle Wei was left in an awkward position. To side (fairly) with his nephew would leave him open to accusations of corruption and engender bad feeling across a number of villages. But to side with them would mean unfairly punishing his favourite nephew.

Uncle Wei surveyed his options and made his decision. It was Sugong who would suffer. He would be conscripted into the army.

It would be a struggle to find any nation that hasn't experienced turbulence in its history, but China does seem to have had more than most. First unified in 221 BC, a consistent feature of its history since has been regular and violent struggles for power. These have been notable for its war-mongers' belief in the expendability of the people, and their ability to replenish numbers lost to slaughter.

As if the Chinese had not ably demonstrated their capability for warfare and bloodshed already, Kublai Khan and the Mongols added their ferocity in the 13th century. The positive to this was the endowment of an external enemy on whom to focus. But once the Mongols were expelled, internal opportunities would present themselves again. Notable among the more recent conflicts was the 19th-century Taiping Rebellion. Astonishing numbers, estimated in the tens of millions, were killed in battles founded on the claims of a man who believed himself brother to Jesus Christ.

The latter part of the century saw the country under siege from colony-happy Britain, France and Japan. If fighting three of the world's greatest powers individually was not bad enough, an anti-colonial rebellion in 1900 saw the invaders unite with Russia, the USA and Germany. The Chinese rebels lost.

Under pressure, and deteriorating in the face of the foreign encroachment, the dynastic system collapsed in 1912. The country had descended too far by this time for a bright, new start and fell instead into chaos and violence.

Money and force meant power and there were plenty willing to fight for it. Small-time bandits plundered their way to the big time, and the most successful assumed the title of warlord. As warlords they fought anyone challenging their interests, from rival warlords to Chinese rebels. The rebels, for their part, were slaughtering Manchurians but were in turn killed by soldiers, who also butchered bandits. And the bandits killed anyone who crossed their path. And then became warlords.

In this power vacuum the Kuomintang (KMT) Party emerged, attempting to restore order and a sense of nationhood. Hampered at first by internal struggles, they began to make progress in the mid-1920s under a new leader, a former general called Chiang Kai-shek. In the first decade of his rule, the warlords were pushed back and a greater control of China won. But in addition to fighting warlords, the KMT had to contend with the Communists. An uneasy alliance, forged in the first half of the twenties, broke down when Chiang made a failed attempt to eliminate them.

A third front of war then emerged when the Japanese launched a full-scale invasion from their Manchurian base. When their external enemy was finally defeated, the KMT and Communists followed historical precedence and turned inward once more. By late 1947, the KMT were fatigued by two decades of fighting and corroded by rampant corruption and the Communists were gaining the upper hand. It was not a good time to join their enemy.

Sugong had no intention of doing so. He had no strong philosophical position on the communist/nationalist debate, certainly not enough to kill others, or be killed, on account of their views. He also knew he would be joining an army whose corruption meant many soldiers went unpaid for their likely deaths. Faced with this situation he made the sensible decision. He ran away.

Running from conscription was a punishable offence and punishment in China was rarely lenient. Furthermore Sugong had few places to go to and he would not be difficult to find.

Fortunately, Uncle Wei had no interest in sending him to battle. The commensurate politician, he had needed to put on a show to keep secure his own position. To the unknowing he would have appeared genuine: a strong official ready to sacrifice his own nephew. In reality he had no greater desire to send Sugong into futile battle than Sugong had in going. He was more than happy to turn a blind eye to his nephew's whereabouts when he disappeared.

Sugong had in fact 'disappeared' to Red-Faced Auntie's village, not too many miles from his own. For the next three months he worked there as an apprentice carpenter until his papers finally came through, seven months after he had agreed to go.

Except they weren't really his. They were Leong Heng Choon's.

A 'relative' of Red-Faced Auntie, this particular Leong had decided to return permanently to China from Singapore. So Sugong got to take his papers. For this he would have to work in Singapore to pay off the debt. Quite what he would have to do was not yet clear.

5

ONE HUNDRED AND EIGHT TRIADS

Leong Heng Choon II set off for his promised land in 1947 on a battered old steam-powered junk called the *Kooi Yang*. Originally intended as a container vessel, she was now packed with nearly a thousand passengers and was hot, stuffy and very crowded. Beds were thin mats laid out wherever a few feet of spare space could be found. The aroma of fresh sea air fought a losing battle against the stench of vomit as the new-to-travel occupants searched unsuccessfully for their sea-legs.

Sugong was oblivious to the discomfort. His mind was preoccupied with dreams of adventure. Any hint of nerves or anxiety was quickly suppressed. He was confident his new life couldn't offer greater hardship than he had endured before. Every mouthful of food he had eaten at home had needed to be earned. The earning of it had never been easy, and what there was, never quite enough. Singapore, he was sure, would be different.

For an untravelled country boy, even the journey was a thing of wonder. The *Kooi Yang* stopped in Saigon after a week to drop off passengers and load rice. Much of the French-controlled city was off limits to the transit passengers, but it was Sugong's first experience outside Fujian, let alone China, and there was more than enough to see. He wandered any areas he was allowed, soaking up the atmosphere of the intriguing city, its strange smells, unusual foods, unfamiliar language and exotic sights.

When the time came to leave he was almost disappointed. No less so when he found out that the space vacated by the departing passengers had been more than compensated for with rice. Furthermore, they were now told they would be making a detour to avoid a typhoon wreaking havoc in their intended path. The delay wasn't so onerous in the travelling time it added. But the enforced stop in Cambodia meant there would be a week's quarantine when they reached Singapore.

This part of the journey was less enjoyable. Sugong, in perfect health until this point, fell ill during their confinement on Singapore's Kusu Island. A high fever developed into a full body rash before it moved to his sinuses, affecting his hearing and balance. It was a miserable start to a dream life. Sapped of his strength, his enthusiasm and excitement also waned and he waited out his fever, despondent and lonely.

After ten long days he was finally released from his enforced captivity. When he arrived on the main island Red-Faced Auntie was there to meet him.

Exhausted and weak, Sugong wasn't in a state for wide-eyed wonder. Which was fortunate, as he found 1940s Singapore not the place to inspire it. At the time it had just become a separate British crown colony, having previously been part of the British ruled 'Straits Settlements'. Due to its ideal location as a trading post between South-East Asia and the Middle East it was a state on the rise and a place where there was money to be made.

It had not yet experienced its economic miracle though, and remained an island whose colonial buildings mostly charmed rather than inspired. To Sugong's disappointed eyes it was less advanced than the city he had left to search for riches. Many streets weren't even paved with stone, let alone gold. But as a young man looking to make good he was willing to overlook his surroundings as long as he had a place to sleep and a chance to earn. All he wanted to do was unpack his bags and get to work.

His attitude suited Red-Faced Auntie down to the ground.

She took him to his new workplace in Duah Poh Market. She owned and ran a shop that rented trishaws. Its home was at the base of a shophouse. A typical shophouse, it comprised a ground-floor store topped by two levels of offices and flats. These overhung the front of the shop by a few feet, supported intermittently by pillars, to provide shelter from the heavy tropical rains. Sugong was to live in a room in one of the flats. Spartan by many standards, it was a place of comfort compared to some of his former dwellings and he had no complaints.

Ostensibly his job would be working in the shop downstairs. In 1940s Singapore trishaws remained a common and practical means of transport. Piloting one wasn't a financially rewarding career, though, and many of the drivers couldn't afford their own vehicle. Instead they would rent them daily. It was Sugong's job to supervise this, from accounting for the ins and outs to providing security and maintaining the vehicles. The work was barely more rewarding than riding the trishaws, but Singapore in 1947 had yet to reach universal affluence and expectations weren't as high. He had a job and he had a bed.

It was a start but he had no intention of it being an end.

It took a full three days before Sugong had his first fight.

Still weak from illness he had been trying to build up his strength. Deciding to kill a flock of birds with one stone, he resolved to do this while teaching himself to ride a bike. This would have the added benefit of allowing him to explore his new home. Not the most adept, he was now able to wobble his way from place to place but complex manoeuvres remained more testing. Swerving to avoid another cyclist cutting in front of him was certainly at the limit of his capabilities. So when he was almost forced head-on into an oncoming car he was far from happy.

The people of Fujian speak Hokkien. Chinese dialects in general are known for their rich vein of obscenities and insults. While Mandarin, the official language, is more admired for its refinement, Hokkien earns respect for its vast and colourful capacity for reprimand. Sugong unleashed some of its potential on the offending cyclist.

Perhaps mindful that he was facing someone built like a mini-Schwarzenegger with an undisguised temper, whose demeanour suggested he was a hair's breadth from resorting to the language of fists, the cyclist accepted the admonishments.

Throwing a final few choice phrases toward the back of the retreating offender Sugong made his way off.

At a nearby coffee shop, his friends were waiting for him as arranged. They had met on the boat and, as they were now 'relatives', a bond was already forming. Sugong hopped up to join them on the back of a parked lorry that sat before a cluster of parked trishaws and they were soon immersed in animated chat.

It didn't last long. Within minutes a group of men wearing traditional wooden workers' clogs approached, the cyclist Sugong had scolded at the fore. The presence of his companions seemed to have resolved earlier issues of assertiveness and his demeanour was far less placid now. His friends didn't look the kind to favour diplomacy either.

Although he didn't know it at the time, Sugong had picked an argument with one of the Triad 108 gang.

Crossing paths with triads would not have been a particularly wise move for a well-established local with ties in the community. It was especially precarious for a fresh-off-the-boat Chinese man whose friends and contacts could be counted on the fingers of one hand. There may not have been a hundred and eight of them, but there were enough to create extreme discomfort.

They ordered Sugong down when they reached the van. He assessed the options open to him as he eyed the group. Self-confident as he was, launching into them didn't seem likely to bring about a happy conclusion. Yet they didn't look open to a chat and the offer of a conciliatory beer. He scanned the area for possible escape routes. Finding none he braced himself and took a deep breath. Then he jumped down.

The moment he hit the ground he knew that reasoning was out. As the first clog connected with his head he darted to the right. His sudden movement meant that the following blows glanced off his shoulder instead of his skull. It also meant that he could grab the large metal padlock he had spotted before jumping down.

He turned and swung it full pelt. He didn't get a perfect connection but it caught one of his attackers flush in the chest, its dull thud knocking him back into two others. The frozen second of surprise gave Sugong a chance to swing out again before he dived between trishaws.

There was now a full-scale commotion. The triads were trying to jump between the trishaws to beat Sugong with their clogs. He was dodging them, ducking behind other vehicles and lashing out with the heavy lock. It was almost comical, Jackie Chan-esque. But without a director to call time it was far more dangerous than a movie set.

The pandemonium did not go unnoticed. From among the heads that poked out from the upstairs window of the coffee shop came a shout.

'Hey, country boy. What's going on?'

In a brief lull in the chaos Sugong glanced up indignantly to locate the voice that had so easily identified him as a new immigrant.

'These bastards think they can beat me up,' he shouted, swinging out with his lock again.

For all of his defiance the chances were that they were right. But luck was on his side. The spectator revealed his identity.

'I'm a police clerk from Telok Ayer station,' he shouted down into the melee. 'I'm calling in an emergency, and I'd say you've got about two minutes before my colleagues show up.'

A catch-up with the local constabulary would have led to discussion about Triad 108's other activities. It wasn't a dialogue they were keen to have. They fled, leaving Sugong with a lump on his head, a sore hand and a sense it could have been worse. He had survived his first run-in with triads in the Malay Peninsula. It would not be the last.

6

FEAR AND LOATHING IN KUALA LUMPUR

I rode in a stuttering, fume-belching bus deep into the suburbs of KL. It had been pitch black when I started off, and the sun remained as reluctant as I'd been to rise. Having managed to get off at the right stop, my butterflies now fluttered toward the training session ahead. As I made my way down the stairs from the street to the basketball court, I hardly noticed the early morning serenade from resident frogs and crickets.

Set down a deep incline from the road, the court was part of a large, square piece of recreational ground bordered by four roads. To the right was a strip of grass with an asphalt badminton court and a children's playground in its centre. In front of it a football/rugby pitch was being monopolised by an elderly man as he perfected his golf swing in the morning gloom. And directly in front of the basketball court was a small white building isolated in a patch of asphalt. It was an area I would become very familiar with in the coming months.

A couple of minutes after arriving I saw a white Mercedes pull up at the top of the stairs. Sugong got out and even my butterflies got butterflies. Despite my nerves, I was temporarily distracted by admiration for his style. He looked pretty cool for an 80-year-old. His loose-fitting polo shirt, sporty plimsolls and easy gait certainly weren't the style of the elderly I knew.

He started to make his way down.

Knowing I'd be coming up in front of my legendary grandmaster I'd been training hard, and despite my short break I was feeling sharp. I was hopeful of making a good impression. Sugong nodded at me, deposited his attaché case at the base of the basketball net, stripped off his polo shirt to reveal his regulation white vest, and we began.

We started with some warm-ups and stretching and a pattern was quickly established. Sugong would demonstrate, indicate the number of repetitions with his fingers, and I would follow. It was a good system and would have worked flawlessly if the Chinese used the same finger signs as us. They don't. Six, I know now, is a fist with thumb and little finger extended. Three is like an ace sign – thumb and index finger joined in a circle, the three remaining fingers extended. Five, the fingers of one hand held in a fist and flicked open, ten the same but with both hands.

In normal circumstances none of this would be too difficult to have a guess at. But the situation was pretty far from my normal circumstances and my powers of deduction had been savaged by jitters. As for Sugong, he appeared to be reserving his tuition for kung fu rather than sign language.

'Oi!' he brought me back to attention. I looked up to see him flashing his fingers unfathomably before turning to take a call on his mobile. A hundred or so one-legged squats later he finished his conversation, turned and looked at me, still bouncing up and down, like I was a complete idiot. As stupid as I felt, I decided it was better to be over-enthusiastic than not keen enough. In any case I was feeling fit and strong and I hoped the unbearably hot, humid weather would hold hidden benefits in advancing my sorry flexibility.

My thoughts were again interrupted by Sugong, this time indicating a stretch. No problem. He opened his legs, spread out his arms with palms facing the sky, and leaned forward. He kept leaning forward. When his nose finally touched the ground he paused for a moment, came back up and gestured for me to take my turn.

My hamstrings have never been the greatest. Hereditary tightness wasn't helped by excessive football playing and un-excessive stretching when I was young. But I had heard of miracle physical feats performed under pressure, the young mother lifting a car to rescue her child. I hoped this might be my moment.

I spread my legs wide and held out my arms. Mind over matter. I breathed in and prepared for the descent. Halfway down and I was still feeling good. Just over halfway down I realised I was full way already. Seeing the floor a foot and a half away I willed myself on, but despite all of my positive visualisation, my hamstrings had given up shop the moment Sugong's nose touched the ground.

As I eased sorely up I caught a glimpse of Sugong's disgusted expression before he turned away.

Training took place in two locations. One was in Sugong's neighbourhood. Although my first session was on the basketball court, it was usually held in the small concrete-floored community hall beside it. The other 'dojo' was the top of a multi-storey car park in central KL. Sugong had helped build it in his contracting days and retained a laissez-faire approach to its use. They weren't exactly grandiose, but as places to sweat, bleed and cry they were more than adequate.

Tuesdays and Thursdays would be in Cheras, Saturday and Sunday in central KL. Or so I thought.

'Sugong wants to know why you weren't here yesterday. He was waiting for you,' said Mr Tan.

'I didn't think there was any training,' I replied.

The reason I thought this was because I had spoken to Madame Quek after we finished on Tuesday and she had made it very clear that Wednesday was to be Sugong's own training day.

'There was. He was waiting for you.'

'Please tell him I'm very sorry, Mr Tan. I'll make sure I'm here next week.'

Mr Tan was one of the Cheras students, but only just. Greeted like a cross between long-lost friend and favourite son, I assumed he was one of the older students but it turned out that it was actually his first day. A fellow Hokkien speaker, Sugong had taken an instant liking to him. Always ready with a smile and a quip, he was quick to charm himself into most people's good books.

Also present was Master Wong, a disciple, but also a master in his own right who had introduced some of his own students, including Mr Tan, to the group. The others were Florence and Ro.

Florence was a sweet, slightly built Chinese Malaysian with a smile that belied her shyness, and a head-snapping kick that contradicted it.

Ro was a German expat looking for ways to squeeze even more into her thirty-six-hour day. Rounding off the group was CG. Asia-Pacific CEO, father of four, you would have thought he too had enough to contend with but he appeared whenever he was in the country, invariably brighter and fresher than me.

They were an extremely friendly, welcoming group who were at pains to make me feel part of the family from the start. But there was a bad cop to their good cop and he had the biggest say.

'Aaahhh!' Sugong grimaced in disgust. 'Ai-yaaah.'

Some curt Hokkien followed, accompanied by a sharp look. It remained locked on me while he shook his head and was only broken at the last possible moment as he turned away. He waved his arm dismissively.

I wasn't sure of exactly what he had said, but the general meaning was pretty clear.

The first week had gone quite well and my confidence had grown. But in the second we hit a block. Whatever I did was guaranteed to drive Sugong to distraction.

Training followed a routine. First up would be stretching. Then chi gung, a kind of breathing-focused callisthenics. When that was finished we would practise forms, the set fight patterns that mimic combat to serve as a teaching and training tool. Last, but definitely not least, was breakfast.

The chi gung I had done previously had focused predominantly on breathing, with movement mainly confined to the upper body to aid the flow of chi (the body's intrinsic energy). The chi gung Sugong taught was called *I Chin Ching*, literally translated as Sinews Transformation Classic. It was based upon the exercises that Shaolin's patriarch purportedly first developed for the temple monks.

It was a much more physical workout than the chi gung I was used to, and involved a lot of bending, twisting and stretching. The Malaysian heat was enough for me to break into a sweat just in the warm-up stretches. After half an hour of chi gung I was ready for my second T-shirt.

Then came the forms. As the newcomer I couldn't just fall into place with the others, so I was separated. This had its drawbacks as well as benefits. On the one hand I had the chance to receive personal tuition from my grandmaster, a great privilege and the kind of instruction that could only be dreamed of. The flip side was the extreme stress that resulted from being the sole focus of his attention.

His style of teaching was certainly different to any I had experienced before. He would demonstrate the steps three times. And that was it. Attempts at clarification were dealt with by a sharply dismissive hand gesture and a fierce look. After the regulation three demonstrations he would be off, to return to other, less stupid students. I would then frantically try to remember what he had shown me and make an attempt at performing it with some degree of adequacy.

Every now and then I really felt I had made a half-decent stab at it. These occasions were more than matched by the times I knew I had something wrong, but couldn't find the switch in my memory to make it right.

It didn't really matter. I was invariably on the wrong end of a scolding however well I thought I'd done. The sharp words would be accompanied by a look that suggested I was trying to upset him intentionally.

It would range from the kind of death stare I would reserve for a person saying something deeply offensive about my nearest and dearest, to something much harsher. Always it would be complemented by bad-tempered, guttural Hokkien and a flurry of angry hand gestures.

By the middle of the second week I was being scolded at every turn. As the days progressed the number of steps I was taught decreased and the anger of my teacher and the ferocity of his scoldings went up.

Things came to a head on the weekend of the fourth week. As usual I was separated from the main group. It was early in the class and Sugong showed me six steps. I was sure I could get them right. I practised diligently for twenty minutes, almost forgetting my fear in the focused repetition.

Sugong quickly dismantled my ill-founded optimism. Disgusted, he berated me loudly before turning to the rest of the class. He gestured toward me, shouted a little more and then laughed derisively. Then with another dismissive wave of the hand he was off.

Three weeks of constant scolding was wearing a little thin. Now I was being ridiculed as well. I was desperate to finish the class, go back to my guesthouse and forget about kung fu. But there was another hour to go and all I had were my six steps, so I kept going.

At the end he returned, watched me and shook his head sadly. His face told the tale. I was clearly trying, with some success, to ruin an art that had survived more than a millennium.

In martial arts there comes a point where a master has enough understanding to change things around a little, making the adaptations he or she feels appropriate. There may even be occasions where lapses of memory can occur in the recollection of something taught decades before. These inconsistencies are not disputed by students. Call it master's privilege.

As a grandmaster Sugong had more than earned the right. He demonstrated again, this time differently to the way he had earlier – the way I was trying to replicate – and walked off. End of class.

It was the low point of my training, but it also marked the turnaround to higher ones. Sugong had been so genuine in his disgust it would not be possible to pass the occasion off as a test of character. But he was of a traditional mind, and he placed great emphasis on respect being shown by students. I had continued to display it under duress and, while he may not have been impressed at their results, he did appreciate my efforts.

'He takes a scolding well' he told one of the others. 'And he practises hard.'

Not exactly high praise, but it was the start of a turning tide.

Finding favour was something of a mixed blessing.

'Sugong wants you to start coming at 6.30,' said Mr Goh, Ji Hang's father and one of the favourite disciples.

As quick to rise from slumber as a sloth, I winced.

'OK,' I replied, unconvincingly.

Even then weeks of punctuality could be undone in a day.

'Sugong says that you're always late,' Mr Goh said, translating Sugong's angry complaint.

'Well, I turned up at twenty-five to yesterday but apart from that I'm pretty good.'

'Come at six from now on.'

I made sure I wasn't late again. I knew that Sugong started around four and I wasn't eager to share his schedule.

The 'reward' for finding favour wasn't just earlier starts. Soon training was up from five mornings a week to seven, and then an evening session was thrown in on Saturday for good measure. It was pretty tiring. So when, a couple of months in, Sugong 'invited' me to a Sunday afternoon session I wasn't entirely delighted. Late-morning snooze and a matinee movie quickly evaporated into unachievable dreams.

'Sugong says you should meet him at the temple at five this afternoon. He's going to take you training in Petaling Jaya,' said Mr Goh, referring to a satellite city of KL.

'Great,' I replied, my false enthusiasm fooling no one. 'Thanks.'

Chow Kit is a neighbourhood that lies in the centre of Kuala Lumpur. While skyscrapers loom at its borders, it is a part of town that remains a little rough around the edges. Nonetheless, I was surprised to see how heavily fortified the temple, lying bang in its centre, was. The reason was later explained. There were a number of illegal gambling houses in the area. If the temple wasn't locked up tight, fleeing gamblers would swarm inside to take refuge at the first hint of a police raid.

I arrived at five as requested. There was no sign of Sugong.

'Sugong? Sugong?' I enquired, using the full range of my Hokkien.

A man pointed around the corner. Following his directions I came to a room and popped my head in the door. Sugong and some friends were playing mahjong. He turned, gave an irritated look and waved me out.

Fifteen minutes later he joined me and we went on our way. Judging from his good mood he must have won, and the music went up a notch or two. He even began to sing along. At least I assumed that's what he was doing; there were vast differences in timing and tone between the recording and his vocals but I put these down to enthusiastic amateurism, rather than sophisticated harmonic improvisation. Half an hour later I realised there was something familiar about the present tune. I looked down at the stereo and saw it was on repeat. Clearly there couldn't be too much of a good thing.

By now we were in Petaling Jaya, or PJ – Malaysians reduce everything to an acronym if possible. Sugong motioned his thumb to his mouth:

'Do you want to eat?'

A shrug, hands gesturing toward him:

'I'm easy – it's up to you.'

I was easy because I'd had lunch a couple of hours before and although I wasn't the slightest bit hungry, I thought he might be. Big mistake. We stopped and he ordered a selection of deep-fried fatty meats. It turned out he was as hungry as I was, but he held a distinct advantage as he had a say in whether he was to eat or not. After a couple of mouthfuls everything was pushed over to me. A finger jabbed in a caringly aggressive way.

'Chia.'

I ate.

When I had forced down the last mouthful we set off and within a few minutes were behind Chin Woo School. Sugong parked the car but instead of going directly to the school he wandered over to a bench at the side of the football pitches. Nice. I followed and made to settle down beside him and let the food digest as we watched the world go by.

'Oi!'

He gave me a forceful shove on the shoulder and gestured at the pitches. It was clear that only one of us was to take a passive role in proceedings.

Whatever my state of fitness and health I have always despised running. With the temperature in the thirties, humidity so high it went beyond tools of measurement and a stomach full of duck fat, I was less enthusiastic than usual. But I thought I could handle a few laps.

Five in I looked at Sugong. He studiously surveyed a lack of activity in another direction. So it was to be ten.

Ten laps down and my T-shirt was soaked through. The duck in my belly felt as if it had been bounced back to life and was making vain efforts to escape. Complete inattention from my grandmaster. Shit. Surely he'd call it quits at fifteen?

It was twenty hateful laps before he finally turned his gaze and gestured for me to stop. If I hadn't been sweating enough to put out a forest fire, I might have spontaneously combusted. My tracksuit bottoms were sodden, even my trainers squelched sweat with each step. Sugong was completely oblivious to my state. He stood up and motioned for me to follow him across the pitches to the school.

I was boiling hot, full-bellied, and looked and felt a disgusting mess. Now to start class.

7

One thousand thunderbolts and a myriad of swords

When Sugong formed a bond with his 'brothers' on the boat from Fujian, he entered into relationships that would stand the test of time. They would not be without controversy. New alien lands provide opportunity for adventure and trouble. As a magnet for the latter this would prove especially true for Sugong. Within a month of the 108 fight he found himself in another awkward situation, this time with his brothers.

It started when he joined two of them one afternoon shortly after his arrival. They met some others and, with no other ideas forthcoming, the suggestion to visit a local temple seemed an innocuous distraction.

They arrived at a complex that had seen better days. Siong Lim was, fundamentally, a fine example of a Buddhist site of worship. Architecturally it was impressive and its craftsmanship was far from poor. But it was in desperate need of repair. While there is something romantic about an old temple showing character with age, this looked more like neglect. In the damaged walls and crumbling paintwork lay a dark tale.

Sugong had arrived in Singapore not long in the aftermath of the Japanese occupation. Distracted by their troubles in Europe, the British had not kept their eye on Asia and they were caught off guard by the Japanese. Sweeping down through the Malayan states, the new Asian power-masters disdainfully brushed aside the old. Britain capitulated and was expelled in January 1942 after seventy days of sub-standard defence.

Despite a none-too-proud record in many of their colonies, the British had not been too bad in Singapore. They were not the first Europeans to arrive – the Portuguese claimed that honour in the 16th century. And it was the Dutch who landed on an island of fishermen a hundred or so years later. But they became embroiled in troubles closer to home in the late 18th century, and turned their attention to fight Napoleonic France. In an act of solidarity, the British offered to take 'temporary' control.

While London may have been genuine in their offer, an ambitious young official had different ideas. For all of his attempts to improve living conditions in South-East Asia, Thomas Stamford Raffles' ultimate obligation was to the British Empire. He saw the potential of Singapore to displace Dutch power in the region and he began to connive.

Finding that the sultan had already established treaties with the Dutch, Raffles circumvented him, recognising his brother as ruler. New treaties, generous in compensation, were drawn up and signed. The Dutch were furious, London was embarrassed, but more pressing issues resulted in further delays. Singapore would remain in the British Empire for the next one hundred and twenty-three years.

Despite residing only briefly in Singapore, Raffles helped transform it and his tenure saw spectacular expansion in population and trade. While the British were not shy to take their share of the money flooding in, there was plenty left for the sultans and ever-increasing migrants. By 1942 it was a trading post the Japanese were more than happy to add to their colonial base.

They too seemed willing to share the spoils, but their relationship with their subjects was inconsistent in benevolence. The British were rounded up and interned. Those who survived the brief resistance suffered three years of treatment only the strictest of fathers would call paternal. The Malays, though, were not abused; the Japanese wanted to encourage cooperation in the other Malay states. Indian immigrants were also courted. By winning their favour the occupiers hoped to incite unrest in the jewel of the British Empire's crown.

But for the Chinese it was a different story. Their long history of rivalry had culminated in Japan's 1937 invasion of the Chinese mainland. Deeply suspicious of the majority Chinese, the Japanese acted ruthlessly to stem rebellion before it could occur.

The result was the Sook Ching (purge through cleansing) Massacre. Guilt was to be suspected of sympathy to China or England. As reasonable suspicion could be as flimsy as a basic knowledge of English, the chances of a just and fair hearing weren't good. They were not bettered by the ability of any soldier to grab a Chinese man and decide on his fate. Between twenty-five and fifty thousand were slaughtered. When they realised that working with the Chinese was essential to running the island, the Japanese eased in their repression. But the battle for hearts and minds was a little late.

Four years prior to Sugong's arrival, a Buddhist abbot had started to provide driving lessons. Although a slightly unusual offering, it was not the kind of activity that would normally have provoked the authorities' ire. There were exceptional circumstances in this case.

When the Japanese invaded China they cut off ports to isolate the country from supplies. One way to overcome this was to deliver by road. One gained particular fame. The Burma Road was an impossibly tight, winding road that wormed its way up the hills of Burma into southern China. A few thousand volunteers risked their lives to deliver supplies to their ancestral home. Of these a third did not live to see it free.

But before they could pitch in, they needed to be able to drive. Which is where Sek Pu Liang came in (*Sek* being the common surname Hokkien-speaking monks take to represent Buddha. In Mandarin it is pronounced *Shi)*. The abbot was asked to make temple grounds available for driving lessons. The Japanese were yet to arrive with their low-tolerance approach to resistance but by all accounts he would have taken the risk nonetheless.

The consequences were dire. If a basic knowledge of English was enough to warrant execution, playing an active role in defending China guaranteed it. In 1942 Sek Pu Liang was taken to the firing squad after twenty-five years service as abbot.

The treatment of the monastery was less definitive, but still brutal, and it emerged from wartime battered and bruised. During the brief defence of the island, the woodland surrounding Siong Lim had been full of allied troops and was heavily bombed as a result. The temple suffered collateral damage. During the occupation it was used as a refuge for the destitute. Although worthy, this placed further demands on the Siong Lim, and when the Japanese were expelled its repairs were low down the list in Singapore's recovery plans.

Temple life did not return to normal immediately. When it opened its doors to the destitute in wartime, Siong Lim had unwittingly left itself exposed. After the war, those genuinely displaced by the troubles gradually re-settled, but some opportunists were happy where they were. They had gained *de facto* control of the land surrounding Siong Lim.

They weren't content just to trespass. They vandalised the temple, harassed female worshippers and disrupted services. The monk who assumed Pu Liang's duties was more than capable of running a temple in normal circumstances. But these weren't normal circumstances and he became increasingly concerned. But he knew of a monk in Indonesia. This monk was a grand-disciple of one of his *siheng* (senior brother in learning) and a man known not to suffer fools. Furthermore he was in possession of unique skills that meant he didn't have to. Sung Huay decided to turn to him for help.

Sugong didn't know the full story when he first visited Siong Lim, but he could see that the temple was some way from its original pomp and glory. He didn't dwell on the topic as he had more pressing matters on his mind. He was more concerned with the activities of his brothers and their friends.

When visiting a temple in a group, Sugong was used to his companions seeking out the area or deity of greatest interest to them. On this occasion, instead of fanning out in their different directions, they were all gathered in one spot. They seemed to be preparing for a ceremony. Sugong had no particular objections to ceremonies but he did like to be given notice if he was to attend one. He certainly wanted to know if he was going to be a participant. And it became clear that he was. His brothers were making preparations for a blood brother initiation.

Modern triads have created negative associations for Chinese secret societies but they have existed in various forms for centuries and the majority were probably not intended for criminal pursuit. More commonly, they started out as a means of mutual self-protection, the poor or socially disadvantaged looking to defend themselves from local power holders or other societies. At the smallest scale they might be founded by small groups of individuals or by the joining of two or more family clans. But they could also be based on geographical location, shared ancestry, or other social and religious ties. Sometimes they would be secret, other times not. Some of the bigger ones were involved in large-scale rebellions at points in China's history, resulting in establishment suspicion and mistrust. But many small societies were of no threat at all.

This didn't mean they were to be entered into lightly. Joining one could mean making a commitment sworn under oath. In a nation where blood letting had not been uncommon over the millennia they were not always for the faint-hearted. Absolute loyalty might be pledged on the understanding that betrayal would result in death by 'a myriad of swords' or 'a thousand thunderbolts'. It was a significant commitment for those that took them seriously.

Sugong did. Seriously enough to have major reservations about pledging himself to nine others, seven of whom he had never met prior to that day.

He had been a victim of circumstance. Among the stupefying array of Chinese beliefs and superstitions, numerology ranks high. Eight, for example, is lucky as it resembles the character for prosperity. Four should be avoided for its similarity to death. Nine was not considered appropriate by the group, and Sugong's brothers proposed him as a more auspicious tenth. They had just neglected to inform him.

Which is how he found himself a reluctant participant. The ceremony began by each brother climbing a tall pole and placing burning joss sticks before a deity on a ledge at its top. Sugong was unenthusiastic but obliging and followed suit, the last to go up.

The oaths were a different matter. He could not reconcile himself to swearing eternal loyalty to this group of strangers. The vows would be hollow. Instead of reciting them in a clear voice, he shuffled to the back of the group and mumbled incoherently.

Although not properly sworn in, Sugong believed in the union, and despite some ups and downs it was one that would remain through the years. The most immediate impact of it was not directly related to this newfound fraternal bond, but its significance would be even more pivotal.

It would again involve Siong Lim, and it would also require pledges. But this time he would make them voluntarily, putting his faith in the hands of the abbot of the temple: a warrior monk.

8

TWO WIVES ON A DOUBLE-CRESTED MOUNTAIN

The history of Shaolin is at best vague. It is based largely on tales recounted through generations, and mainly supplemented with legend rather than fact. This results in very few definites and a lot of mights and maybes.

There is general agreement on some grounds. The Shaolin temple would appear to have been founded around AD495, and there is one real certainty in its location: Song Shan (Mount Song), Henan Province, north central China, where it still stands today. (Song Shan lies in the middle of China's 'Five Peaks' and was considered the centre of the world by the ancient Chinese.) Somewhat disappointingly its name doesn't bear reference to great warriors or martial arts phenomena. The most common and likely explanation has it named after newly planted saplings that surrounded the temple site; the characters 'Shao' and 'Lin' literally translating as 'Young Forest'.

A more intriguing claim bases itself on the delicate diplomacy required by an emperor's domestic arrangements. Unlimited in the number of wives he was allowed, he judiciously decided to settle two apart. He gave them residence on the two peaks that make up Mount Song: Mount *Taishi* (first wife) and Mount *Shaoshi* (second wife). Shaolin Temple was built on the second forested peak.

According to folklore, it was not particularly notable until an Indian monk called Bodhidharma (Tamo to the Chinese) arrived in AD527. It has been claimed that Bodhidharma was an Indian prince. Irrespective of his background, at an early age he decided to give up his claim to things material and devote himself to Buddhism. In the 520s he is said to have travelled overland to China.

The arrival of an eminent monk was guaranteed to elicit imperial interest, and Bodhidharma received a summons. The emperor was a devout Buddhist in his own way, making personal sacrifices and encouraging Buddhism in his subjects. Yet he followed the Buddhist path partly in hope of what he would stand to gain in return. To Bodhidharma, good deeds were an end in themselves, and the emperor's intent nullified his endeavours.

Holding the all-powerful title of emperor, the present incumbent was used to having people literally kow-tow before him. Bodhidharma was an eminent and straight-talking monk with a possible royal heritage of his own. He was not the kow-towing type.

When the emperor enquired into the merit his deeds had earned, Bodhidharma was less than diplomatic. He bluntly told the emperor that he would have none. It was not a meeting of minds and the monk was dismissed.

As fate would have it, the Shaolin Temple was situated near the northern court and Bodhidharma headed to it. But when he arrived, he did not settle within its walls. One suggestion has it that he did not share the current abbot's ideas on the path to enlightenment. Never shy to express an opinion, he apparently developed relations on a par with those nurtured with the emperor.

For whatever reason, Bodhidharma decided to step back from society in search of personal enlightenment. To this end he climbed Mount Song, found a cave in which to shelter, and sat down to meditate for as long as the endeavour required. Nine years later, with the intensity of his meditation having supposedly burned his shadow into the cave's wall, he was ready to descend.

He returned to the temple flanked by a one-armed disciple called Huike (who had apparently lost his arm when he cut it off in an enthusiastic gesture of sincerity to Bodhidharma). There he proceeded to lay the foundations for Chan Buddhism – more widely known by its Japanese alias, Zen – and Shaolin martial arts; reasonable achievements by any standard.

In terms of martial arts, most accounts don't suggest Bodhidharma introduced a fully-fledged system of fighting. Martial arts of some sort were quite possibly practised at the temple already as banditry was rife, and knowledge of self-defence would have been a sensible precaution for the oft-travelling monks. Had he really descended from royal ancestry it is possible that Bodhidharma did know some fighting arts but the more common claims suggest an impact that was influential rather than all-encompassing.

Bodhidharma's primary focus was on non-martial aspects of Buddhism. Having convinced the Shaolin monks of the benefits of meditation as a way to enlightenment, he was apparently disappointed to see them fall asleep in the middle of it. One particularly unlikely story claims that after suffering a similar episode in his cave, he cut off his eyelids to avoid a repetition. (It has been said that, when discarded, they sprouted into shoots that became the first tea plants.) He was less drastic with his disciples. To remedy their sleepiness, and ensure their muscles didn't disintegrate, he was said to have devised a series of callisthenic movements. These acted as a catalyst for the martial arts forms that would evolve over the coming centuries. And Bodhidharma became the figurehead and inspiration for Shaolin.

Legendary institutions by definition require legends on which they are based. More recent investigation suggests that many of Shaolin's may, in fact, be myths. There is very little historical detail on Bodhidharma, but it has been suggested that he was an influencer, rather than the originator, of Chan Buddhism, and the sect didn't significantly establish until more than a century after his death.

His patriarchal role in the martial arts is even more questionable, with one of the foundations on which it is often claimed – the *i chin ching* chi gung he introduced and passed on in manuals – a proven 17th-century fraud. In fact, the historian Meir Sahar suggests that prior to the manual's popularisation of Bodhidharma as patriarch, the monks venerated a warrior deity, Vajrapani (Narayana in Chinese), as the inspiration for their art.

If not shocking enough to Shaolinophiles that their founder was not their founder, there are also claims that their art was for a long time not an art. While there is evidence that Shaolin monks were involved in military battle from as early as the seventh century they may have been co-opted to boost militia numbers rather than for a specifically defined art.

They supposedly did seek out great masters to advance their fighting skills in the Song dynasty (960–1126), but written evidence of a unique Shaolin style emerged only in the second half of the Ming (1368–1644). This isn't to say that there wasn't a specific style earlier, but there is no conclusive proof that there was.

However, in the Ming period the Shaolin style did become famous. Intriguingly it may have coincided with a move to supplement the staff fighting that was so practical in close-combat warfare (for which they were renowned), with empty-handed techniques and chi gung. Which begs the question why?

There is a line of thought that Shaolin forms – the series of movements that mimic combat as a teaching and training tool in many martial arts – were partly developed as a form of moving meditation for their synthesis of the mental and physical. This would make them an ideal complement to Chan Buddhism and a perfect explanation for Shaolin kung fu. However, that the origins of Shaolin martial arts would appear to have been more practically focused raises questions whether this line of thought emerged some time after the early generations of Shaolin fighting monks.

Shaolin's open mind to evolution also saw the temple welcome outsiders to train. While the majority were there to learn, an information exchange with the more advanced saw a range of unlikely individuals, from bandits to generals, make contributions to this holy art. But the monks did not appear content to just absorb and develop in their spiritual home. As they travelled they spread their kung fu to other areas. Further Shaolin temples may even have opened and of these the most famous – and contentious – is South Shaolin.

Unlike the Henan Temple it no longer stands, and there is dispute not only over its location but whether it existed at all. Whether the temple was real or mythical, a distinct south Shaolin style of kung fu did emerge with the most obvious difference to the north being the emphasis accorded to hand instead of foot. The south became renowned for its bias toward punching, while the north accorded predominance to kicks. Various reasons are provided for this, from differences in anatomy between north and south – the northerners being supposedly taller and therefore suited to high kicks – to claims of narrow town passageways in the south, or of injuries to southern monks' legs in battles with pirates, both of which supposedly led to greater reliance on punching. Just as possible, the styles may have diverged without particular reason.

It was likely in the south that an abbot named Sek Hui Jing learned his art. Very little is known about the abbot beyond his lineage as a forty-eighth generation Shaolin monk. He took on only four disciples. Three died before the 20th century reached its mid-point, leaving just one guardian of the art. His name was Sek Koh Chun.

9

A WARRIOR MONK

Although he was born nearly a millennium and a half after Chan patriarch Bodhidharma, information on the life of the monk Koh Chun is hardly more forthcoming. It is possible he was born in Huay An, Fujian Province on 27 December 1886. After this, information on him becomes less clear.

When taking the vows of monkhood, Buddhists move on, to some extent, from the life they led before. Relegating the importance of their past does not help in the re-telling of it and Koh Chun's disinclination toward reflection further muddied his history's waters.

As with Sugong, Koh Chun was the second of four siblings. Unlike Sugong he got on well with his elder brother. This good fortune did not balance the tragedy of his parents' death while he was a young boy, but it at least meant that he had a loving family to care for him while he grew up.

It was not a privileged upbringing however. His brother was a labourer and the rewards for his efforts were as low as the work was hard. Their impoverishment was far from unique. As the Ching dynasty collapsed and Chinese society imploded, poverty and suffering were features of rural life. Yet sharing the misery did not lessen the stresses and burdens on their lives.

Like Sugong, a generation later, Koh Chun was fascinated by martial arts from an early age. He left his village at thirteen when he found his first master, a man named Chow Piao. Chow Piao was a *piu si* – an escort charged with ensuring the people and possessions under his protection reached their destinations intact. With law and order crumbling, piu si were much in demand, and Chow Piao's reputation was good. To be alive and employed, while bandits repeatedly tested a piu si's skills, was testament to this in itself.

For more than three years the young Koh Chun learned Ngo Chor kung fu, the same style Sugong later learned as an apprentice at Kai Wan Temple. Koh Chun also benefited from some extras Chow Piao had picked up along the way; secret weapons and techniques his master had found beneficial to extending both his career and his life.

Koh Chun returned home at sixteen. His brother and wife had decided to emigrate to Singapore and Koh Chun agreed to join them. Much like Sugong some fifty years later, in Singapore they saw a resolution to their poverty and a foundation for future happiness.

It started fortuitously; Koh Chun's brother found work as a boatman, ferrying passengers and goods from port to port. While riches remained beyond their reach it did seem as though they had escaped the worst. But fate held a cruel twist and their optimism was razed by disaster. It was the job that Koh Chun's brother had been so happy to find that was the cause. After less than three years on the island his boat was caught in rough seas and he was swept overboard to his death.

Koh Chun was devastated. Underpinning his martial inclinations was a sensitive soul. The suffering of those around him had always affected him and the death of his brother, whose love and affection had never been fairly rewarded, drove him close to despair.

From his struggle to cope with the loss came a resolution that he would not resign himself to it. His response would be to confront suffering and help others escape its clutches. With his mind set, the eighteen-year-old returned to China and made his way to Ching Sing Temple. There he had his head shaved by his new master, Shing Liang, and agreed to enter the monastic way of life. These first steps in the process to becoming a monk were followed by two years in which he had to prove himself capable of following the necessary edicts. Only then would he be allowed to join their ranks. When he had shown himself worthy he was finally ordained a monk of the Caodong Buddhist sect.

Koh Chun remained at the temple for a couple of years. But his was a restless spirit and he was not content to restrict his learning to a single location. He left for Indonesia, staying at a sister temple for a year, before travelling the country for one more. Returning to China, his thirst remained unquenched and he began to plan his next trip. Not one to set his sights low, he decided this journey would see him seek enlightenment from the four corners of China.

Travelling the length and breadth of a continent-sized country deficient in transport would be a substantial undertaking at any time. But Koh Chun set off in 1912, just as China ended two millennia of dynastic rule and just as it entered one of the more chaotic and violent periods in its violent, chaotic history.

But Koh Chun had not chosen monkhood as a form of escape. He had a genuine desire to help others and he was prepared to put himself at risk in the course of this quest. With four brother monks he set off.

At the turn of the 20th century martial ability had clear practical benefits. As power was decided by the law of the fist, making sure one's own were capable of administering justice was a sensible precaution. Shandong had a particularly strong reputation and outsiders were said to exercise caution even when dealing with the province's women and children.

It was here that Koh Chun and his companions found themselves in the first year of their trip when they heard of a violent dispute. Two villages with a history of discord were generating enough bad blood for the entire region. Whether there was a specific spark point for the latest round of feuding was unclear. But when the West Village came across a renowned fighter they sensed an opportunity to inflict a defeat on their rivals. They set up a *lei tai*, a raised platform used for fighting, and issued their challenge.

The tradition of lei tai goes back centuries. The setting up of one could arise from a variety of circumstances. A master might want to assert personal dominance or the supremacy of his art. A rival, dubious of another's claims, could wish to issue a challenge. Or a personal dispute might act as catalyst for lei tai's pugilistic mediation.

One thing was certain: a lei tai champion needed to be a supreme fighter. Lei tais followed winner-stays-on rules. Someone wanting to declare and then assert their superiority could be challenged by tens of opponents. It might take weeks of challengers, sometimes on a back-to-back basis, before a master's primacy could be declared.

There were very few rules. No holds or strikes were barred. The only regulations applied to the ending of battle – a fight was considered won if a fighter was forced from the stage, submitted or became incapacitated. Over the course of a lei tai, countless fighters could be injured, some maimed, and an unlucky few might even lose their lives.

The West Village had not set up a sporting competition. Having secured a lethal fighter, their intention was to inflict a devastating blow on the neighbours they despised.

A great deal is made about face in Asian cultures. The concept is not alien to countries outside the region, and in essence the mix of respect, honour, dignity and pride is common to all. But despite the similarities there is a difference, and it lies in the significance that is attached.

To many in Asia it would be considered an honour to pick up the tab at a restaurant for the face it would bring, even if this meant being left out of pocket. An undesirable home that could be hidden from others might be considered acceptable if it afforded a prestigiously branded car that could be displayed to all. And an impossible challenge might be accepted if this averted the loss of face declination would bring.

And so it was that the East Village felt compelled to send their martial artists into battle when challenged by their enemy. They weren't ignorant of the champion's reputation and they were aware of the negligible chances their fighters had. But they would sacrifice these young men before they surrendered the honour of their village.

The West Village's fighter made his living on lei tais. Success for a travelling lei tai fighter could be measured in his continued ability to breathe, walk and talk unimpaired. Early retirement was forced on all but the best. This man not only remained in rude health but he brought with him a particularly brutal reputation.

Known as *Tai Hor*, literally Lei Tai Tiger, receiving his punch without parry was said to result in certain internal injury. And while there may have been dispute over the numbers it was generally agreed he had dispatched opponents from life as well as stage.

While the Shandong grapevine could not be believed without question, it appeared that the first few days of the lei tai had seen him add one more to his tally. But the East Village had their face to maintain. They could not back down from their bitter rivals. So the destruction meted out by fist and foot continued. It was in the midst of this violent carnival that Koh Chun and his entourage arrived. The dispute was the talk of the province and the villagers were delighted to find virgin ears to hear the tale.

Life was not easy for a Shandong peasant and a juicy vendetta was a welcome distraction from their daily toil. The monks were less enthralled by the scandal. Instead of revelling in the feuding, they felt obliged to resolve it. They hastened to the village the next day.

As a predominant belief system in China, Buddhism, and by extension Buddhist monks, were generally treated with respect. But the villages were immersed in their hostilities and afforded more reverence to the feud. When the monks made their well-intentioned intervention they were given a blunt response. If they wanted to involve themselves in the villages' affairs they could prove themselves worthy on the lei tai. If they were unwilling or unable they should leave the villagers to settle the dispute in their own way.

It was clear from the stories swirling through the province that to enter the lei tai would expose the monks to danger. Furthermore, the East Village had not done much to suggest they were deserving of protection, despite their obvious need. Yet the monks were of a mind. Unnecessary suffering was being inflicted and they had the capability to put it to an end. Their obligation was clear.

The task before them was not easy. That evening the first monk took to the stage. He had years of training behind him and was an accomplished fighter. In the opening minutes his light-footed technique was the more impressive and murmurs could be heard in the crowd as they sensed an upset.

But a gap in his defences allowed one of his opponent's sickeningly heavy blows to land in his ribs. Momentarily doubled over and defenceless, he was brutally dispatched.

It took a brave man to follow the champion's display of power. Koh Chun's fellow monk was such a man. Unfortunately he was no more able to repel Tai Hor's strength and he too was expelled without ceremony.

His was the last fight of the night but the following evening's hostilities started with equally bad fortune for the wandering monks. Two others were struck with such venom they suffered internal injury. The second of them would later die as a result. Of the five, only Koh Chun now remained.

Quite what he must have felt on entering the lei tai is unknown. He must have known he was possessed of exceptional ability and he must have held the confidence that this brings. Yet his brother monks had been far from unaccomplished and witnessing their demolition was surely as demoralising as it was distressing.

Whatever the emotions stirring within, Koh Chun did not hesitate when it was his turn to step into the ring.

The best fighters are the ones able to adapt to their opponent. In theory that is straightforward; in a duel it is more easily said than done. From the imprecise accounts there are of the battle it would seem that Koh Chun took some punishment in the early stages. To the onlookers it looked as though another holy man was going to go down as he parried and manoeuvred in search of his opponent's weakness. But they underestimated Koh Chun, for he was one of those with the physical and mental ability to change tack during a fight.

From fighting in a conventional style he switched to lohan monkey, incorporating the power of the lohan style with the trickery and agility of monkey. [Lohan – or *arhat* in Sanskrit – represents a high-level Buddhist who has achieved enlightenment. In acknowledgement of lohans, the word also represents a powerful Shaolin style.]

The exact details of the fight are not on record. One story has it that the monk lured Tai Hor into launching a punch, only to collapse down and deliver a telling blow to his opponent's groin. What is known is that by using his amended technique it was Koh Chun who was left standing at its conclusion, and he who 'owned' the lei tai.

With his victory Koh Chun gained the attention of the province. Kung fu fighters were to China what the gunslingers were to the American West, and he found himself the subject of great acclaim. But it was not this he was seeking. His only goal had been an end to the villagers' battle, and with a peace of sorts achieved, he set off on his quest again, now alone.

10

RIGHT. EVEN WHEN WRONG

In his pursuit of knowledge, Koh Chun made good on his pledge to travel the length and breadth of his country. He visited the Five Peaks and studied in numerous temples along the way. What he learned and where he learned it is for the most part undocumented but some of the monasteries he visited were famed for their medicine and martial arts and it is likely he made the most of his opportunities while he was there.

It's doubtful Koh Chun expected the trip to get easier after its hazardous start but if he did this belief was to be frequently disproved. Wandering through land they considered their territory he was at the mercy of bandits and he was forced to resist attacks. The worst of these was in Sichuan Province when he was hit by a poisoned dart with only his medical training to save him from an unpleasant death.

But four years into his odyssey, his travels were adjourned. The reason was a monk called Huay Jin.

Even less is known about Huay Jin than Koh Chun but his martial arts were proclaimed to be without equal. Koh

Chun himself had already progressed to an advanced level, so for him to present himself as a potential disciple is an indication of Huay Jin's ability. Yet it almost didn't happen.

Huay Jin was a highly principled man, and an extremely strict master. As with many of the traditional sifus he appeared to have a complete disregard for egalitarianism when it came to kung fu. Only those possessed of innate and exceptional talent would receive his tuition. Even then ability alone would not suffice. Huay Jin's demands for unswerving good character and impeccable morality ruled out others who might have expected to find a place in his set.

Koh Chun met the requirements and was taken on as a disciple. But after accepting the new monk, Huay Jin began to harbour doubts. His concerns were founded in the newcomer's character. He did not question his goodness or his compassion but he did worry that Koh Chun's will was too strong and his temper too quick. Until his unease was dispelled he decided to provide spiritual teaching only to his newest disciple. Koh Chun would not learn kung fu.

As setbacks go it was formidable. But as usual in the face of adversity Koh Chun did not allow himself to be disheartened. Instead he grew more determined. He resolved to learn covertly.

As he was staying in the temple it wasn't difficult to manoeuvre himself into proximity to his master and sihengs when they trained. Koh Chun surreptitiously watched them, memorised their steps, and waited. When night came and temple life was at an end he would sneak into one of the courtyards and practise what he had observed.

While enterprising, it was not a plan without flaws. The logistics in particular were decidedly imperfect. The temple's living quarters lacked en suite facilities and it was never free of some comings and goings whatever the time. In such conditions regular night-time practice was unlikely to remain secret for long and Koh Chun faced a quandary in the balance of risk to reward. He was deliberately disobeying his master and the consequences of discovery were not something he wished to dwell on.

It was not long before he was forced to. When word of Koh Chun's clandestine activities found their way to his sifu he was summoned to the chambers of the head monk. Gossip flares in temples no less easily than it does outside them and he received a warning he was facing expulsion. Had he considered it earlier he would probably have concluded this was the most likely scenario arising from his actions. But he had been painstakingly avoiding such deliberation and now, confronted with the possibility, he was distraught. He made his way to his master, desperate to avert the likely outcome.

Faced by a particularly stern-looking Huay Jin, Koh Chun knew there was credence to the rumours. Before an explanation could be demanded from him, he threw himself upon his sifu's mercy and begged his forgiveness. A master is always right, even when he's wrong, so even if Koh Chun's actions had been defensible, by disobeying Huay Jin his behaviour was nonetheless amiss.

Apologies complete, Koh Chun hastened to convince his master of the merit of his conduct before Huay Jin could intervene with a dreaded edict.

His explanation was one of almost complete conviction. His love of Buddhism and martial arts was deep-rooted and genuine. Having found a master whose knowledge of both he revered, the news that he could only learn one had been a major blow. Despite his desire to follow his master's direction to the letter, doing so would have forfeited the knowledge he so valued and desired. This dilemma had erroneously led him to stray from his master's directives.

Koh Chun also raised the dangers he was exposed to when collecting alms for the temple. As he was a target for society's less scrupulous, skills with which he could defend himself were a necessity. Given his existing ability the second part of his defence may have been somewhat disingenuous. But as he listened Huay Jin's expression began to soften enough for Koh Chun to at least hope that he might avoid the worst.

Koh Chun's task was helped by his other conduct. This particular insubordination apart, he had proved himself a diligent and hard-working disciple. Even his extra-curricular night-time study, although unacceptable in its disobedience, held a positive in the dedication it revealed.

At the end of his exhausting defence Koh Chun was not spared a savage scolding, but at its end came a reward. He would not only be permitted to stay at the temple, Huay Jin declared he would be allowed to learn. But it was on a proviso. He would not have permission to teach anyone else.

For the next eleven years Koh Chun dedicated himself in his entirety to his studies, practising relentlessly. At the end of the period he was a formidable exponent of Shaolin kung fu.

11

PASSING ON THE ART

After such an extensive amount of learning many people might consider their education complete. But Koh Chun's wandering spirit took him off again, this time to South-East Asia. As he travelled through Indonesia, Burma, Thailand and India he would again have reason to be grateful for his martial arts.

Crossing a river one day in Burma, the boat on which he was travelling was stopped by *er pah* – extortionists who claimed 'taxes' for entry to 'their' territory. They were demanding payment for the passengers to disembark and did not grant exemptions to monks.

As a monk, Koh Chun asked for alms only as necessary and was rarely in possession of money. Unable to make payment even had he wished to, he directed the boatman to set off again and dock further downstream. If they did not land in the er pah's territory, he did not see how they could make claim to any taxes. It was not a view they shared.

Not long after disembarking Koh Chun realised he was being followed. He quickened his pace but to no avail. His pursuers soon caught up and surrounded him. Again a demand for money was made and again Koh Chun explained he had none. Yet they remained determined to get something from him. He could pay from his pocket to sate their greed or pay with his well-being to satisfy their violent intent. With the money not forthcoming they decided to make their claim on his health. It was a mistake.

Dim mak, when translated literally from its Chinese characters, means 'press meridian'. More famously it is known as the death touch. As the nickname suggests it is a formidable skill to possess. Its fundamentals bear relation to acupuncture. But whereas acupuncture uses small needles to clear acupoints and enhance energy flows in the body's meridians, dim mak uses pressure to attack them. It is claimed that an accurately administered attack will block these points, disrupting the body's flow of energy and even blood. This can result in paralysis or even death if vital organs are deprived of their needs.

Koh Chun knew dim mak and he accepted the responsibility that accompanied the art. It was a weapon of last resort. Surrounded by a group of agitated er pahs he decided this was an appropriate occasion. As the first man to attack came forward, instead of stepping away Koh Chun moved in. Avoiding his opponent's strike, he countered with an iron-hard finger which stabbed at a meridian.

To the rest of the gang it was not clear what happened. They saw one of their number move in as they had seen others do before. But this time, in a flurry of robes, the attacker and not the attacked went down. And he went down hard, collapsing as if dead. Most unsettlingly, he did so without any apparent strike; no punch, kick or claw.

The collective momentum of the group halted as abruptly as their compatriot's collapse. They were violent men more used to inflicting blows but they were not afraid of being hit. But to see one of their group taken out so efficiently and with such little effort by this unassuming monk caused a frisson of fear to course through the group. They fled.

With the stakes of its application so high, knowing how to undo the effects of dim mak is as important as learning to administer them. Once the danger had gone Koh Chun turned his attention to the prone man. Applying his knowledge of remedy, he revived the er pah and sent him on his way.

After a year travelling through Asia, Koh Chun's travels ended in Indonesia. His first master, Shing Liang, had died while abbot of a temple in Medan and Koh Chun was asked to replace him. For the next twenty years it would be his base.

Koh Chun's achievements were notable in the circles in which he moved and he would have lived on in the histories of the temples to which he contributed. But his story would probably not have reached a wider audience had he not made a momentous decision fourteen years into his stay at Medan's Chn Yuen Kung Temple.

By 1941 there were few corners of the world not engulfed by the horrors of the Second World War. Having devoted his life to countering misery, Koh Chun felt despondent at the suffering being inflicted beyond his control. While unable to make a difference in the grand scheme of things, he was determined to affect positive change in his own realm. His belief in the benefits of kung fu remained unswerving. But his sihengs had all passed away and he was ageing himself. It was time for his master's art to be passed to a new generation.

But he had made a vow to Huay Jin twenty-five years earlier and it was one he could not break without his sifu's blessing. This was a complicated undertaking; Huay Jin had already passed away and was unable to attest to the increased emotional maturity of his disciple. Koh Chun wrote instead to one of Huay Jin's siheng. Only a trusted brother from his sifu's generation could carry the authority to grant Koh Chun's request.

The wait for a response must have been agonising. Yet it can only have increased Koh Chun's joy when it came. Huay Jin's siheng had agreed to Koh Chun's appeal. His master's legacy could now be continued.

12

THE FIFTIETH GENERATION

Sek Koh Chun and Sugong's paths crossed as a result of the blood brothers. Two that Sugong met on the boat started training soon after their arrival. Knowing of Sugong's passion for martial arts they encouraged him to join.

It wasn't as easy as signing up to a modern-day school. When the brothers had approached Sek Koh Chun they found him seemingly more interested in turning them away than taking them in.

'How many of you want to learn?' he demanded.

'There are four of us, sifu.'

'If I decide to teach you I'll devote a great deal of time and energy. I'll expect even more from you in return. You'll have to train hard and you'll have to make sacrifices. Are you ready to do that?'

'Yes we are.'

A glib promise was not going to be enough.

'There are terms to which you must agree if I am going to teach you,' he continued. 'If you accept me as your master you must promise to train seriously for at least three years. Once you enter the temple you will not be

80

allowed out. I'll make an exception if you have to work or have family commitments. Then you can go to your job, but you must go there directly from the temple, and come straight back. If you can't stay in the temple you'll need to come here before work, report back immediately after and go home only to sleep.'

The potential disciples had not been lying when they affirmed their commitment but they had not quite expected this. They looked at one another nervously, before their question-and-answer exchange of glances and nods resulted in consensus. They agreed.

'You must be prepared for hard work,' Koh Chun went on. 'And you need to know its benefits won't be immediate. For the first three months you'll do only the basics: stance-work, foot-work, running, punching and kicking. You will learn more after that but don't be mistaken; it will get harder, not easier.'

Again, after some concerned glances, the young men concurred.

But just because they felt themselves capable and appropriate, it didn't mean that Koh Chun did. He took them individually to another room and grilled them, enquiring into their backgrounds, their families, their hopes and aspirations. Even then they did not find out if they would be accepted.

'Come back on Friday. I'll tell you then if I'm going to teach you.'

Only on their return were they allowed to become disciples.

A few months later it was Sugong's turn. After announcing his presence, he sat down to wait for the man he hoped would become his master. After Sugong had nervously fidgeted for a few minutes Koh Chun appeared.

Sugong was immediately struck by his domination of the room. It wasn't that he was a physically imposing man. He was not much taller than Sugong and what the slight monk had in additional height Sugong more than compensated for in brawn.

The most immediate way in which Koh Chun's presence asserted itself was through his face. His dark eyes were not unusual in shape but they were striking in their intensity. From the fiercest stare to the friendliest of looks, once caught in their sights it was impossible to evade their compulsion.

The impact of his eyes was accentuated by the eyebrows that capped them. Thick and black, they lent further authority to his countenance, their vitality contradicting the sixty years lived by their owner.

His other features were not exceptional individually. His nose was a fair size, his lips were thick and their facial housing notable only for a lack of wrinkles. But when combined and commanded by their owner's strength of character they came alive, unique in malleability and the force of personality they expressed.

When looking to make a lifetime commitment to a master, the goal is a sifu who knows what he stands for and has the strength to stand for it. In Koh Chun, Sugong got the sense of such a man.

Before he could be accepted as a disciple he had to go through his screening. As they made their way between rooms he felt the burn of Koh Chun's eyes. He later learned this cursory physical assessment was enough to have potential students rejected. Koh Chun might be willing to make some exceptions to imperfection if he felt someone especially worthy but this flexibility was not applied to character. Perceived shortcomings here met with outright rejection.

Koh Chun evidently had no such reservations with Sugong. Unlike the first batch, he was not subject to a nerve-jangling wait to find out his fate. A brisk order – 'Follow me' – and they were on their way. Koh Chun led him to the main hall, seated himself on a chair and motioned Sugong to kneel on the cushion he placed before him. The hall's large Buddha looked on.

A temple employee hurriedly brought in tea and oranges before taking similarly quick leave. Sugong set both down at his side, composed himself and began. He held out the cup of tea with outstretched arms and bowed with the word 'Sifu', an acknowledgement of the role the monk would hold for life. Sek Koh Chun received the tea and placed it at his side. Sugong then repeated the motions with an orange, also ceremonially received. His final bow was performed with his hands empty, palms pressed together.

He remained on his knees when he straightened from the last bow. The ceremony was not yet complete. He now had to swear to oaths that would form the moral guidelines of his new life. They included, among others, vows to develop the good within him and relegate the bad and to be loyal and righteous toward friends, students and his master. Altogether he made thirty-six pledges.

The last vow made, Sugong was now officially a disciple of Koh Chun. But his sifu was not quite finished. He strode off, leaving Sugong to again hurry in his footsteps, this time to the Bodhidharma altar. There were no further oaths required here but both men pressed their hands together and bowed in respect to the patriarch of Shaolin.

Sugong was now his descendant, one of the fiftieth generation of Shaolin. The western calendar recorded the year as 1948. To Sugong it was year zero.

13

AUNTS, AUNTS AND OPIUM

Sugong may have felt that life's foundations had been ripped up and relaid, but others were less willing to acknowledge the quantum shift that had occurred. He had stopped working in Red-Faced Auntie's trishaw shop after a few months. There was a fee for relocating Chinese to Singapore, and in Sugong's case his monthly 'Straits Settlement money' came to far more than he could afford. Earning nowhere near enough to pay his considerable sum he had found work at the port as a labourer. Although the money was slightly better, a further three months down the line he was still way behind in his debts. Red-Faced Auntie came to find him.

To be an economic migrant is to be a target for society's less scrupulous. Modern people-smugglers entrap their victims into servitude through debt and threat, and things were no different in 1948. With a low income and a large liability, Sugong was short on options. So when his creditor told him she had work for him he wasn't in a position to refuse. The job was bike couriering.

Compared to some of the jobs migrants were forced into it didn't seem too bad. But the devil lay in the detail.

Sugong wasn't to ferry documents between corporations. He would have to deliver opium.

It was not an assignment that pleased him. In terms of self-preservation it was far from ideal. Fresh-off-the-boat immigrants were unlikely to have their stays extended if caught up in crime. As delivery boy, Sugong stood at the sharp end of the risk and the blunt end of reward.

He also had personal objections. While not adverse to bending a few rules, he had always made an effort to adhere to his own moral framework. Opportunities for ill-gotten gain had been available to him over the years, and he had taken pride in turning them down. Now he was to be forced into exactly the kind of work he had avoided, with Red-Faced Auntie the only beneficiary.

For all of his objections the work itself was straight-forward and not particularly taxing. He would load his bicycle with a bundle at one address, cycle to another and make the delivery. But bicycles had not proved auspicious for Sugong and their curse would persist.

After about three months in the 'job', he arrived laden at a junction where a policeman was directing traffic. Had he continued as he was there would not have been a problem. But uncomfortable in his predicament, and by no means a natural in the saddle, Sugong panicked.

Greater cycling abilities may still have seen the situation pass without incident. But nervous and highly strung, he twitched at the handlebars, unintentionally jerking the front wheel to the side. Sugong continued on the trajectory the bike had been following. His cycle, however, clattered to the ground. With his forward momentum now executed *sans* bike he was catapulted head-over-heels to land in an undignified heap.

When his tumble was complete, Sugong did not share the amusement of the giggling onlookers. As he had gone airborne, his delivery had followed suit. It now lay halfway between him and his uniformed nemesis. He scrambled forward terrified and bundled it back up, looking anywhere but at the policeman. He flung the parcel in the bike's basket, leapt back on and pedalled away as fast as his incompetence would allow, the bike weaving wildly in his frenzy.

Expecting to be pursued and caught at any moment, he pushed the vehicle to its limits. Tyres squealed in protest as he mounted kerbs and skidded around corners and Sugong's lungs soon burned with the ferocity of the wheels. When he had still not been detained after a couple of minutes, he allowed himself a glance behind, certain it would reveal a horde of gaining pursuers. But he found no sign of a chase. Relieved, his heartbeat eased and his senses returned. A more extensive scoping of his surroundings brought comfort through familiarity. If he continued in the same direction he would arrive in Hong Lim market. This was a stroke of luck as he had an auntie, a real one, who lived nearby.

On arriving he flung down his bike at the gate, flew into her yard and pounded on the door. When it opened, he burst in, slamming it shut behind him. Sweating, gasping for breath, his eyes wild, Sugong was quite a sight. Used to his temperamental behaviour, Auntie Quek fixed him with a weary stare and awaited the explanation.

Had he been in the frame of mind to come out with an excuse it would have needed to be a good one to justify his entrance, his appearance and an armful of opium. He wasn't. As he blurted out the truth, Auntie Quek's expression turned from quizzical to something more reproachful and her lips pursed ominously.

The Quek temper was not unique to Sugong. His aunt had mastered its nuances years before he was born and she wasted little time in giving him the benefit of her experience. With his ears ringing from the rebuke, Sugong still found himself in possession of an unwelcome stash of opium. Circumstance would combine with his blood auntie to rid him of it and any future bundles.

News of the commotion spread, and rumour soon had it that Sugong was in custody. With delivery failing to reach client and Sugong nowhere to be found, Red-Faced Auntie assumed that he had been caught and the opium confiscated. This opened the door to some business on the side.

But despite the temptation, Sugong was far more keen to rid himself of the opium and its associations than he was to become immersed deeper in its world. He had further encouragement in the form of an angry aunt. As pro-active as she was fierce, she had a message conveyed to Red-Faced Auntie. The unwanted stash was to be removed from her home. Immediately.

The bundle was worth considerably more than Sugong's debt. By returning it, he felt a repayment of sorts had been made. Auntie Quek was of the same mind and expressed the view to Red-Faced Auntie with no little force. Faced with facts and a lady as formidable as herself, Red-Faced Auntie agreed. Sugong was debt-free and at liberty to retire from his servitude.

Although extracted from one delicate situation, Sugong lived in an environment where it would only be a matter of time before he became embroiled in another. He didn't want to be a drug courier. He didn't want to be a pimp. And he didn't want to be a gangster. All he really wanted was to be able to earn enough to eat, and to train. But life in the less prosperous corners of Singapore did not afford dreams easily in the 1940s, even if they were as limited as Sugong's. As things stood he could only see two scenarios: prison or the temple.

In terms of austerity there wasn't much between them. But the temple had kung fu, and it had Sek Koh Chun. He chose Siong Lim.

14

AN ANGRY MONK

Training with Sek Koh Chun was not easy. Sweat would be broken before dawn did. Warm-ups would involve the disciples running around the temple roofs in the stifling Singaporean heat with weights strapped to their legs. Then the hard graft would begin. And when training had finished for the morning, it was off to the port for a day's labour. Back-breaking work complete and there would be a further three hours with an angry monk.

For the blood, sweat and tears were the easy part. The real problem was Koh Chun's temper.

It was not an area where Sugong was easily impressed but in the head monk he recognised a man on another level. If there was one thing that surprised him more than his master's fierceness it was the manner in which it was expressed. Koh Chun had an unexpectedly rich and extensive understanding of the more colourful corners of the Hokkien language. And he would unleash it without mercy on the unfortunate cause of his ill-humour.

The abbot's lack of patience and demanding standards were a challenge to all of his students. But just as difficult were his teaching methods. A demonstration of steps and stances is a common way to teach martial arts, but while Koh Chun would sometimes perform the moves in an explosion of swirling robes for the most part he was having none of it. He would sit and direct his disciples verbally from wherever he was perched.

'Forward stance, grasp with the left, punch with the right. NO, WITH THE RIGHT. What's the point in you being here if you're not going to listen to my instructions? Are you stupid or are you trying to see how far you can push me?'

The scoldings were applied liberally and they were dreaded. Even worse were the times when a mistake resulted in a turn of the head, a dismissive wave of the hand and the quiet but firm order:

'Go.'

It didn't get much easier for the students when they were on the right path. Those hoping an accurate interpretation of his instructions would result in inversely proportionate praise were disappointed. A brisk 'Yes, that's right' was as effusive as it got.

Patience did not appear to be a virtue in the eyes of their sifu. After teaching something, Sek Koh Chun would expect it to be mastered quickly. And once it was taught that was it. No more instructions; no hints or reminders. From then on it was to be performed without flaw. Students were taught only once.

Anyone thinking himself lucky to see Koh Chun begin meditation during practice was also in for a rude awakening. With the master's eyes closed and his focus apparently elsewhere, it appeared an opportunity to escape a tongue-lashing. This was not the case. Even the smallest of mistakes would still be caught by the fiery monk.

'Why haven't you been practising? Why should I waste my time teaching you if you're not going to put in any effort?'

Converting the monk's verbal instructions into physical actions was extremely difficult at the best of times. Some just weren't capable. The presence of their terrifyingly bad-tempered sifu upped the ante and even students with the capability could go to pieces. They were scolded until they improved or left.

The more fortunate departees went of their own accord. The less lucky were denied the choice. If Koh Chun felt the requisite effort was not being exerted, the disciple would be dismissed and told not to return. Once the door closed it didn't open again.

Even personal practice was problematic. Koh Chun would not accept that in the course of memorising a sequence, speed and power might be sacrificed while the movements were drilled into muscle memory. Another scolding would ensue. The disciples soon learned to do their own training on the grounds outside the temple.

When they trained inside it was a sight to behold. Koh Chun had a formidable knowledge of Shaolin and this gave him an array of options. When presented with a new student he would size them up and consider their stature. Someone small and nimble might specialise in monkey-style. Another, more powerful and imposing, tiger.

Groups of students or individuals would be stationed in different areas of the temple grounds, each practising their own thing. Some would have sandbags tied to their legs as they jumped up courtyard walls and ran around the temple roof. Others would be in a corner, forearms thudding against one another's, as they conditioned their limbs. More still would be stationed in the halls and courtyards, practising their forms.

There were a few universals all knew to follow. Not slacking off was a given. Scoldings were harsh enough when they did try to follow instructions. The students also knew not to question their sifu. They were to do what they were told until they were told not to. Answers would either be found through practice or provided by their sifu; but only when he decided the time was right.

Just as importantly, they should mind their own business. They would be taught what was appropriate when it was appropriate, and it would be Koh Chun who made the decision. Sticking their nose into their *hengdai*'s business was not tolerated. (A hengdai is a brother in learning, the seniority of whom is not indicated.)

Koh Chun showed no inclination to explain his reasons for his segmented teaching. One possibility was likely to have been the time and care he took tailoring his teaching to an individual. His efforts would be undermined by the same student trying to develop his own curriculum.

Tradition and history may also have played a role. The repute of the Shaolin Temple meant it held an allure for those wanting to achieve martial excellence. At times a martial arts swap-shop of sorts, the alumni ranged from generals to rougher sorts whose interest lay in one-on-one warfare. With students not always matching high Buddhist ideals, it is said that knowledge was imparted carefully. The higher arts were supposed to have been taught only to long-term disciples who had proved their genuine intent through the years.

It was a practice that endured at Siong Lim. There would be no fast-track.

Koh Chun's teaching methods created a diverse and varied training ground, and enabled him to pass on a wide spectrum of knowledge. They also contributed, unintentionally, toward a competitive atmosphere of an unusual kind.

That there was a degree of rivalry was unsurprising. The temple was filled with young men fanatically dedicated to learning their art. In such circumstances it was inevitable that some would want to be recognised as the best. But making that claim was difficult. There were standard forms that were practised by all of the students. But when it came to the more specialised they were unable to compare like-for-like with their hengdai. It wasn't just that they were taught different forms, they weren't even supposed to watch the others as they practised, let alone cast judgement.

But there was a hierarchy. Koh Chun had numerous duties at the temple and he had to be frugal with his time. This resulted in him focusing his attention on a select group, disciples he had identified as the best. Only they would receive extensive personal tuition. The others would still be taken on as disciples, they would sometimes be supervised as part of a group, and on occasion they might even be taught directly. But the majority of their tuition would come from the seniors.

For the monks it must have been a surreal experience. Siong Lim was not even a Shaolin temple, but one from the Caodong sect. (While Koh Chun was a Shaolin disciple of Huay Jin, he was ordained in Caodong and it was through this lineage that he was invited to Siong Lim. While separate to Shaolin, Caodong is a sect of Chan Buddhism.) The monks had been carrying out their duties in conventional Caodong manner before Koh Chun took charge. Now they were suddenly faced with swarms of kung fu disciples running around the courtyard, jumping walls, hitting bags and breaking bricks.

Training was open to them but only one or two accepted the offer. Fortunately many of their number were young men who shared similar backgrounds to the disciples. So despite their different motives for being in the temple, good relations and friendships developed. They lived in the same compound, shared the same facilities, and would eat and chat at mealtimes like any other group of friends or colleagues.

The monks also knew they had Koh Chun to thank for the rescue and rejuvenation of the temple, and the presence of the disciples for its continued protection. Even if they did have objections they would have taken care in the way they chose to air them. The importance of temple discipline wasn't relevant only to the martial arts disciples, and they were not the only ones wary of his temper.

Despite the hardship, learning from Koh Chun was a joy. For all of his fierceness he was revered. Those able to live with his scoldings knew they were his way of raising their levels and that kindness and affection underpinned them. When he wasn't admonishing them into shape, he treated them with the fondness of extended family and he expected fellow students to view one another in the same vein.

There was also an unswerving belief in the art he taught. It's a common feature of students to believe their school or system to be the best. In a way they are all right; martial arts tend to share at least some common traits and the style that suits an individual is likely the best for him or her.

What created such appeal in the branch of Shaolin Koh Chun taught was its lineage. The fact that it had remained in the hands of so few in its recent history undoubtedly gave it allure. Its breadth and depth made it even more appealing.

China is a huge country, and kung fu has a long history. (The Chinese characters for 'kung fu' literally translate to something more like 'excellence' or 'skilled activity'. They can in fact be applied to any art or application. While Chinese will refer to the martial art as *wushu*, 'kung fu' is used throughout this book as it has come to be understood in English.) Numerous styles have emerged from its different regions as a result. While a martial art such as taekwondo has relatively few main branches, kung fu lives a far less regulated existence.

With its long history, evolving nature, and migration to far-flung lands, Shaolin diverged from a single unified existence. Further to the different broad lines of development in north and south, a huge range of specialised styles emerged in both. The broad, elegant moves of white crane (peh hok) contrast with the explosive power of lohan. Mei hua (plum blossom) can be slow and fluid in style (although this differs by school), while tiger powerfully rips and claws all before it. There are tens of different variants, each with their own distinguishing techniques.

Originally, most would have been the preserve of monks (although some were created by laymen). But over time they spread and developed among commoners, reaching a level of specialisation which led many schools to focus on just one particular style. The refinement of their martial art meant that some Shaolin monks may also have devoted themselves to a specialisation. But by living and training at the source of many of the others, it is likely they had both the opportunity and an obligation to learn at least the fundamentals of a larger range.

Shaolin temples accepted lay disciples. They also had monks who left for lives outside the clergy. But while Shaolin kung fu did not remain the sole preserve of monks, some of the secrets probably did not leave. These were passed down only to monks. And only ones that had proven themselves over long, hard years.

With the turbulence inflicted on Shaolin in the first half of the 20th century, finding such a monk was not an easy task. Sek Koh Chun was one. When he finally started to teach, it wasn't for money as he did not charge for lessons. It wasn't for glory as he had no desire for that. He taught because he loved the art and wanted to propagate it and ensure it prospered.

An angry monk

Many teachers may be forced to compromise to attract students, maintain school numbers and earn the money they need to survive. Koh Chun had no such inclination. He was well aware of the worth of his endowment and he had no interest in playing to weakness or whims.

Someone wanting a hobby or a boost to their ego? Prepare for a tongue-lashing before expulsion. A desire to learn and a willingness to work hard? Good. They could learn. But it wouldn't be easy.

15

Less isn't more

Michael joined me a couple of months into my stay. After seven years killing himself for a Japanese bank he had decided to take a year off, travelling the length of South America to recharge his batteries. When I set off on my kung fu sabbatical it didn't take much to persuade him to extend his trip for a couple of months.

Normally of reasonable intelligence, when together we were reduced by our pursuit of *est*. What est it was didn't matter. Whether eating a hamburger in the fewest bites or tackling the hottest chillies in the Brick Lane Curry Eating Competition it only mattered that the other didn't achieve it.

Finding ourselves in one another's pockets for near-on twenty-four hours a day wasn't the best way to curb our stupidity. Before long any activity, from speed of eating to length of massage, became occasions of winners and losers.

Fortunately we found an outlet where we could unite.

We adhered to a strict policy of first in, last out. We had grudgingly accepted that, short of stopping our training to concentrate solely on weights, there would always be bodybuilders to out-lift us in the gym. But the sauna was different. It was the great equaliser. It didn't care about size or stamina. It was all about attitude.

We had the added advantage of being the only ones aware of the competition. Two scoops of water on the coals would hot things up and weed out the young, weak or sick. A couple more would be added in heat-resistant company.

A six-scooper would be saved for only the most demanding of circumstances, requiring, as it did, a towel to be placed over our faces to prevent our lungs being burnt by the resultant steam.

It ended as quickly as it began. Having happily seen off a novice we eyed the Malay man suspiciously on entry, his self-confidence troubling to us both. Turning to the coals he spread open his towel with the enthusiasm of a first-time flasher, remaining static for five minutes of slow-roasting. Curious needs sated, he towelled up and departed without any acknowledgement of unusual behaviour.

Competitive sauna was never mentioned again.

The reason we were able to indulge our sauna peculiarities was the central role the gym played in our schedule. We might not have been at work but we certainly weren't on holiday.

Our daily routine would see night prematurely invaded by 'day', with the metallic tones of a phone alarm inducing distraught semi-consciousness at five. By 5.30 we would be roadside at Jalan Pudu to hail a taxi. 5.31 and a first would be dismissed for a ridiculously inflated price. 5.32 and a second would have waved us away, the district of Cheras where Sugong lived notorious for its morning traffic. By 5.35 we would be off, bounced around in the back of a plastic-seated Proton (Malaysia's much-maligned national car), suspension squeaking and brakes straining as the driver attempted to reach our destination and turn back as quickly as he could.

At 6.00 we would unlock the doors to the hall, switch on the lights and fans and sweep the concrete floors. As we did a cockerel would cheerfully remind us of the ridiculous hour.

Then some stretching, and a greeting to Sugong as he invariably switched off the fans and our only chance of salvation from the heat, the breeze they provided apparently damaging to chi.

'Sugong, cha' (Good morning, Sugong) was quickly followed by hellos to CG, Mr Tan, Ro, Master Wong and Florence. Then training would start.

By 8.30 we would have gone through a couple of T-shirts, our extensive fluid intake outpaced by overworked sweat glands. Just before the point of evaporation, Sugong would replace his watch, pull his Montagut over his vest and we would know it was time for breakfast. (Montagut is a French brand of polo shirt seemingly only available in the East. To Chinese men of a certain generation it holds the allure of Prada, Armani and Gucci all rolled into one. Sugong was of the generation and ensured every one he owned was of the brand.)

Breakfast itself could last almost as long as training, especially if Sugong was feeling playful. When he was, neither Michael nor I were safe from impromptu demonstrations. They inevitably ended with us rubbing fast-reddening hands while Sugong beamed, satisfied his iron palm had lost none of its efficacy.

By ten we would be off in Mr Tan's car negotiating the traffic to the centre of KL. The city's approach to urban planning involves the approval of all and any high-rise buildings (assuming the appropriate palms have been suitably greased). Phase II seems to consist of some hastily crossed fingers, and prayers the city will naturally evolve to cope with its new demands. The road department's response is a new artery or two to the already clogged heart of the city.

As a result morning rush-hour lasted about four or five hours and evening six or seven. We were usually caught in the jams that accumulate at the point they meet.

KL isn't London, New York or Tokyo. While Malaysia has set its sights on being a developed nation by 2020, a decade ahead of deadline, its capital remained a bit crumbly at the edges. Balancing the Twin Towers, the other skyscrapers and the futuristic monorail were the rats scurrying through discarded rubbish in side streets, pre-war buildings that looked like they struggled to make it post-war, and the hawkers and vendors that scrambled to claim whatever street space they could grab. Yet it was this that gave the city its character (maybe not the rats), preventing the perceived sterility of its prim neighbour, Singapore.

Home for us was a condominium in Bukit Bintang – we later found out it was directly opposite a building where Sugong had once run a school – and we would usually return around eleven. Bukit Bintang is set in the centre of KL's 'Golden Triangle', the heart of the city's entertainment and business zone. The main streets' glistening malls and skyscrapers reflect this stature but the neighbourhoods in between are indicative of the hustle and bustle of the city's natural character. Our nearest streets were a hive of activity with restaurants, hawker stalls and pirate DVD sellers all frantically plying their trade.

On our return there would be time for a quick shower before a return to bed. An hour or two later and we would groggily make our way out for lunch in the adjoining roads of Tengkat Tong Shin and Jalan Alor. Lunch finished and after a quick retreat to an internet café, we would head to the gym.

You could have called the gym our second home. Except with more waking hours spent there than at our apartment it was more like our first. The most regular clients, we were treated royally by staff desperate for company during the mid-afternoon hours when the gym was at its emptiest.

Ostensibly, our purpose was to practise whatever we had been taught in the morning by Sugong. But after a couple of hours in the studio we would be ready for the real business: pecs. From the Pyramids to the Empire State Building, man has always yearned to build big. Hard-wired into the psyche is a desire to be imposing on a personal level. Having grown up watching kung fu films that saw small Asian stars annihilate disproportionately large westerners, I had assumed the belief would hold that bigger isn't better. I was wrong. Whoever we trained with was unfailingly impressed by Michael's size – 6ft 3ins and broad – annoyingly I never seemed to make the same impression. The rationale was obvious and the implications of an extra foot in height and stone in muscle plainly visible in their minds.

Sugong was probably the exception. In the same way that I was never sure if he realised he had passed thirty, I don't think he knew he was not a towering 6ft 6ins. While anyone else with a similar relationship between size and attitude might have been accused of a Napoleon complex, Sugong seemed blissfully unaware of any need to compensate for a lack of height. And I don't think anyone had dared to tell him.

He was keen that we beef up, though. A man who would have been aghast at the suggestion that less is more, he wanted us to have more bulk, more power, and if there was anything else we could think of we should have more of that as well. Which was one reason we were working out. The other was the primeval instinct of size.

The most immediate manifestation of this is the common denominating desire among men: an unusually imposing manhood. But this is determined pre-birth by genetic lottery. Pecs are a different matter altogether and Michael and I were determined to help Mother Nature. Not the most scientifically advanced of body-building programmes, our pec-based workout involved heading straight to the various chest-building machines. In the recovery periods between alternating on these we would work on other muscle groups before returning for more.

Upon completion of our various gym-based stupidities we would head to a hawker stall to eat. Then we would make our way home for a DVD if we were in lively mood, or an early night if we were particularly tired. We usually skipped the DVD.

It wasn't the kind of life I imagined for myself looking on from the age of eighteen. Balancing the demands of family, influence and riches would have been more aligned to my youthful expectations. But it was a schedule we were happy with and it would have worked... if it hadn't been for the World Cup.

To me it was the start of a four-yearly paradise. Even Michael, a footballing non-enthusiast, was excited. In theory it was perfect – the ideal reprise from a punishing daily schedule, a connection to home, and the satisfaction of seeing others push themselves to physical extremes. In reality, the six-hour time difference to the host nation Germany had the effect of depriving us of essential sleep and taking our tired bodies to further levels of distress. Getting up at five is not fun at the best of times. It was significantly harder when half the night had been spent watching TV.

We watched the games at a local *mamak* stall. Mamak stalls are a cross between an Indian-run restaurant and hawker stall. Some of their tables and chairs are indoor but the more popular seats lie under whirring fans that hang from corrugated tin roofs outside. They offer mostly

North Indian, Muslim fare including tandoori chicken, curries and Malaysia's adopted national dish, *roti canai*.

Pronounced 'janai', the roti is a bread made by kneading dough with oil. After being subjected to pizza-base-like swirling, it is folded, fried in yet more oil, and served with a bowl of dhal for dunking. It is entirely unhealthy, has a significant impact in reducing life expectancy, and tastes so good it's worth it.

Another common, and in this case more important, feature of the mamak stall is a profligacy of large screens dedicated to sports. Our local had a huge screen set up in the outdoor section at the far wall. And like every other mamak stall in Malaysia it was completely packed from June to July in 2006.

We would fight our way to a couple of chairs and then wait for the action to begin. As often as not this was in the crowd. The English are spoilt for footballing choice with strong local teams completed by a talented, if under-achieving, national one. But the Malaysians benefit from neither, making them the most excitable of neutrals. To the majority supporting the underdog is for losers. Support the team that wins; and if that means changing at some point so be it. But with so many teams in the World Cup, and a lot of them not great powers, there was confusion about who to go for. To see a restaurant full of Malaysians going wild for a Togo goal against Trinidad and Tobago when they knew none of the players in a game that meant nothing was entertainment in itself – if it hadn't been for the morning after.

The matches started at 9pm, midnight or 3am Malaysian time. We tried to schedule our sleeping hours around them, either getting extremely early nights or a couple of shifts before and after a game. But it was no good. We fumbled through most days like a couple of jet-lagged zombies and were inevitably scolded for our lacklustre, error-ridden performance by Sugong.

Less isn't more

Training with Sek Koh Chun might not have been easy. But being taught by his favourite disciple wasn't exactly a walk in the park.

16

Blooding the art

In an ideal world, Sugong would have dedicated 100 per cent of his time to training. Circumstances meant this was not possible. He had to eat, and to do this he had to earn. With his trishaw career at an end, and in possession of no formal qualifications, he was not in a position to cherry-pick the ripest jobs. Which meant that he continued, for the time being, as a coolie at the port.

He kept his eyes open to other opportunities though, and when he heard about a job at a rubber factory he leapt at it. Depending on your expectations of job satisfaction it wasn't much to jump at. It was hard on labour and easy on fulfilment; his role was to carry large rubber sheets between the factory sections for the majority of his day. But it paid considerably more than either of his last two positions and that was all the satisfaction he needed. For Sugong had a plan.

Used to surviving on the most meagre of incomes, Sugong intended on using his new-found 'wealth' to open up opportunities. His debts settled, he could now send some money home, but with Sek Koh Chun's less than liberal views on partying there weren't many other avenues where the remaining money could be spent. So Sugong saved.

He saved well, hoarding away a considerable amount of money within a couple of years. When he thought he had enough he triggered his plan of action. He moved out of the temple and bought three motorbikes: a 500cc Triumph, a 650cc Norton and a 500cc Harrier.

While he loved each like the children he was yet to have there was a business plan behind the purchases. He had found a good spot on Xiamen Street where he could put them on display and he began hiring them out at S$2 an hour.

It started promisingly. For the first couple of weeks they were on constant loan and the money rolled in. Sugong's only complaint was not being able to spend enough time with his babies. The police soon gave him cause for more. Getting a young business registered was a difficult, costly and time-consuming process; one Sugong had not gone through. So when the police came past after a few weeks he had a problem. His situation became trickier still when he was unable to talk himself out of it and the day ended with one of his bikes in the police compound (the other two were fortunately on hire). A vicious cycle began.

Sugong would rent out his bikes from the roadside with a wary eye alert to the sight of his adversaries. He accepted that some level of disruption from the local constabulary was now unavoidable but he hoped that he could earn enough to pay the fines from his profits, an operating cost of sorts.

He would begin work with a prayer that the day would end with the bikes still in his possession. But if his unwelcome visitors arrived he was forced into damage limitation. He would escape on one bike while the others, if not on hire, were grudgingly sacrificed to the pound. He would pay the fines and collect them with an insincere promise not to err again. Then the cat and mouse games would begin anew.

It was not the blueprint on which bike-hire businesses are modelled. Sugong's 'operating costs' soon began to eat into and beyond his profits. Increasingly demoralised – this was not what he had in mind in his pre-venture dreams – Sugong, instead of becoming the Hertz of Singaporean bike-hire, sold the bikes and moved back to Siong Lim.

During the period outside the temple training had remained Sugong's core concern. He didn't have much choice in the matter. But rather than being scared off by his fearsome sifu he had begun to win his respect. It started in the preparations for a demonstration Koh Chun committed to in 1951. It was an election year and as a pre-election event Siong Lim's disciples were asked to show off their martial arts.

Having taught just a handful of forms in a couple of years, Sek Koh Chun fired into action. Of the main disciples he identified a core of five. Each was taught ten forms in the six months prior to the demonstration, every student's different to the others'. It was the opportunity Sugong had been waiting for and he practised like a man possessed. It showed.

On the first day of the demonstration he did a two-man form with one of his siheng. Sugong took the empty-handed side of the combat sequence, his partner the double-sword (a broadsword in each hand). As accomplished and practised as his senior was, Sugong was the more prepared. By the end of the set his siheng's hands were swollen and bruised from Sugong's hard blocks. He was unable to take part the next day.

One of Sugong's *sidai* (junior brother in learning) took his place. He had even less of a chance. To make matters worse, this time Sugong also had a weapon, the three-sectioned stick – three short sticks inter-joined with short lengths of chain – to oppose the junior's staff. Halfway through the form Sugong dodged the blow of his sidai's stick as they had practised, before snapping back his counter-attack, also as planned. But Sugong was faster than his partner and by the time the latter raised the staff to block, Sugong's strike hit him squarely on the head. Blood flowed and the display came to an early end.

After the performance Sugong awaited his master's response in dread. He wasn't sure how Koh Chun would react but he had a fair idea.

He was pleasantly surprised. Instead of the scolding he expected, Sugong found himself the subject of compliments from his delighted sifu. Koh Chun was not a violent man despite his lethal skills, and he took no pleasure in seeing his students hurt, but his view of Shaolin kung fu was not that of a game or a sport and a few cuts and bruises were not going to distress him.

He was more preoccupied with Sugong's progress. Teaching him every day he had of course witnessed an improvement. But it was only the fresh perspective of his performance on stage that revealed the full extent of his development. Koh Chun was more than a little pleased with the fruits of their joint labour.

Having endured a sleepless night of worry at the prospect of a furious Koh Chun, Sugong was delighted to be first greeted warmly and then singled out for praise. Not content to reward his disciple in words only, Koh Chun bestowed favour in deed as well. From that point on the range of forms Sugong would be allowed to learn extended greatly. To a man generally undemonstrative of fondness, it was the greatest sign of affection Siong Lim's abbot could make.

Inevitably it led to some tension with one or two students in the competitive atmosphere of the temple training ground. Koh Chun had no time for the arguments and wrangling.

'What's there to be envious about? He gets up earlier than anyone else and he trains. He gets back from work, and he trains. All he does is train. He trains harder than anyone else. He trains longer than anyone else. What right have you to resent him?'

There were no takers for the chance to answer his rhetorical question.

'And even if you did have the right, are there any of you who wish to question my judgement?'

The monk's stormy expression cast all other eyes down. Agreed with, resented, or not, the decision would stand.

17

MEE HOON MEDIATION

The most overt way in which Koh Chun revealed feelings of trust and affection came through teaching. In Sugong's case, he made another display: he gave him a special room in which to stay. This was a more complicated gesture of goodwill.

When thinking of Sek Koh Chun there are two parts to be considered. First and foremost was the Buddhist monk, a man of compassion and enlightenment whose desire to relieve injustice led him to a life of self-imposed deprivation.

While his martial arts may have been more headline-grabbing, he was renowned for his kindness in Singaporean society, as in China and Indonesia before. He may have had a certain fierceness when imposing discipline on his students and disciples but when it came to the community at large he was more obviously benevolent. The doors to the temples he headed were always open. If there was an accident and someone required bone-setting, he would tend to the break. If internal ailments or injuries needed treatment, he would make an assessment and prepare a herbal remedy. And when those without influence had their rights ignored, Koh Chun would intervene quietly with others who held sway.

When it came to the time for thanks he would deflect their efforts.

'There's no need to thank me. Thank Buddha.'

From the wealthy a donation to the temple would be accepted. From the poor, gratitude and goodwill to Buddha sufficed.

He was a well-versed Buddhist, greatly respected by fellow monks. He was a highly regarded medicinal practitioner, turned to by doctors as well as the sick. And he was a man of compassion.

Then there was the warrior monk.

The very concept of *wuseng* (warrior monks) is contentious. Although they have existed outside of Shaolin, the acts of heroism associated with the order are probably the best known. The first notable example came in the 7th century with the reputed intercession of thirteen monks in an imperial struggle. Their assistance to a prince helped him to become emperor and they gained his appreciation, as well as widespread renown, for their influence on the dynastic succession.

The victorious emperor acknowledged this with land. Complimentary edicts that permitted the consumption of alcohol and meat among others may also have been granted, although there is debate over whether these are story-tellers' inventions.

The incident was not an isolated encounter and Shaolin's reputation flourished with each new tale of patriotism. They were lauded for warding off Japanese pirates and gained further esteem for other rebuttals of invasion and insurgency in the centuries to come.

Yet the combination of monk and martial art was, and remains, an apparent paradox in a belief-system famed for pacifism. To excel in a deadly art is a seeming contradiction to the prohibition of violence and a belief in the sacrosanctity of life.

It has been argued that the origins of Shaolin kung fu lie not on martial foundations but in a desire to facilitate enlightenment through a combination of spiritual and physical pursuit. There are also suggestions that when turned toward pugilism the art does not necessarily lie at odds with a Buddhist path, protecting the faith, others, or even oneself being justifiable acts of compassion as long as the force is minimal and used as a last resort.

Koh Chun was never called to the defence of his country. But when his safety or that of others was threatened and benevolence and reason were not enough he was ready, willing and able to apply his skills. Although it was something he was reluctant to do, it was not a course of action of which he felt ashamed. As for his students, while he did not encourage belligerence he was not teaching for their gratification. If required, they too should be ready to defend those in need. Sugong was an enthusiastic adherent to this line of thought.

Sugong was a Buddhist. He was not flawless but he believed in the guidance of Buddha and he revered his master. So he tried to abide by Buddhist principles and the precepts and tenets to which he was pledged.

Yet he remained mischievous and he still had an innate ability to attract trouble. Fights in particular kept calling. His wasn't a desire to inflict violence; unless in real danger he would never focus on vital points, instead preferring to take out an opponent's legs and put him to ground.

He did find excitement in the thrill of combat and its test of will and skill but neither was to be found in bullying. So while he may have been prone to react a little quickly he would try to avoid being the cause of a brawl.

But if someone came looking for trouble he would provide it, with a little extra in return.

Beneath the prickly outer shell lay a softer core. Those who negotiated the exterior would themselves become part of a strong relationship. If at any time they were wronged they would have an ally ready to do all he could to make things right. With nearly a hundred fellow students in the temple, wrongs needing righting came about with more than normal frequency.

A hengdai coming away badly from an argument turned physical knew Sugong would make himself available to settle the dispute. Another pressured by triads could rely on Sugong to enact a resolution. Their confidence was not misplaced. And if Sugong had to apply what he had learned while straightening affairs then so be it.

This willingness won him favour with his hengdai. It was less appreciated by others in the community. A coffee shop owner who found his store a temporary gangster re-education centre was unlikely to be delighted. A restaurateur whose head waiter's eyes were blackened might not share the Siong Lim students' admiration. When they wanted to air their grievances they came to the temple.

It was Koh Chun who would have to hear their complaint, placate their temper and bring the issue to an accommodating end. As with all great problems in Chinese society the best start was over tea.

'Let's go to the back,' he would say, gesturing toward the dining area. 'We can have some *mee hoon* (a dish of fried noodles) and get this resolved.'

Sugong would be summoned from his room, the one nearest the dining area his sifu had conferred on him in recognition of the frequency with which he was called. They would all sit down and discuss the problem over the plate of noodles, the quick-tempered monk displaying his contrary powers of diplomacy and charm. By the end of dinner an agreement would have been reached. They would know where responsibility lay and the identity of the apologising party would have been decided. Whereby the complainant would leave and the matter be considered settled.

Again Koh Chun's reaction did not run according to expectation. Barring the odd exception, his most tempestuous disciple was not berated. Instead Sugong would find himself the recipient of generous praise.

The indirect nature of Chinese social interaction sometimes precipitated Koh Chun from openly expressing contempt for others in society. But there would be no mistaking the pride in his voice when he called for *mee hoon* prior to a table talk with a triad boss and his bruised underling. When it had finished he would refer to Sugong by a nickname, based on his given name of Chong Tze, and admonish less active students.

'Ah Chong not only trains hard, he puts what he learns into practice,' he would scold. 'What are the rest of you doing?'

Just as Koh Chun had clear views on the rights and wrongs of fighting, he had no doubts in regard to its outcome. The art he taught was only to be used when necessity required. But when that time came, losing was unthinkable. He wasn't the disciple of a millennia-old order who would ruin the credibility of Shaolin by allowing his laymen to be punched around.

The result was a certain fluidity in Siong Lim numbers. Anyone losing a fight would be summoned by the abbot, whose disgust would be palpable.

'You've disgraced me.'

Lecture over, the student was now an ex-student.

This posed a problem. The number of fights involving students was reasonably low. But when battle occurred, the result was not always a clear-cut, easy victory. Turning up for training, a bruised fighter would be hurriedly ushered out of sight by his more experienced siheng. They knew his battered features could arouse enough suspicion for, at best, a scolding and extra training; at worst expulsion. Until his warrior markings had subsided the student would need to train secretly, out of sight of their sifu. Training with Sek Koh Chun was indeed not easy.

18

FRIENDS WITH THE ENEMY

When his bike-hire business ended, Sugong once more needed to find work. Undeterred by the lack of success in his last venture, he decided to put faith in his entrepreneurial spirit again. He would open a gaming shop. The game itself was similar to pachinko, the slot machines that are so popular in Japan. In both small metal balls are fed into noisy one-armed bandit style contraptions. At some mysterious point, winnings are paid out if the unfathomable rules are followed and the player's luck is in.

Sugong's dilemma was that it didn't appear very Shaolin. In fact, despite being at the more game-like end of the betting scale, it still seemed to be in conflict with the tenet that advised against gambling. However, all oaths and scriptures are open to a degree of interpretation. It is said that intent is everything and in this case Sugong interpreted it as 'Do not gamble for your own gain.' Which suited his purposes.

Subsistence living to his eyes did not qualify as gain and he had committed to supporting the temple's finances with whatever was left after costs. Siong Lim relied on donations that had not been particularly forthcoming of late.

Having learnt carpentry during his stay in Red-Faced Auntie's village, building basic premises did not pose a problem. Finding a site did. He searched high and low for somewhere suitable but when one couldn't be found he reverted to plan B.

The frantic pace of change Singapore would see in the 1960s and 70s had yet to lead to the expropriation of Siong Lim Temple's land and it was still generously endowed. Sugong constructed his premises on some unused land just beyond the very fringes, crossed his fingers and opened for business.

Despite his hopes and plans he didn't prove lucky. Another idea, good in principle, proved imperfect in practice. Sugong's intention was for a small enterprise on his doorstep requiring limited attention. He hoped it would provide him with a basic income, the temple with regular donations, and still leave him free to train. He would supervise from a distance but someone else would look after the day-to-day.

To this end he hired a couple of local girls. They were sharp, bubbly, and very pretty. Seemingly ideal for the job, he hoped they would attract attention to the venture.

They did. The shop's rise in popularity was meteoric but a problem lay in its patrons' interest. They fed money into the machines as he had hoped, but it was usually with one eye on the manageresses. Before long there were squabbles and these soon turned into fights. Once they did, police attention became inevitable.

Sugong's hope for limited involvement began to look unrealistically optimistic. With tills ringing and fists flying he was forced to spend increasingly long hours at the shop. Operating hours ended around midnight and his 4am starts became increasingly hard.

Sugong was sixteen in this, his earliest picture. He would soon be kidnapped in a family feud.

Meanwhile, Koh Chun was head monk at the Chn Yuen Kung Temple in Medan, Indonesia, and had recently begun to teach Shaolin kung fu.

Slightly less well-known than lion dances, dragon dances are also performed at Chinese festive occasions. Above, the Binjai Chinese Wushu Institute that Koh Chun started pose in full regalia.

Siong Lim Temple did not escape unscathed from World War II,
but at the time Koh Chun and Sugong arrived it would
have looked something like this 1930s postcard.

Sek Koh Chun ascended from head monk to abbot in 1954. Dressed in
his robes, he is seated in the middle of the front row of this group photo with
his kung fu disciples to commemorate the occasion.

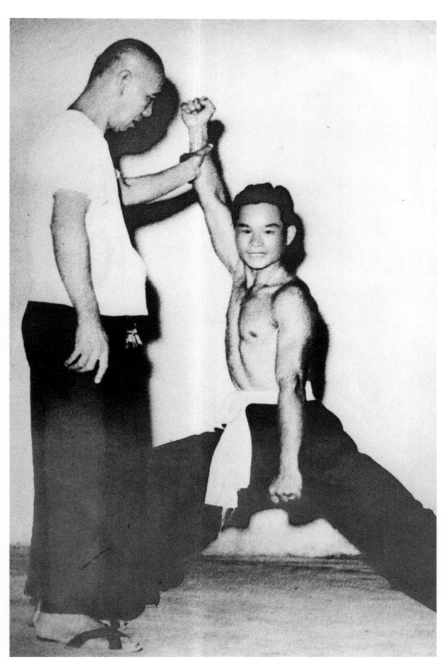

Sek Koh Chun was not often photographed in unofficial settings and this is a rare picture of him teaching a student, a young Sugong around 1950.

Different lohan have different characteristics. In this series of pictures Sek Koh Chun captured their expressions with startling effect. Lohan forms feature in the

Complete Encyclopedia of Shaolin Temple Martial Arts written by Shi De Qian of the Henan Shaolin Temple, in which Koh Chun himself is mentioned.

Sek Koh Chun in more contemplative mood during his tenure
as Siong Lim's abbot.

少 靈 山 醫 局

SAO LENG SAN MEDICAL HALL

(CHINESE PHYSICIAN)

星洲大坡道拉實街門牌五十三號

No. 53, TRAS STREET, SINGAPORE 0207.

TEL: 2219602, 2215751

本 局 廿 餘 年 臨 床 經 驗
專 科 ： 跌 打 風 傷
特 製 ： 丹 膏 丸 散
專 用 ： 科 學 針 灸
治 療 百 病

鄭樹祥醫師

Kung fu represented only one aspect of Koh Chun's teaching. This advert, promoting Siong Lim student Tey Soo Siong's clinic, indicates another key area.

For all the rivalries and competition, relations between the *hengdai* were ultimately strong. On a trip to Penang's Kek Lok Si Temple, Sugong stands second to the left.

Different animal styles require different hand positions for their strikes. Here Sugong avoids a two-open-fingered attack that mimics the forked tongue of a snake. The *hengdai* he is practising with was a nephew of Koh Chun.

Koh Chun was not a man for granting much free time. Sugong practises diligently with a *dan dao* (broadsword).

For reasons unclear, Sugong and his *hengdai* often dispensed with the need for training gear when performing for the camera. In this impromptu series of pictures at the Penang Buddhist Association, Sugong remains resolutely well-dressed.

In 1959 Sek Koh Chun was in his last year of life, and beginning to grow frail.

Thousands lined the streets to pay their respects before
his funeral procession in May 1960.

While Sugong's wardrobe was not normally one of suits and ties, he was willing to dress up for a studio shot.

Penang bustled in the 1950s and 60s, but life could be
complicated behind the scenes.

Sek Koh Chun founded the Nanyang Siau Lim Guo Shu Chiong Hui (South-
East Asian Shaolin National Art Association) in 1958 to head up the schools of
Singapore and Malaysia. Sugong was sworn in for a term as instructor in 1967.

(above) In the same year, some of the Association's finest demonstrated to celebrate the inauguration of the Singapore National Wushu Federation. Sugong stands at the back right, Ng Ser Kow is third right in the front row.

(right) They destroyed a selection of hard objects as part of their performance at the Happy World Stadium. Right, a stick is broken on Sugong's outstretched arm.

The May 13th Incident would have short-term consequences for Sugong and long-term implications for Malaysia. In this image, a soldier surveys the wreckage in a Chinese part of town.

Sugong (front row seventh from right) opened the Quek Heng Choon Institute for Physical Culture in KL's Bukit Bintang in 1970 in a building owed by relatives of Master Lai.

Despite high standards and uncompromising teaching methods, places in Sugong's schools were highly sought after.

Master Lai began training with Sugong in 1967 and gained senior instructor status in 1975. Here Sugong's *hengdai*, Lim Ah Hor, presents him with his certificate.

As well as training them in martial arts, Sugong also wanted his disciples to become teachers so they could pass on the art. Sifu crouches to Sugong's left with the other instructors.

David Niven, star of the film *Paper Tiger*, provides the laughs as he plays around with weapons. Sixteen of Sugong's disciples, including Sifu, participated in the action scenes Sugong choreographed for the film.

There are eighteen traditional Shaolin weapons but there is a belief that anything should be usable in a fight, hence the use of less obvious arms such as umbrellas and benches. When pressed, Sugong would narrow the range of years he considered himself at his peak from 20–60 to 40–50. He is pictured training with a selection of weapons at the age of forty-five.

Never a huge drinker, Sugong would join in festivities if the occasion warranted, as it does here, celebrating his fiftieth birthday with family and friends.

By ANNA CHEAH
Pix by NG AH BAK

Quek still has his marbles

26 JAN 1986

I. STAR

Although he only taught chi gung in Taiwan, Sugong's own kung fu practice did not diminish during his time in the country.

Having taught for such a long time, he featured in a number of articles in Malaysia's press. This feature was written as he made a trip back in 1986.

Sugong's return to Singapore at the end of the 1980s allowed him to re-live old memories with his *hengdai* at Siong Lim. Sugong stands centre left.

Sugong took on disciples while teaching at the Koh Chun Men school in Singapore. His *hengdai*, flanking him on either side, could be relied on to support the occasion.

When Sugong returned to China in the 90s to build his parents' shrine, he took the opportunity to renovate his house. Here he is surrounded by the women of his extended family.

With a scolding never too far away, any time spent as Sugong's sole focus of attention was unsettling, especially in my early months.

Breakfast bore little resemblance to any I'd had before. Fish-head soup was far less challenging than it sounded, and tasted as good as the other regular fare (with the exception of intestines).

Our training venues were not ones of luxury but they did provide a good back-drop for a picture. CG stands far left, Mr Tan is third from left, next to Michael, and Ji Hang is fourth from right.

While the years took some toll on his stamina, Sugong's physique was unrivalled for his age (above) and his vigour and enthusiasm were undiminished in short bursts (below).

Any breaks from training caused a build-up in energy which sought frantic escape in a flurry of flailing arms and pointing fingers.

Pained expressions at dawn on Michael (left) and me on our trip to China in the knowledge that the next twenty-four hours will see a repetition of the last.

Quek Junior (left), Master Wong (right) and I all enjoy the moment at a Fujian temple. But Sugong is distracted by thoughts of the next destination and the need to hit the road once more.

Information was not always readily available on the trip. The significance of Kai Wan Temple was revealed only in passing about a year after our visit, although Sugong's high spirits on the day provided a hint of its importance.

At our farewell dinner, Sugong decided to hold an unplanned tea ceremony where, contrary to normal procedure, we were taken on as grand-disciples rather than disciples per se. Mr Goh (left) and CG assist.

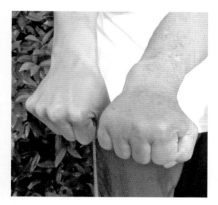

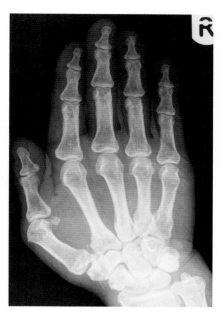

Sugong's hands may not have been at their peak in his eighties but they remained pretty impressive, dwarfing the foot-taller CG's. An x-ray revealed healthy joints and a bone density comparable to a man in his twenties.

And Sugong showed just what they could do to a concrete block in London during a trip to Master Lai's Nam Pai Chuan school in 2009.

Our farewell speech had been translated into Hokkien,
unbeknown to the gathering, and our pitiful attempts
were the subject of general amusement.

Sugong went easy on my not-so iron stomach in a demonstration in Malaysia.
The reason for my apprehension can be seen overleaf.

The police attention was even more unwelcome. Fights inside the club's premises were rare – Sugong's reputation saw to that. But while they took care not to incur Sugong's wrath within the club's walls, the love rivals took their arguments outside. Reports of disturbance made their way to the police, who in turn followed them to the proprietor, a man known to his patrons as Quek Chong Tze.

But Quek Chong Tze was not going to be so easy to track down. In fact he didn't even exist. When the police called around, Sugong would bring out his registration papers and deny any knowledge of the man. He was Leong Heng Choon, and he had the documents illegally gained for his entry to Singapore to prove it. Despite their well-founded suspicions, the police could do little but accept it. But as their visits became more frequent their patience wore increasingly thin. Repercussions began to look more and more likely.

Which is when Sek Koh Chun stepped in. It is probable that he was initially unaware of Sugong's activities as the disciple did his utmost to limit the club's exposure. But when word came to him of police visits, the limits to how far even a blind eye could be turned were breached. The club had to close. And so less than six months into his second business operation Sugong shut up shop once more.

Although he had stopped working on the docks, Sugong still had friends there and in free moments he would head down to meet them. One afternoon he arrived to find a group killing time before their evening shipment arrived.

He found them in the middle of a heated debate, banter flying. Sugong settled himself on a pile of crates and, unable to miss out on a good argument, was soon at the centre of the dispute. He was sat across from a man who gave such a good account of himself that Sugong couldn't help but take to him despite his contrary views. Before he could find out the man's name there was a call from the area foreman and the impromptu gathering broke up.

As they walked away Sugong asked his old workmates about the man, thinking he was new.

'Him? No, he's been around ages. But he used to work in Boat Quay. He's only just come over here,' said one. 'He's called Leong Tat Keng.'

Sugong stopped abruptly and asked him to repeat the name.

'Leong Tat Keng. I think he's from near Xiamen back home.'

Sugong had turned before the sentence was complete. He strode back the way he had come and, as he passed a container, he saw his long-time adversary, the cause of his kidnapping, stepping out of a warehouse fifty metres away.

'Leong Tat Keng!'

His shout had the desired response and his unknowing antagonist looked toward him and broke into a grin. The smile was not returned. When Sugong reached him and introduced himself, Leong's face reverted to seriousness just as quickly. Sugong then announced his purpose for being in Singapore; to avenge the beating Leong's family had given him. His words hung heavy in the air.

'And that's what you still want to do?' his adversary finally asked.

It had been the motivating factor for Sugong's upping his training ten years earlier, and he told Leong as much.

'You should know that I had nothing to do with all of that,' said Leong. 'That was a dispute with my family and yours. I didn't know anything about it and I played no part.'

Sugong remained as he was, expression unchanged. Leong was no less ready to back down. He gestured to the men around them, who were now eyeing the confrontation.

'You do what you want but I'm not going to sit back and take a beating. And they won't just stand around either.'

When it came to fighting, Sugong wasn't overly concerned with long odds, particularly when blood had already rushed to his head.

'Never mind them,' he said. 'You've got a debt to pay.'

With the face-off continuing, the tension mounted and a physical conclusion began to look inevitable. Instead Sugong spoke again.

'Come to Killiney Road Coffee Shop when you've finished your shift.'

The suggestion to move a fight from the secluded environment of the docks to a coffee shop was an unusual one. Leong was caught by surprise and momentarily allowed puzzlement to show on his face.

'You're going to have to buy me tea before I consider this matter settled,' concluded Sugong.

Again Leong looked bewildered, until he realised an olive branch was being held out and he once more broke into a grin. That evening, instead of going to battle they shared a beer. And instead of gaining revenge on his erstwhile enemy, Sugong took the first steps to the making of an unlikely friend.

19

IRON VESTS, DEATH TOUCHES AND THE ART OF STEALTH

Martial arts have always been accompanied by mystery. The exploits of their legends may only have travelled west in the last half-century, but in the east they are as old as the arts themselves. Despite existing within the scientific realm, martial artists' skills can appear to reside beyond possibility. And when coupled with the exaggeration that often accompanies excellence, a delicate balance can be tipped.

Technology may have allowed movies to catch up only recently but magical powers have been associated with martial artists for centuries. Fighting on the leaf-tips of a bamboo tree may be going further than any credible person would be willing to suggest. Yet people, apparently rational in every other aspect of their thinking, are willing to extend seemingly outrageous claims to their sifus, sigungs [although I referred to Sugong in Hokkien, the Cantonese, *sigung*, is more widely understood. Similarly, sifu is pronounced *sufu* in Hokkien] and martial arts ancestors. The reason is *chi*.

Chi is not unique to the Chinese and similar concepts exist in other cultures. In Sanskrit it is known as *prana*, in Japanese *ki*, and related notions were even espoused by the Romans and Ancient Greeks. The problem, perhaps, is not so much whether it exists, but what it is, what it does, and the extent it can influence and be influenced by man.

Defining chi is not a simple task. Although imperfect, it is most easily likened to the intrinsic energy of the body and the world around. Science is not particularly comfortable with the concept but that doesn't preclude chi. Science is not always perfect, being taken as fact only until the latest science proves it wrong. It is not definitive, for example, in explaining why some people are more vibrant and others have a sparkle in their eyes. Chinese might attribute it to chi.

Scientists are happier to accept that electrical energy helps drive our systems and enables us to move. The benefits of some 'alternative' medicines such as acupuncture are also becoming more widely proclaimed. Yet accepting one or both of these makes possible a bridge to believing in chi.

Extending this admittedly simplistic line of thought would see the debate move on to one based more on the form chi takes, and the extent of its power: whether it is no more than the flow of energy through the human body in a form accepted by western science under different terminology, or if it is something more potent that can be cultivated and utilised by those who have learnt how.

Many martial arts, particularly Chinese, view chi as something we are born with, something that exists around us, but something that needs to be developed to deliver its all. The most well-known method of doing this is probably tai chi. Sometimes misunderstood as a light-impact workout, its focus is on increasing the body's levels of chi and improving its flow. Doing so to benefit health forms a partial reason for practice, but the foundations of the art, and a continued purpose, lie in the enhancement of martial ability.

Tai chi is far from being the only method of developing chi. Chi gung is a form of breathing exercises that traces its history back to Bodhidharma's supposed callisthenics and beyond. Outside martial arts, there are numerous other activities, such as yoga, that are also energy-focused. As the characters for *chi gung* can be translated as energy through breathing, it could even be argued that some cultivation of chi is gained in any form of exercise when attention is paid to one's breath.

The greatest benefit is arguably to health. Those practising chi-based arts often claim healthier organs, better blood circulation and generally superior well-being. Studies may not be able to prove exactly why, and disputes continue on the concept and existence of chi, but they generally concur there is a positive result to practising activities that focus on its generation.

The other main advantage is martial, and here conjecture is even more pronounced.

As many martial arts confer importance on chi, one of the factors that differentiates them is the extent of their emphasis. Arts such as tai chi that focus heavily on cultivating chi are known as internal. Shaolin kung fu, along with arts like karate, taekwondo and muay thai, are referred to as external.

The terms are somewhat erroneous. The kicking, punching and grasping of Shaolin also share space with chi gung.

Likewise, tai chi is not static and while its movements may often be slower and the focus more on generating internal power, it shares physical elements with its 'external' relatives. While clumsy, the definitions enable a quick understanding of a martial art's accentuation all the same.

While martial arts all have their own methods of developing chi, there is a degree of commonality. Foremost is the theory of the *tantien* as the engine room of the body's chi. The tantien is situated about an inch and a half below the navel and an inch or so inward. (This is sometimes known as the lower tantien, with a middle tantien around the solar plexus and an upper between the eyes. There is also more than one *chakra* – a similar concept to yoga.) It is not a physically identifiable organ like the heart or lungs but it is seen as the point from which chi is generated, stored and pumped around the body.

Although there are static exercises, chi is most often developed by callisthenics that combine the physical and mental. On the physical side, movements of the body are usually coordinated with controlled breathing. The mind is commonly focused either on the tantien or the parts of the body to which chi is to be directed (although meditation, focused on neither, is also claimed to achieve results).

Even when practised martially, there are different objectives to the development of chi. The most obvious would be the generation of greater power when kicking, punching or pushing. But it can also be used to gain greater stability (often referred to as 'rooting' due to an ability to seem rooted to the ground) and enable a fighter to break another's root. Others use it to build resistance to blows, hence the references to iron vests and the like.

All of these skills are impressive when executed correctly, and at the highest levels they can appear to exist beyond science. Common to all is a tendency for exaggeration and fallacy. The most extravagant claims are usually made with the benefit of separation, be it geographical, or, more commonly, through time. The greatest masters are always dead; and when they were alive the accolades were most likely bestowed on ancestors before them: Legendary masters able to jump thirty feet from a standing start; fighters whose punches could pierce hard ground to their elbow; others whose chi reserves were so great that vehicles bounced from their torsos.

At the start of the 20th century a Chinese secret society called *I Ho Chuan* (The Righteous and Harmonious Fists) decided to rid the country of colonialists. While their intentions had some merit, the foundations of their physical uprising were a little shaky. Many were martial artists and they believed their powers so great that, when combined with Taoist charms, they could repel the intruders' gunfire.

The slaughter of thousands in the massacre that ended 'The Boxer Rebellion' – martial artists were referred to by westerners as 'boxers' – should have been a definitive rebuttal of chi hyperbole. But memory dies as fast as a misconceived martial artist. Which is not to say that all stories of chi are false. But an element of scepticism must be retained for some of the more outrageous claims. It is probably prudent to reserve judgement on thirty-foot leaps until unpropelled men start flying through the sky.

And so the legends of Sek Koh Chun must be approached.

There are claims that he was able to break objects from a distance, projecting his chi through a pointed finger. He was supposed to have been seen jumping the twelve-foot walls of the temple on a regular basis. He was even meant to have contracted his bones in a demonstration to celebrate the opening of a studio in Penang.

'Rubbish,' was Sugong's response. 'I lived and trained with him for over ten years. Do you not think I would have seen him jumping over walls?'

But to complicate matters, while disagreeing with the tales, he concurs on some claims of extraordinary abilities. Assessing the ability of a man who never demonstrated publicly has obvious complications. Yet it is not impossible, for a teacher leaves his imprint on his students, and some judgement can be made through their passion and prowess.

There can be no doubting the fervour Koh Chun inspired, with schools tracing their lineage to him crossing continents. The reverence in which he was held by his direct disciples can be attested to by the number of those alive who still carry his picture, despite being in their seventies and eighties and their master dead for more than fifty years.

There also seems little room for debate in terms of prowess. With so many styles to kung fu it is common for masters to specialise. One may have expertise in white crane, another praying mantis or monkey. Koh Chun had such students and some of them received acclaim for their skill. Yet the fact that they specialised while he mastered the spectrum is indicative of a superlative ability.

Beyond his excellence in the external arts, Koh Chun's long years of learning gave him great depth in the internal. He knew soft chi gung, hard chi gung (used for the iron body techniques), chi gung derived from animal forms and he was a long-time practitioner of meditation and likely much more.

He also knew *nei gung*, literally translated as internal skills, which help generate internal energy and can also be used to withstand blows. And he was a master of *ching gung*, literally 'light skills' used to lighten the body or at least make it more nimble. While the exaggerations of the film industry take things too far it apparently allows an expert to cross short distances more quickly, jump higher and land safely from greater heights.

And of course there was dim mak.

While all of these abilities may have been of a science that is debated and not agreed upon they were, for the most part at least, explainable though biophysics. Others were less so, and ranking high among these were his skills of fate-reading and invisibility.

The 'invisibility' needs qualifying. It was not the bandage-wrap-requiring kind that would provide competition for The Invisible Man. It was more akin to an art of stealth. However, it had greater complexity than an ability to sneak around very quietly or walk very carefully on tiptoes. Whether it was related to chi or ching gung isn't clear, but whatever techniques and abilities were used, Koh Chun was apparently renowned. Sugong is adamant that when he wanted he could enter and leave rooms and buildings unobserved.

Koh Chun's fate-reading was not based in the martial arts. During his trip around China he learned how to create protective talismans from one of his grandmaster's sihengs and the fate-reading may have been related to this. This ability apparently enabled him to read the future and even change people's destinies. Yet just as impressive was his aptitude to see the past. Whether the vice was gambling, drinking or women, any disciple straying from his Shaolin oaths remained very wary of their sifu.

Whether real or perceived the ability would certainly prove of use.

20

AN ABBOT, AN OFFICER AND SOME GANGSTERS

As Siong Lim Temple grew in the number and renown of its disciples so did misunderstandings about their activities. Some were innocent, others more calculated. The earliest weren't directly related to the martial arts students; it was the monks who came under fire. The problem dated back to the unwanted post-war occupiers of Siong Lim. Koh Chun's reputation had reached Singapore before he arrived in 1947. The temple's trespassers did not leave immediately when he appeared and their offensive behaviour did not instantly become pure. But they were wary of the new head monk.

His aim was to re-build the congregation. He evidently believed a united front would better rid them of menace and go further toward achieving harmony rather than a one-man martial mission to dispose of the problem.

Faced with the new mass resolve that Koh Chun led, the trespassers were eventually forced to accept defeat, but they did not do so with grace. Their revenge was an attempt to disparage the temple. They spread rumours of womanising monks from a temple housing secret passageways and traps to abduct and hold hostage their female prey. Based on the tales of an unrelated book the stories were manifestly untrue. Yet they provided compelling gossip.

There was little the temple could do but continue in its functions and attempt to dispel the rumours through good deeds. With the temple open to the public, the lack of tunnels and the like was obvious and easy to disprove, and the whispers gradually subsided.

The kung fu disciples were at the centre of the other main controversy. This contended that they contained gangsters in their number. There was irony in the suspicion as Koh Chun detested the activities of criminals. As a man devoted to helping the underdog, he viewed the mobsters that fed on them as parasites. Furthermore, through his tuition, young men who might otherwise have bolstered gang numbers were offered an alternative path. If he felt an existing or past gangster was redeemable, Koh Chun might accept them on the understanding their illicit activities were a thing of the past. But if their actions were in the present there would be no place for them in his school.

To prevent erroneous entry, prospective students often required nomination from an existing disciple. Even then, if Koh Chun suspected deception they would be quickly dismissed. It was always possible for one or two to slip through the net and another might succumb to temptation after starting to train. There would be no compromise for either from their sifu. A disciple found to have gangland connections would be out. Even one or two from the favoured senior students left under such a cloud.

Yet to Koh Chun, gangsters weren't completely without merit. There was one benefit to their existence – practice.

The martial arts of Shaolin are claimed to have developed partly in response to attacks by bandits. Their monks, including Koh Chun, had been able to hone their skills repelling them. While there were no bandits attacking the temple in Singapore, there were enough villains to allow the tradition to continue. In particular, the area in which the temple was housed, Toa Payoh, had yet to be absorbed by the city and was notorious for being home to numerous gangs.

Siong Lim's disciples were by no means allowed to swagger the streets of Singapore picking fights, but if someone needed protecting, or a gangster invited a lesson through threats and aggression, they were not discouraged from providing the necessary tuition.

There were a number of skirmishes involving disciples and gang members as a result. Unfortunately, to those unaware of the temple abbot's attitude, the brawls appeared to be fights between gangsters, instead of the battles against them they really were.

Among the number who misconstrued the situation was a faction in the police force and eventually they came calling. While Koh Chun had no patience for errant disciples, he was fiercely loyal to those who had proved themselves to him. He had no intention of allowing them to be unfairly harassed.

It must have been a quiet time for Singaporean crime, for when the police came they did so in numbers. The officer in charge, an Officer Yew, ordered the disciples out.

The students nearest to Koh Chun saw his eyebrows furrow and his eyes darken in anger.

'Go up to the roof.'

At the order just under a hundred disciples broke from their training and scurried into the eves of one of the temple halls. As they huddled there, three Buddha statues were on hand to pass judgment of a higher kind.

Koh Chun strode to the temple gates.

'What do you mean by this nonsense?' he demanded of the officer.

'You're housing gangsters,' the officer shot back. 'Send them out.'

Koh Chun was furious.

'Don't be ridiculous. I wouldn't let any gangsters come near the temple and I certainly don't bring them in. My disciples are trained to defend themselves and others and nothing more.'

Koh Chun's disdain for the officer was not concealed.

'In any case, there's no one here today. You can look for yourself,' he concluded, gesturing towards the temple's gates.

The police entered the temple but, finding the abbot's claim apparently true, they soon made their way back out.

Officer Yew was not happy. He warned Koh Chun, threatening to return and arrest him should he get the chance. The words were not the kind that could normally be expected to lighten Koh Chun's mood. But he appeared distracted and when he spoke again his tone had changed.

'You've no cause to arrest me,' he said. 'But instead of trying to intimidate me I think you need to pay more attention to yourself.'

Officer Yew's eyes widened.

'Are you threatening me?' he demanded.

'Not at all,' said Koh Chun. 'You're going to face danger in the next few days. I don't know what, but you need to take care.'

Made without any suggestion of malice, the officer found the warning unsettling. As his character was inclined, he compensated for his discomfort with aggression and eyeballed the monk belligerently before storming off.

Four days later he was back, this time unaccompanied. Koh Chun found him waiting politely in the temple. His attitude when he addressed the abbot was much changed. He began by apologising for his previous behaviour, taking Koh Chun by surprise. The apology was accepted, but still Officer Yew remained where he was.

'Thank you, Sek Koh Chun.' He bowed his head and when he continued he was even more hesitant than before. 'But I was hoping you would also be good enough to let me show you my true character.'

He stopped, looked down for a moment and when he brought his head back up he asked to be allowed to join as a student of Koh Chun. The request was a bigger surprise than the apology.

'Could I ask what's brought about such a change?' Koh Chun asked.

Officer Yew then explained the events of the previous day. He had clashed with a triad, with whom he had had prior run-ins, and been forced to flee when the man pulled out a gun. While escaping, one bullet had come perilously close to hitting him and he had been unable since to banish Koh Chun's warning from his mind.

Koh Chun paused in thought at the end of the officer's tale. The policeman waited for him to speak.

'Officer Yew, I will admit that I was not impressed with your character when I met you and while your scare has moderated your excesses I doubt you are an altogether changed man.'

Koh Chun words were even and considered.

'However, I'm willing to give you the benefit of the doubt. I don't intend to make you a disciple but I will teach you as long as you agree to abide by my rules.'

Officer Yew eagerly accepted the terms and, bowing his head again, bade his farewells.

With his acceptance Officer Yew became the first policeman to enter the auspices of one of Koh Chun's schools. He did not become a senior student and he did not attain any importance as a martial artist. But with other officers following in his wake, his entry did initiate a modern tradition of sorts. Their presence put to bed rumours of gangsterism in the temple, a repayment of sorts for the magnanimity of the abbot. Their influence would also come to the assistance of one of his disciples at a later date.

21

THE RED FACE OF RAGE

As a senior figure in society, it was almost inevitable Sek Koh Chun would have his run-ins with the establishment. But one of his favourite disciples was not going to be outdone when it came to getting in trouble. For it was not only Sugong's fists that led him into difficult situations, his love life did too. Again Red-Faced Auntie was involved. Again it wasn't really Sugong's fault.

This particular situation dated back to the time he spent in Red-Faced Auntie's village while in flight from army enlistment. He was hard-working, not deficient in personality, and of more than able body; Red-Faced Auntie decided she had found good stock. She travelled to Sugong's village and quickly came to an agreement with his mother. He was now engaged to Red-Faced Auntie's daughter.

Not having actually met the girl, his feelings on engagement were not those one might find in a modern-day fiancé. In place of heart-pounding ecstasy stood ambivalence. But he was now twenty-one and old enough to get married. And in his village an acceptable match between suitable families was of greater importance than passion and romance.

Having little interest in the whole affair, Sugong had left the arrangements in the hands of others. After the opium-couriering incident he naturally assumed the engagement was at an end.

He then found out that Red-Faced Auntie was not of the same mind. Which was a problem. Expecting an annulment, he had started courting another girl, Ah Peng. But, as an agreement had been made, he was obliged to start seeing Quay Kim, the daughter of Red-Faced Auntie, as well.

If he had been exhausted combining hard labour with the demands of Koh Chun in training, it was nothing compared to doing the same while dating two girls. Especially when Ah Peng's views on partying were considered; a quiet stroll in the park wasn't her thing. Even in a good mood Sek Koh Chun would only consider sanctioning non-temple activities at the weekend, so something had to give. Master or girlfriend.

Sugong was bemoaning his circumstances one day to one of his sihengs, Ng Ser Kow. Ng was going through a lean spell.

'You're better off having problems with two than trouble with none,' he joked. 'I'd be happy to take one off your hands.'

Said in jest, it wasn't received in the same vein. Sugong immediately offered Ng the chance to step in. Unable to believe his luck, his brother jumped at the opportunity and Sugong's problems were halved to just one. It was a difficult one though. Not expecting to be overcome with love, Sugong at least hoped for compatibility with the person with whom he would forever commit. But he just couldn't get on with Quay Kim.

So rather than anger or a sense of betrayal, Sugong felt relief when he found out that a blood brother, Lee Cheok San, had fallen for her charms. He was happier still when told the feeling was mutual.

Unaware of Sugong's attitude toward the situation, Lee was agonising over his quandary. Not only had he fallen for a brother's fiancée, he had fallen for the most quick-tempered of them. He didn't train in martial arts, and it was with some trepidation that he approached Sugong to make his confession.

The response was not what he had expected.

'That's great,' said Sugong, thudding a slap on Lee's back.

'It is?' asked Lee, confused.

'Really. I'm delighted for you.'

Bearing in mind their turbulent history, Red-Faced Auntie was not devastated to see a switch in partner and she reacted quickly, severing ties with Sugong, and transferring affections to Lee. It appeared a happy solution for all.

Except a significant minority were left displeased. When the other blood brothers heard, strong objections emerged. While the path of righteousness might not have been one that they followed without divergence, there was an implicit agreement that it not be strayed from, within their brotherhood at least. They were aware Sugong had given his blessing to the arrangement but some could still not accept it. To one in particular, Teoh Tai Seng, an oath was an oath and an oath should be binding.

'A younger brother should never take the woman of his older brother. It goes against all rules,' he admonished Lee.

Lee was distraught. He was deeply in love with Quay Kim but he also had grown up in the same code-obliging society as his brothers. He tried desperately to reconcile his conflicting emotions and convince his brothers of his case, but to no avail. After hours of increasing despair he gave in.

'I didn't mean any harm. I only considered it because I knew Ah Chong had no feelings for her and I made sure that he had no objections. But I'm as righteous as any of you and I value our brotherhood just as much. If you all agree that this goes against our oaths and I am wrong then I will break the engagement.'

Sugong was blissfully unaware of the commotion. He had not wasted any time moving on and was more than happy with his lot. One of Ah Peng's workmates was a girl called Ah Koo Kiah (a nickname translating literally as 'Little Puppy'). He hadn't been able to make a move while courting Ah Peng, who coincidentally disliked her, and even when things weren't going smoothly with Quay Kim he had remained faithful. But when his constraints were lifted he swiftly secured a date.

So he was a bit taken aback when he heard that Lee had broken the engagement. While he had sympathy, he felt the situation was now beyond him. He had done all that he could in giving his blessing. If Teoh and the other brothers felt the marriage should still not go ahead it was their decision. The matter was over from his point of view.

Red-Faced Auntie did not concur. She was furious. Ending an engagement was a serious business and for the girl it had massive repercussions. Society's expectations were for good Chinese girls to remain 'pure'. Anything that cast doubt on this purity threw a shadow over her character and with it her future prospects. No greater doubt could be engendered than in the breaking of an engagement.

Questions would be asked. Why had he dumped her? Had she had an affair? Did he discover her virginity was not intact? These would make it difficult to find another husband. Equal opportunities were not yet a concept for consideration and the extent of many girls' ambitions was to find a good husband from a prosperous family. If they were unlucky they would find a lesser man. Not finding one put them in an unenviable position. They would struggle to find a role in society, their families would not receive a dowry and they would lose considerable face.

Sugong wasn't the cause of Quay Kim's dilemma but, not knowing the chain of events, it was natural for Red-Faced Auntie to believe that he was. Finding out he had started courting Ah Koo Kiah did nothing to quell the bad feeling. To Red-Faced Auntie it appeared that Sugong had moved on but was denying her daughter the chance to do the same out of spite.

'You've ruined the future of my daughter,' she screamed when she had tracked him down.

He tried to explain the situation but was unable to interrupt the verbal onslaught before she stormed off, leaving his ears ringing with threats. He knew her well enough to know they would not be empty.

He first became aware of her acting on them when a hengdai stuck a newspaper under his nose. An advert with him in a starring role stared back. Leong Heng Choon was never a part of the Leong family, it stated. He had never been betrothed to Quay Kim and a good-for-nothing like him, scrounging his way in the Siong Lim Temple, never would. Rumours to the contrary were just lies.

While Sugong could understand Red-Faced Auntie's desire to clear Quay Kim's name he was not happy to be sullied in the process. But if it would bring matters to a close he decided it a price worth bearing.

A few days later he went to visit a fellow student who ran a medical clinic in town. Happy to catch up, his siheng made him a snack while they chatted. Before Sugong could take a bite from his food he heard a bike clatter to the floor outside.

'Ah Chong, get out,' shouted a friend as he burst through the door. 'The police are coming for you.'

Sugong bolted, making it to the end of the road and around the corner just in time. Arriving immediately in his wake, the police ransacked the shop. With considerable irony, Red-Faced Auntie was trying to set him up as an opium dealer. It was clear that she would not stop at clearing her daughter's name. Red-Faced Auntie wanted revenge and Sugong knew he had to defend himself. Fortunately his 'aunt' had provided the ammunition he needed in her newspaper ads.

Sugong spoke to a student called Leong (no relation to his auntie) and together they took action. Sugong threatened to sue Red-Faced Auntie for defamation and accused her of creating confusion around his name. Unknown to her, he had already changed his surname back to Quek. Leong would also sue to say that, as a Leong training in the temple, his name had been tarnished by her malicious accusations.

Knowing they would win their cases, Red-Faced Auntie was forced to put corrective adverts in the paper. She formally cancelled his debts and paid him compensation. It looked as though closure had finally been reached on his association with his birthmarked relative.

It hadn't. The trouble surrounding the incident was creating quite a stir. It was not something Koh Chun wanted associated with the temple. His ultimate responsibility was to Siong Lim and he was obliged to maintain its reputation. To prevent the cloud of controversy surrounding Sugong from engulfing the temple as well he could see no alternative than to cast out Sugong.

It was not a decision reached easily. For despite their sometimes shared fierceness and quick temper, Sugong and Koh Chun had developed a close relationship. Koh Chun had taken his vows at the onset of adulthood and with them had passed up the chance to have a son. Sugong already had a father but their relationship had been so fractious it really existed only in name. In each other Koh Chun and Sugong found a like mind and a surrogate for their missing kin.

It became Koh Chun's habit to visit Sugong's room on his end-of-the-day rounds. They would chit-chat about minor things, or if Sugong was down or had problems Koh Chun would console him and offer sage advice. The contrast to the spikier sides of both men could not have been more striking.

In the early hours of the morning Koh Chun would often call by Sugong's room, this time to wake him. This done, he would move on to meditate, while Sugong struggled into the new day, if it could be called that at 4am. In an empty courtyard he would practise alone before Koh Chun, meditation complete, came to supervise.

As with his own master, Siong Lim's head monk did not practise a policy of equality when it came to teaching. The most talented and hard working received the greatest share of his attention; the others got less. Geography played a further role in his bias. Students from his native province of Fujian had a head-start in his affections, and they would benefit for their understanding and use of Hokkien. With a tick in all boxes, Sugong was one of those who benefited from personal tuition.

So his banishment was not a happy arrangement for either man. Furthermore, he remained under threat of arrest. The police earned their meagre salary pursuing criminals in traditional manner. Some supplemented it chasing citizens deemed outlaws by virtue of an enemy's bribe. Punishment for ordinary criminals followed the standard arrest, prosecution and detainment model. Justice for wrong-doers identified by market forces was more succinct. It was administered through beating, the severity of which was determined by the desire and payment of the sponsor. It was imperative to Sugong's safety that the police be called off his back.

As money could influence the police force, so could power. Koh Chun made efforts to affect the latter. He contacted a local politician to arrange a sit-down with Sugong and, respectful of the head monk, the man agreed. He was also a Leong and therefore 'related' to Red-Faced Auntie. At their meeting Sugong seized on the fact. After explaining the course of events to the politician he appealed to his fair-mindedness.

'Your Leong family are trying to get me arrested but what have I done wrong? I haven't committed any crime. I haven't even acted badly.'

Whether in testament to Leong's impartiality, Sugong's persuasiveness or the influence of Koh Chun, the politician concurred. Within a week the police were pulled off Sugong and an agreement was reached with the Leongs. He and Red-Faced Auntie's family would sever all contact. Sugong was finally free to return to the temple and could go about normal life without fear of repercussion.

On his return Koh Chun took him aside.

'Now you're back and you have some money,' he said, referring to the compensation, 'it's time you settled down and stopped getting in trouble. You should get a wife, build yourself a home and calm down.'

Sugong remained as ambivalent to marriage as he had been before. But as it was his master making the suggestion he would listen.

'I've seen you making eyes at that pretty girl next door,' he continued, referring to Ah Koo Kiah, whose family lived next to the temple, unaware Sugong had started the ball rolling. 'I'll speak to her parents and see if something can be arranged.'

Sugong was happy enough with Ah Koo Kiah as his wife-to-be. He was even more touched by the honour and affection implicit in his master's offer to act as a go-between.

'Thank you, sifu,' he said. 'I would be honoured to have you as my *hm lang*.'

It was not long before Sugong was engaged to Ah Koo Kiah. Yet marriage did not follow engagement as quickly and before Sugong entered its institution he would find himself in a different country and a new set of troubles.

22

Eating tea in a coffee shop

What's that?' asked Michael.

'Chicken. Have some, it's good,' I replied.

'Ah, mate,' said Michael through a mouthful of bones. 'It's only half eight in the morning. I wouldn't want to be eating this shit at a reasonable hour.'

Sugong looked over. Michael pushed the rest of the chicken's feet in front of me, pointed in my face and made suggestive expressions.

'CG, could you tell Sugong that Nick loves the chicken's feet please.'

Sugong beamed, let out a happy cackle and ordered another two plates.

'Yeah, nice one Michael. That one's for you.'

Even if it wasn't lost to translation I think Sugong would have been confounded by the half-empty/half-full conundrum. To him there was no such thing. The glass was either full to overflowing or so empty it might evaporate. There was no in-between; literally no half-measures.

Sometimes I wondered whether he practised martial arts as an excuse to release some of the pent-up energy caught in a constant struggle for escape from imprisonment in his body. When we trained, he would sit and watch the class for as long as he could restrain the forces within. Then he would be up and on his feet, waving his arms and correcting or scolding, depending on his mood.

He would pace in front of the group shaking a hand, lashing out an arm, or jabbing a finger in tandem with the choice words being barked. In a good mood this would be accompanied by wide, open-mouthed grins and the finger pointing would be friendly – 'you so-and-so' kind of thing. In a bad mood he would pick up on a fault that had irked him to distraction and be unable to leave the scolding, wheeling back to deliver it in another form of words and actions.

And all the time you could sense his energy, independent of his conscious, dragging him forward by a thrust-out chest. Propelling itself down his arms in its search for freedom, his limbs would be overcome in an involuntary whirr of grasping, flailing, pointing and circling. His face was not spared and it was no less animated, veering wildly from joy, to indignation, and then despair, just in the course of a sentence. It was exhausting to watch. How he got through the day without collapse I didn't know.

The breakfast table was the place most likely to witness this gamut of emotion. Breakfast was very important to Sugong; just how important could be judged by its near equal status with training. Considering martial arts practice had constituted the majority of his waking hours for the past seventy-three years, that was a high ranking.

The arrival of breakfast would be announced by his putting on his watch and rings, pulling his T-shirt back over his vest and pointing his thumb to his open mouth.

'Yum-cha, yum-cha.'

Literally translated as 'drink tea' from Cantonese (I don't know why Hokkien wasn't used here but it usually wasn't), it meant we could stop training, get changed and devour some food.

But breakfast wasn't just for eating. Sharing tea (the term, confusingly, often including food) with your seniors is a sign of respect in Chinese society. By joining Sugong for breakfast we were giving him face at the same time as satisfying his restless, sociable character. A couple of rushed slices of toast while running out of the door was definitely not his thing.

And it was at the breakfast table that the stories would emerge. I would get edited highlights at the end but, like opera, a great deal of enjoyment could be gained from just sitting back, watching and letting it wash over you.

The morning meal also gave Sugong the chance to indulge in his secondary speciality – sports nutrition. It was a role he took seriously, although his direction was slightly different to the accepted wisdom of the west.

'Sugong wants to know why you're not eating properly.'

'I have had twice as much as everyone else, Mr Goh.'

'Yes, but he says you're training hard and you're too thin. You should be eating more. Here, have some pork.'

With that a full plateful of pork fat with trace elements of meat was doled onto my plate. Putting aside the health considerations, I have always had a real dislike for fat.

'Thanks.'

Every race and culture attaches importance to food. Dining sees family bonds built, business deals done and new loves ignited. But Malaysians are more obsessed with eating than most, and of the Malaysians those of Chinese origin take some beating. In addition to all of the ordinary reasons is the chance to combine one favourite pastime with another, in this case medicine. While efforts are made to align eating with health consciousness in the west, the relationship between food and body is even more prevailing in the eyes of the Chinese.

'Have this soup. It will help your circulation.'

'Drink this – it detoxifies the blood.'

'Eat these. They'll give you power.'

I was happy to go along with it for the most part but on some occasions the suggestions were less welcome.

'Here, have some of this, it's good for your joints.'

I looked at the meat-veined fat that had just been put on my plate. I could see no reason why the health of my joints would be improved by eating it.

'I'm not sure Albert. If I eat any of that I'll probably die of a heart attack before I get the chance to worry about arthritis.'

'No, no. It's OK. Have some Chinese tea. It breaks down the fat.'

Fortunately, or unfortunately, I had come out a couple of months before Michael joined the party and so I got to experience the food first. Breakfast was almost always noodles, usually in a soup, except on special occasions when we would have dim sum (with obligatory chicken feet; double portions after Michael's moment of genius). Just to confuse matters, morning tea, which involved eating, would be taken in a coffee shop.

Malaysian coffee shops have a few universals. They fill a large corner unit of a shophouse block and are unfailingly furnished with round plastic tables and chairs (always old and weather-beaten). Hawker stalls ring the perimeter, of which at least two sides are open to the street. The stalls themselves consist of a metal base topped with a glass fronting that reveals the different offerings.

The walls of the coffee shop are always lined with old tiles, even if the coffee shop itself is new, and the floor gradually accrues cigarette butts, the odd tissue and a bone or two during the course of the day.

I was intrigued by the bones at first, being more used to cutting away meat from bone and leaving the latter on the side of the plate. The prevalence of the chopper in Chinese kitchens, however, means that any mouthful has a higher chance of containing bone than a traditional western cut. Armed only with chopsticks, bones are more difficult to deal with before entering the mouth so there is a tendency toward negotiation afterward when they are expelled with varying degrees of refinement.

The sophistication of Japanese food presentation and the rituals behind its consumption can make one fearful of defacing the presented work of art. Having spent a couple of years there, eating Chinese-style came as a bit of a shock. Here, a more pragmatic approach was taken to dining. Priority was definitely accorded to the act of consumption with far greater laxity granted to how this was achieved.

'So Nick, what would you like?' asked Master Wong in my first week.

'To be honest I can't work out what anything is, Master Wong. Just order me what you're getting please.'

The noodles tasted pretty good but I wasn't too keen on the thick meaty tubes.

'So Nick. How do you like the intestines?' said Master Wong with complete innocence.

Aargh. For God's sake, what was wrong with these people?

'They're er, they've got quite a strong flavour, haven't they? I think I might just have the vegetable one next time.'

'A lot of protein. Good for power.'

23

THE PRETTY GIRLS ARE IN PENANG

By 1954 Koh Chun's renown was starting to create problems of a sort. The numbers of prospective students grew too large for the facilities at Siong Lim to accommodate.

His solution was a school outside the temple and Sao Hua San (Shaolin Chinese Mountain) was duly opened by a group of senior students. It was the first of what would be numerous Koh Chun related schools, although, while he sanctioned them, he limited his own tuition to the temple.

Allowing branch schools to further permeate the art was an extension of Koh Chun's desire to bring it to the masses, to preserve and strengthen the branch of Shaolin to which he was duty-bound. So when he was asked to oversee the restoration of Siong Lim's sister temple in Penang it seemed logical to open a school there as well. In order to do so Koh Chun took along with him one of his most senior disciples.

The arrival of warrior monks was no more common to Penang than it had been to Singapore and on the first two nights large numbers turned up. The third brought less welcome guests – the police.

Kung fu was often associated with triads. Various secret societies claimed a shared history with Shaolin and martial arts skills were useful to their operations. This meant that local police might be interested when a new school appeared. Whether it was master or student that had overlooked the bureaucratic detail, the fact remained that the necessary registration papers had not been acquired for a new school. The police made their presence known and their displeasure felt before they left.

The situation was not ideal. But having literally fought for his life during his marathon quests across Asia, Koh Chun was not unduly disturbed by such minor niggles. His student was less comfortable and wanted to avoid any run-ins with the police. The difference in outlook meant it was not long before a displeased monk and his disciple made a return trip to Singapore. Waiting for them was Sugong.

For some people trouble is a choice; they either follow the path that may lead to it or they take another. Sugong never found the fork in the road. Koh Chun had his man.

Before they left Sugong had some business to take care of. He needed to convince his fiancée of the benefits of joining him once he settled in Penang. Not overwhelming in her enthusiasm, she was at least not against the idea. Her parents were. Never one to let a major obstacle stand in his way, Sugong bade his farewells with a promise to convince them of the move's merits on his triumphant return.

Satisfied with a situation resolved, they were off. It was the middle of 1956 and after nine years in Singapore Sugong was once more on his way to pastures new.

Siong Lim's sister temple, Siong Kheng, was not home to Koh Chun and Sugong for long. With the temple about to be extensively refurbished, the pair were forced to move out after a brief stay. Their eviction turned out to be a blessing for Sugong. He put his carpentry skills to use and built a wooden shelter to serve as their temporary home.

Sugong's skills were competent but he had not yet reached the heights of master craftsman. In any case, the resources at hand made the building of a palace difficult. But both men came from humble beginnings and both had slept their fair share of nights with only a blanket of stars. Neither was concerned with their basic dwelling.

Sugong, on the contrary, was delighted. Their 'house' was essentially an upmarket hut of sorts. It was a stilted construction with the kitchen and eating area among the stilts, and the 'living quarters' – a simple rectangular room – above. For all of its simplicity, the time spent in the hut was a period Sugong would cherish.

Living in such proximity to Koh Chun strengthened an already close personal bond. As a further bonus it encouraged the elder of the pair to impart more knowledge to his eager disciple. The extent to which Koh Chun taught depended on his mood and the ability of the student before him. During this time both were good and Sugong benefited.

Both were busy men. Koh Chun was tested by the problems that came from overseeing a temple renovation; Sugong was learning and practising while simultaneously teaching and preparing to set up a studio. For the time being his classes were taught in the grounds of Siong Kheng. But long-term they would primarily take place at the school he had been tasked with establishing, the Penang Shaolin Gok Su Gen Sin Sia (Penang Shaolin Athletic Association).

Four months after arriving it was ready, its home a shophouse in the centre of Georgetown the capital of Penang. As a general rule shophouses are quite narrow and arguably not ideally suited for martial arts schools. But there is a theory in Shaolin that where there is enough space to accommodate an ox there is room to train. While that may be pushing things a little, kung fu schools were not prosperous ventures and the Penang shophouse provided a better home than most. It was certainly more than satisfactory to Sugong and Koh Chun. As student numbers grew it appeared to be a view the city's inhabitants shared.

Koh Chun was the sifu but in practice he only taught at Siong Kheng. It was the chief instructor, Sugong, who taught at the Association. So although not 'his', responsibility for the school fell largely on Sugong's shoulders.

It was something he relished, providing him with two aspects previously missing from his life – pride in his work, and a steady and reliable income. With a satisfying job and a loving fiancée, it seemed as though he was finally settling down to the uneventful life his sifu had demanded.

It may be his character that made such a thing impossible or it could just have been bad luck. But it was not long before events turned and his life's fortunes began to swing up and down once more.

It started with Ah Koo Kiah. Six months after the school opening, and now settled in Penang, Sugong felt the time was right to fetch his fiancée and tie the knot. Koh Chun was due to make one of his regular forays to Singapore so they set off together.

Sugong started the journey in high spirits but he quickly found them ill founded. He had hoped Ah Koo Kiah's parents would relent in their opposition when faced with his success. But he found them no more enthusiastic on his return. He spent a few days trying to persuade them but to no avail.

Sugong's romance with Ah Koo Kiah had never been one likely to rival Romeo and Juliet. He liked her and had been happy to date her. And when Koh

Chun had acted as intermediary he had been deeply affected by the honour. But the relationship had always been more about expedience and less about love. All the same he wasn't delighted at this unsatisfactory conclusion. Koh Chun noticed his low spirits. 'What's wrong, Ah Chong?' he asked.

'Sifu, I think it's over between me and Ah Koo Kiah,' a downcast Sugong replied. 'Her parents won't let her move to Penang so the only way I can marry her is if I stay here.'

Koh Chun again revealed his pragmatic side.

'Is that it?' he exclaimed, with no attempt to conceal his surprise. 'What are you worrying about? There are plenty more girls in Penang. She's not that pretty anyway – you can do much better when you get back.'

By this time Sugong knew his master's character well and he had come to expect his penchant for the unpredictable. But it was still not the response he had anticipated.

'Sifu, it was you who suggested the marriage, you acted as *hm lang* and you were witness at the engagement ceremony,' he said, shocked. 'Anyway, you said she was pretty. Now you're saying she's ugly and I should find someone else?'

'Yes, well, I thought you were in love and I didn't want to discourage you,' said the monk a little sheepishly, before brushing the comment aside. 'But what does it matter – she can't come with you, and the fact remains that there *are* prettier girls in Penang. Come on, stop messing around. Let's go.'

So they went. And Sugong's second great love affair came to an end.

In early 1957 Malaysia wasn't yet Malaysia. It only became a country (Malaya) when it achieved nationhood later that year. Previously linked but independent states with their own ruling sultans, they joined a British administered union after the war.

Historically, its location, between the Middle East and China, had made this collection of states a prosperous trading post. The early centuries of the second millennium saw Islam adopted from the Middle East; its latter half saw colonial interest exported from the west. As in Singapore, the Portuguese came first, followed by the Dutch with whom they fought.

The British displayed an uncharacteristic reluctance toward profiteering and became involved only at the request of a northern sultan anxious to protect his state from Burma and Siam. They were rewarded with the island of Penang in 1786 for their help. To this they added Malacca, swapped for Indonesian interests with the Dutch, and with them formed the Straits Settlements along with Singapore and Port Wellesley in 1824.

Despite their independence, the Malay states shared a common language, religion and traditions. Their predominantly agricultural life was welcomed by the sultans as it allowed them to own and rule the land. The expansion of tin mining in the first half of the 19th century added a new dimension as it required extra immigrant hands. These ambitious Chinese would prove less reluctant to seek control and by the end of the century they managed large sections of industry and agriculture.

Increasingly, the British became involved in the affairs of other states as sultans sought administrative and protective assistance. In 1896 ties were made formal with the creation of the Federated Malay States (affiliated with the British) alongside the Straits Settlements and the Unfederated Malay States (the unaffiliated remainder). The structure of the 'country' would remain until World War II.

Despite their failings in the war, the British were welcomed back at its end. But while most colonial countries faced problems trying to turn the clock back, the British encountered resistance when they tried to move it on.

With Chinese and Indians now making up the majority of the population, the British tried to extend native privileges to them, shocking many Malays. The sultans had been happy for large sections of the country's economy to be in the hands of foreigners, as long as they retained political control. It now appeared that this would be lost. Ordinary Malays were concerned they would become second-class citizens in their own land, outnumbered and without control of economic or political power. It seemed as though the premises of British–Malay rule had been betrayed.

Resistance to the Malayan Union grew quickly and the British backed down. A new union was proposed. The new concept was a Malay nation into which other races would have to adapt, not the multi-racial Malaya previously proposed. Stricter rules for citizenry were introduced and Singapore excluded to offset its large numbers of Chinese. On this unstable footing the Federation of Malaya was formed in 1948.

24

A SHARK IN MURKY WATER

It didn't take too long for Sugong's spirits to pick up when he returned to Penang. He had liked it from the moment he first arrived, the outgoing nature of its majority Chinese complemented by the Hokkien they spoke. Coming back was like coming home. He quickly settled back in, his engagement soon fading into memory.

It was a period of calm that should have served warning of a storm. Within a couple of years Sugong would find himself at the centre of a love triangle, the target of a female gangster, and worst of all, persona non grata with his sifu.

The seeds of trouble had been sown before he arrived. As fundraising began for the Siong Kheng project, volunteers stepped forward. One was a lady called Lang Soh. She proved enthusiastic and able, helping the group cause by raising funds and support for the renovation. As she went about her tasks she came into contact with some of the students. Which is how she entered Sugong's life.

Lang Soh certainly appeared to be an honourable woman, showing virtue in her dedication to the temple cause. Without a view beneath the surface of Penang society it was an impression that would not be challenged, which was fortunate for Lang Soh, because it was here that she truly lurked.

Sugong, however, was teaching the locals, young men from varied walks of life. He gained a perspective on the different shades of Penang quite quickly. It wasn't long before he began to hear rumours about the apparently upstanding benefactor. The best thing to do when the whispers reached his ears would have been to speak to his sifu. As is often the case with best things, Sugong followed an alternative path.

Lang Soh's intentions when she put herself forward were not motivated solely by philanthropy. As her assistance led her to meet students, she moved closer to more practical concerns. For her real business was loan-sharking. While a profitable trade, it was also precarious. Rivals jostled for the chance to muscle in and debtors were sometimes unwilling or unable to make good on their arrears. The importance of good strongmen was unquestioned for both and Lang Soh was in search of a supply.

There was a flaw to her plan. Teaching was still in its early days and many of the students were raw. Sugong on the other hand had been training for most of his life. It was natural that Lang Soh turned her attentions to him.

Her loan-sharking operation was a family business. With Sugong still largely ignorant of their activities, she and her husband started to nurture a relationship, paying him well for small, legitimate tasks and inviting him to a store they owned for meals.

Life in China and Singapore had been austere. To Sugong it appeared as though a corner had been turned. As he received good money for legal graft, the lure of comfort and prosperity closed his ears to whispers about its source. For in addition to her murkier activities,

Lang Soh had legitimate businesses, and it was around these that Sugong's tasks revolved. He helped with shop deliveries, made repairs to her premises and provided general assistance when he was asked. But this innocent debut to her employment was part of a plan to reel him into greyer terrains. It began with him accompanying Lang Soh on her collection rounds.

Sugong justified his activities to himself. The money they collected wasn't protection money and there was never any violence or threats. He sought to persuade himself that she was just an entrepreneur who made her living providing finance to people who couldn't get loans from the bank. But to Lang Soh, Sugong's accompaniment was a first step and a show of force, a message to all that she had the backing of one of Penang's toughest.

The situation grew murkier and Sugong soon found himself questioning his stance. His doubts began when Lang Soh called him one day to rescue her nephew. He had been trapped at a club by some rivals and was in need of extraction. Concerned at the threat to family 'friends', Sugong went to help, only to find when he arrived that the gangsters had already left.

He still sought to argue his actions were just the help of a concerned friend. But it was becoming more of a struggle. If accompanying Lang Soh on collections had confirmed reality in some rumours, this was the moment he should have assessed the truth of the rest. But Sugong was yet to make the breakthrough, something he would bitterly regret.

25

Two girls in a too-small town

To complicate matters Lang Soh had a daughter, Pek Lian. Entangling them further, she wanted her to marry Sugong. The reason this was a complication was his lack of complementary desire. But Lang Soh saw a valuable asset she believed could achieve full potential through a union with her family. She did not readily accept Sugong's refusals.

One of their legitimate businesses was a supplies store, and she would sometimes invite Sugong over for lunch. Increasingly he would find himself seated next to Pek Lian. Around this time a siheng of Sugong's visited from Indonesia. Batai, nicknamed for convenience after the area he was from, was an enthusiastic tourist and set to work on Penang with his camera.

While not exactly a new invention, cameras were still a luxury to men of Sugong's background and film was not easily spared. This rarity of images meant that pictures were usually saved for special occasions and often had the significance this attached. A photograph of a man and woman together for example, could hold connotations.

'Batai, won't you take one of Pek Lian and Ah Chong together?' Lang Soh asked innocently one evening. 'The light behind them is so nice.'

Sugong immediately protested, arguing he did not want to waste Batai's precious film on insignificant pictures. His siheng, recognising Sugong's discomfort, politely concurred with a claim he was running low on film. But Lang Soh was not easily dissuaded and insisted a picture be taken. The argument was settled when she sent her son to the shops for more film for Batai.

A picture of a chubby, beaming Pek Lian sitting next to a decidedly awkward Sugong was duly taken.

'Wonderful,' said Lang Soh.

Lang Soh hoped that by maintaining pressure and generating momentum for the marriage, she would precipitate its occurrence. But Sugong had not proposed and he was adamant this was a situation that would not change. Unwittingly, Lang Soh threw in an obstacle at the very time she was trying to clear a path.

At the lunches to which Sugong was invited, he sometimes found a girl at his other shoulder. Like Pek Lian, Su Ching worked in the supplies store. Unlike Pek Lian, she was good-looking. Whereas Pek Lian could at best be considered a bit chunky, Su Ching was petite and had a graceful gait. Her eyes were a deep brown and, when turned to someone she liked, they were very effective in holding their gaze. Pek Lian's was a plain face of big cheeks that was not especially attractive, even if it was one of jollity and smiles. By contrast, Su Ching's serious expression only enhanced her beauty when she allowed a rare smile escape.

Sugong found himself the recipient of more than a few and he was generous in reciprocation. When she started to bring breakfast over to the studio in the mornings the possibility of romance became clear.

'Ah Chong,' she asked one day, 'do you want to see a film this weekend?'

Sugong instinctively sensed the trouble this might bring.

'I'd love to, Su Ching,' he replied, just as intuitive in his inability to avoid it. 'I'm a bit busy at the moment though. Could you pick up the tickets?'

He handed her some notes.

'Get the evening show, and I'll meet you at the Cathay Cinema at seven.'

So it was that Sugong found himself in the Cathay foyer, spruced up and ready to unleash an avalanche of charm.

'Hi Ah Chong, sorry I'm late.'

Sugong turned to greet his sweetheart.

'Er, Pek Lian, so pleased you could make it,' he said, confused to be stood before the less favoured of his admirers.

'Su Ching,' he nodded a displeased greeting at the other, standing at her workmate's shoulder.

They went in.

That Sugong found his arm clenched by a love-struck Pek Lian while Su Ching sat four rows back was the consequence of a busy day. Instead of buying the tickets herself, Su Ching gave the money to one of the other girls in the shop with instructions.

But Lang Soh was a formidable lady, able to instil fear in debtors and gangsters alike. Her workers were certainly no match for her and Su Ching's colleague was far more willing to end a friendship than to antagonise her boss.

When Lang Soh was told about the tickets she acted quickly to nullify the threat.

'Su Ching, Li Yan tells me you're going to the cinema with Ah Chong,' she said to Su Ching, who had been summoned to her office.

Su Ching knew of her employer's desire to marry Pek Lian to Sugong and was aware she stood on dangerous ground.

'That's right, Madame,' she said innocently. 'We were talking about the movie and realised that neither of us had seen it so we thought we may as well go together.'

The infrequency of male/female friendships at the time made this unlikely.

'Of course, of course,' Lang Soh said just as sweetly. 'I don't think Pek Lian's seen it either. How nice it would be if you all went.'

'Yes, wouldn't it,' Su Ching replied, her smile etched painfully on her face.

Sugong didn't know any of this. All he knew was that he had landed in exactly the position he had been so studiously avoiding. He made his escape as quickly as possible at the conclusion of the film.

The next day Su Ching came to see him. She was angry.

'I saw you with Pek Lian all over each other,' she said. 'You pretend you're interested in me, but really you're just after whatever you can get.'

Having stewed overnight, Sugong had not started the day happy. Now he was almost speechless with rage.

'What are you talking about?' he exploded. 'I thought I was going with you. What were you doing bringing her along? And why did you sit so far behind?'

Su Ching back-tracked and explained what had happened but Sugong was not appeased.

'You want to go to the movies with me – buy the tickets yourself.'

He stormed off.

With a few days to cool off it's likely the flames of love could have been rekindled with Su Ching. But Sugong wasn't given a few days. Encouraged by her perceived progress, Pek Lian turned up at the studio the next day with two tickets to the following weekend's show.

Sugong wasn't in a mood for subtlety.

'I'm busy next weekend.'

'What about the one after?' Pek Lian enquired, undeterred.

'I'm busy then as well. In fact I'm busy now. I've got to go.' He turned around and left Pek Lian. Distraught, she turned on her tail and left in tears for the comfort of her mother, a mother more capable than most of fighting for her cubs.

26

POISON IN A MASTER'S EAR

Entangled romances weren't Sugong's only problem. And just as Lang Soh lay at the centre of his relationship difficulties, she could be found at the root of his other ills. After the incident with her nephew, Sugong had returned home troubled. He had been in enough fights not to be worried by one he had avoided but he was concerned about the direction he felt himself being dragged. He resolved to confront Lang Soh.

Lang Soh's instinct for manipulation was finely tuned. The next day she was nowhere to be found but she managed to pass on a message asking Sugong to help out at the shop. At the end of the day his finances were strengthened and his resolve to challenge Lang Soh had moved in inverse decline. Lang Soh kept presenting obstacles to confrontation over the coming days and when Sugong finally found himself in a position to confront her his inclination had waned.

When the next emergency call came he was ready to act against his better instincts. Once again a relative of Lang Soh was in trouble, this time her son. Again, Sugong convinced himself he was on a mission of friendship. As before there was no violence but this time it was a much closer call.

Lang Soh's son had gone to make a collection. When he saw a group of rivals making their way down the street he had locked himself in the shop, wary of the coincidence. His call to his mother had led to hers to Sugong. When he arrived, Sugong found the gangsters outside the shophouse door. By this time Sugong had been involved in a few altercations in Penang. The reputation he had gained when he emerged favourably was supplemented by the renown he had as an instructor of a kung fu school. It was enough to ensure that only a very few in Georgetown would dare to challenge him. He gambled that these gangsters were not in their number.

He walked past them to the door and called Lang Soh's son out. There was a great deal of tension when he reluctantly emerged. Death stares were directed but Sugong's presence ensured he was not touched. And for all the posturing and threats of 'next time' no attempts were made to prevent them mounting the waiting trishaw and leaving the scene.

Still Sugong attempted to defend his involvement but it was an argument with himself he was beginning to lose. Within he knew he was getting submerged in an unsavoury world and he knew he had to get out. His problem was how. He was not intimidated by Lang Soh or the people she had around her. What concerned him were the consequences of his master finding out.

One of Lang Soh's businesses was a nightclub and Sugong would sometimes help out with security. While he was unaware of who ran the club, Koh Chun did know that gangsters were often to be found not too far behind. He did not want Sugong entangled. The situation started to put a strain on their relationship.

'Ah Chong, have you been helping out at that club?' Koh Chun would demand, knowing it to be the case.

'Sifu, I did go down to help out last week. Hok Long was ill and they didn't have anyone to cover.'

'Did you not hear me when I told you that I don't want you involved?'

Chastened, Sugong would apologise. But he was more worried about what his master didn't know, even if it wasn't true. Although he had only entered the peripheries of her world, Sugong had a sense of Lang Soh's power to twist and manipulate. He was worried about the rumours she could start, and the poison she might pour in his master's ear.

One evening Lang Soh asked Sugong to join her on a collection. Sugong agreed. He had decided to stop working for her and this would present an opportunity to resign she could not avoid.

They were due to collect from a barman. Not keen to discuss business in front of customers, colleagues and his boss he had arranged to meet them in an alley at the back of the bar. On the surface it had looked to be a collection no different to others on which Sugong had joined Lang Soh. Uninterested in proceedings with the debtor, Sugong kept a lazy eye on the alley as he mulled over what he would say to Lang Soh.

But her discussions with the barman became increasingly heated and Sugong was surprised by a sharpness in her voice he had not heard before. Then she ordered him to hit the barman. It was a demand that shocked him despite the vague language she employed. When he didn't comply she turned on him.

'Don't come all innocent with me,' she snapped. 'Where do you think your shop wages come from? Without collections you don't get paid.'

It was the first time a collection had involved anything more than collecting. Stunned, Sugong still didn't move.

'Do I need to remind you of the things I could tell your sifu?' she hissed. 'I know it would upset him to hear what you do.'

Until this point the barman had remained static, confused by the unorthodox collection service before him. With Sugong frozen to the spot he took his chance to run. His movement brought Sugong back to life, and he grabbed at a flailing shirt-tail. The barman reacted by swinging a punch at Sugong's head. Ducking the blow Sugong instinctively hit back, knocking the man to the floor.

The punch cleared the fragile web Sugong had strung across his conscience. When stripped of her veneer of charm, Lang Soh was just another gangster. By joining her on her rounds he was a henchman. But he differed from others as he had a master to betray and an art to defame.

27

RUMOURS AND LIES

The day after the incident with the barman Sugong went to find Lang Soh. His mind had been in turmoil at the end of the previous night and he had not told her of his decision. As was her way when she anticipated an awkward situation she proved elusive.

When she gauged enough time had passed for the waters to settle she reappeared. She asked Sugong to accompany her on another collection, her tone coaxing and friendly once again. This time Sugong declined. Hoping to make the break cordial he claimed he needed more time to focus on his teaching. It was not news Lang Soh wanted to hear.

'That's how you want to make your living?' she asked sarcastically, an edge to her voice. 'That's not how you've made it before and I heard no complaints when you collected your wage.'

Sugong did not rise to the bait. He continued in his efforts at an amicable parting, but Lang Soh was not willing to give up her prize without a fight. She started to make veiled threats about what she could tell Koh Chun. At this point Sugong grew riled and their argument became heated. It ended with Lang Soh walking out, leaving her threats to hang in the air.

A few days later Sugong met a friend at a favourite coffee shop. His route home took him through some side streets and alleys. As he was making his way down one he saw a familiar figure step out ahead. It was the barman, now accompanied by friends. Sugong stopped and began to edge back.

A warning shout made him turn just in time to see a chopper flashing down at his head. He instinctively blocked up with his left arm and the blade sank deep into his forearm. Despite the wound, he managed to grab his attacker's wrist. As he brought it down he smashed with his other hand and heard a crack.

The man was not alone but Sugong landed heavy blows with his right fist and elbow on both of the others as they moved in. As they flailed he ran between them back the way he had come and toward the trishaw whose driver had alerted him to the attack.

The danger did not immediately subside when he leapt in. As the vehicle attempted its slow-accelerating escape, his pursuers made ground. But just when it looked as though they would catch up the trishaw found its rhythm and the distance between them stretched out again. By the time they reached a turn in the road the chase had been abandoned, the threats of his pursuers lost to the ambient noise of the city streets.

In the Penang school's early days the coaching staff had been temporarily bolstered with the arrival of another Siong Lim student, Boon Kiek. When he left, another disciple, Diong Hor, came to take his place. Having never opened and run a school alone before, Sugong was grateful for both the support and the additional time it gave him for his own training. Now Diong Hor's presence provided assistance of another kind. Sugong was anxious not to let his latest set of troubles tarnish the Association. The only way he could think of ensuring it didn't was to resign.

But Koh Chun used to divide his time between Singapore and Penang and he was in Singapore at this point. Which meant that Sugong's resignation had to be delayed. On his return the surface relations between master and disciple were no different. But Sugong's emotions were in tumult as he fretted over how to deliver his news. Yet it was Koh Chun who sent for him after a few days.

'What's this nonsense I hear about you and that girl?' he demanded, his features stern.

At times progressive in his thinking, Koh Chun could as often be of traditional mind. He held firm views on how a man's affairs should be conducted. While Sugong's thoughts had been focused on explaining his decision to leave the Association, Lang Soh had thought only of revenge. Using Batai's picture she had provided 'proof' of Sugong's efforts to woo her daughter, before revealing he had been trying to court others as well.

Sugong tried to defend himself, but he had been out-flanked. He knew there was nothing that could be said to Koh Chun when he was in this kind of mood. Reasoning that he could not upset him any further, Sugong took the opportunity to tell Koh Chun of his intention to leave. The darkened brow of his sifu was evidence that Sugong had misjudged his capacity for displeasure.

Once again Sugong found himself on the defensive as he desperately tried to justify his decision and tell Koh Chun of his aspiration to set up a new school. His arguments did not convince.

'Go,' said Koh Chun in dismissal, waving his hand and turning away. Sugong trudged disconsolately from the temple.

But he was determined to win back his master's favour. When he felt the time was right he set about establishing a new studio and within six months the Siow Hua San school was ready to open. It was far from the first Koh Chun affiliated school, as in addition to the Penang Athletic Association and the original Sao Hua San, a number of others had opened in Singapore. Yet in the present situation it had complications that were unique.

Having opened the Athletic Association and been its instructor, Sugong had built relationships with and won the loyalty of its students. As Siow Hua San was a sister school and not a competitor, some of them decided to return to their former teacher at the new Koh Chun branch. The resultant reduction in Association class numbers, however, could make Sugong's intended homage look anything but.

Sugong endeavoured to avert this potential threat. As at the Association he assumed the title of instructor. Similarly Koh Chun was identified as sifu, and it was before him that students were taken to kneel to become disciples. As their number increased and Sugong's sincerity was demonstrated, Koh Chun's displeasure subsided and relations between the two began to improve again.

Sugong was delighted to re-establish this bond. He was equally happy to forget his relationship with Lang Soh. She was not of the same mind.

Lang Soh's activities did not diminish in any way after Sugong left her employ and her methods became no softer over time. One episode in particular gained local renown. In a dispute over money, Lang Soh had sought to expedite matters with a direct approach to diplomacy. Unfortunately for her, her adversary held some influence of his own and from the hospital bed where he lay post-beating he called in a favour. Yet he had underestimated Lang Soh.

Through her own contacts and some judiciously placed payments, the police investigation was stymied and Lang Soh found herself free to continue as she pleased.

It was Pek Lian who came to Sugong with an invitation for dinner. Sugong was initially cautious, happier to be out of her family's reach. But when she explained the reason for the celebration, he reacted in typical haste, less judiciously than hindsight would suggest ideal.

'You want me to celebrate because your family had someone beaten up and got away with it?' he said sharply. 'I stopped working for your mother already. When are you going to realise I don't want anything to do with any of you?'

Pek Lian left in tears.

Sugong realised his reaction would draw a response and Lang Soh played her hand quickly, visiting Siong Kheng within a few days. There, she sought out Koh Chun. When sitting down with him she voiced her 'concerns', having apparently found out that the school Sugong ran was a front for gangsters. When Koh Chun asked for her suggestions on what he should do, she implied that the art that he was abusing be used to teach him a lesson. When pressed for clarification, she did not expand on the violent implications, but still left the temple confident her work had been done.

Her scheming proved counter-productive. Koh Chun was familiar enough with Sugong's impetuous nature to know that where there was smoke he would likely find fire. But this did not sound like the kind of blaze he was usually liable to start. Curious as to the cause of Lang Soh's meddling, Koh Chun made enquiries of his own. The more he found out, the less he was impressed. The rumours surrounding the beating led to stories about her other activities. When it became clear that this past benefactor was not as righteous as she had indicated, it was made clear that any future offers of assistance would not be required. Conversely, Sugong and Koh Chun's relations continued to improve and it began to look as though there would be a happy end to an unpleasant episode. But Lang Soh's tentacles had reached deeper than that.

28

KUNG FU AND KARAOKE

The first wake-up call was at 5am and didn't even chip at the log I was sleeping like. The second came at 5.30 and was more persistent than the automated phone call.

'Nnnnrrr,' said Michael.

'Mmng,' I replied.

After a minute, the banging on the hotel door became more unpleasant than the act of getting up and Michael answered it.

'OK, OK, coming,' I heard him say.

He stumbled back into the room proper.

'It's Junior Quek,' he said, referring to one of Sugong's great-nephews. 'We've got to go.'

I had already drifted back toward unconsciousness and the resumption of conversation was proving far too much. My body's instincts kicked in.

'Yi'llcomeinabit,' I heard myself mumble before welcoming the darkness of oblivion again.

Bang. Bang. Bang.

At first I thought my head had begun pounding audibly. Then I realised the door was being hammered on

172

again. I looked at the clock. 6am. What was wrong with these people? I almost managed to stand up out of bed before the combination of an explosion in my head, and the buckling of my weakened legs, tripped me head first into the wall. I dragged myself up it and went to the door. Junior Quek again.

'Ah yes. Just coming,' I said, trying to stop my eyes rolling wildly. 'Just wash my face. Then come over,' the words accompanied by gestures.

He nodded and turned away down the hall. I sagged, and collapsed back into bed.

BANGBANGBANGBANGBANG.

I was jolted upright and a flash of indescribably bright light burned what little was left of my brain to a crisp. 6.30. I half-crawled to the door. Junior Quek looked less than impressed.

'Ah yes. Just wash my face. Then come,' I said, not sure if I was suffering from déjà vu, a bad dream or a more unpleasant reality.

Junior Quek nodded and walked into the room. He had obviously received stricter instructions, most probably accompanied by a scolding for coming back without his prisoner. He wasn't going to be fobbed off so easily this time.

I shuffled, stooped, into the bathroom, my body assuming a curved upper torso to ensure my mouth didn't reacquaint itself with the previous night's alcohol. Perhaps splashing some water on my face and brushing my teeth would bring about a miracle cure.

Out in the scalding heat of the Chinese summer, each new step brought a fifty-fifty chance of vomiting and a fresh rebuttal of my vain hope. I struggled onto the pillion position on his bike and we took off on the five-hundred-metre, sickeningly bumpy ride on a path through the fields to Sugong's house.

Eyes burning, I clambered heavily off the back and rounded the corner to a glaring Sugong. He didn't appear to be in the mood to acknowledge his part (suggesting the night out) or his family's (serving the alcohol) in my condition. But despite standing before one of the fiercer of his repertoire of scary looks, I had my first good feeling of the day. Over his shoulder I could see the others sweating away at a form; Michael looked particularly green-faced.

The smugness that temporarily distracted me from my unhappy existence quickly disappeared. Sugong motioned for me to sit and ordered me to eat. I looked at the deep-fried bread and the glass of milk and my body sagged around its churning core. My mouth was bone-dry prior to eating the bread. After two mouthfuls any moisture that remained in the rest of me had also been leeched away. I gulped thirstily at the glass. It turned out to be soya milk and tasted about as good as the vomit I was trying to hold down. It distinctly lowered my chances of success.

But just before I cracked we were off, traipsing heavily back through the fields to the hotel. My head felt like an ant caught in the burning point of light from a magnifying glass held to the sun. 7.00 and we were back in the room. I failed to see the purpose in my two-minute attendance. If I had been allowed to sleep I might even have felt part human. Whatever. Bed.

Bangbangbangbangbang. 7.30. Oh God. Have mercy...

It had seemed a great idea. At the end of our time training with Sugong, Michael and I planned to travel around China for a month. It so happened that Sugong was returning to his village for a couple of weeks at the same time.

'Sugong wants you to visit his hometown with him,' said Mr Tan.

'That's great, Mr Tan,' said Michael. 'But what about the language barrier?'

Expansive Hokkien debate. Lots of hand gestures.

'Well, I'm sure you could muddle through,' came the response.

There was a pause as we imagined muddling through in a small, rural Chinese village with no English speakers for hundreds of miles.

'Look, why don't you join us?' asked Michael.

Mr Tan's face reflected deep deliberation for about a second. Then he broke into a huge grin.

'Of course I'll come along. Why not?'

Delighted, we all high-fived each other. Sugong sensed something happening, and excitement began to swell the energy levels of his body to bursting point. Head rapidly turning from face to face in an attempt to work out what was going on, he clearly needed to be put out of his misery. Mr Tan quickly translated.

Sugong's beaming smile lit the room. He looked like a child told his next ten birthdays and Christmases had just come at once. No longer able to restrain his body, he leapt to his feet and started high-fiving everything in sight. I got the impression it was his first experience of the high-five but he got full marks for enthusiastic application.

A quick chat with Master Wong and four became five.

We were ready to go.

In advance of our trip we read the guidebooks like any good traveller. Not for us the ignorant tourist unaware of the customs and traditions of a country. One of the more interesting observations we noticed was on the Chinese avoidance of arguments and confrontation. They did this to save face.

Ten minutes after arriving in a boiling hot Xiamen and we were in the middle of our first screaming match. We were at the airport and stuck in a packed lift. In contradiction to the laws of physics or common sense, a family of four was trying to squeeze themselves and their full trolleys into a non-existent space. Halfway in and as far as they could go they stopped, as though a force of nature would make possible the impossible. There was a brief pause to allow simmering tempers to reach boiling point, before the inevitable row erupted. Sugong's nephew Quek Junior (Junior Quek's uncle – it was all very confusing), who had met us from the flight, had clearly inherited the family temper.

And so the scene was set for our experience of conflict resolution in China. It wasn't the last time we would witness people 'saving face'.

We arrived in Sugong's village to find that it had now been almost consumed by a small town. The town itself centred on the T-junction of two large 'highways'. That they were highways should not have been in doubt, as with three lanes in either direction they would have fitted the normal definition of the word. Where they differed was in their usage.

You normally expect a highway to be the epitome of driving regulations, the high speeds and densities necessitating a set of common rules. The Chinese do not agree. In KL the 'rules' of the road are seen as more of a guidance system to be ignored when inconvenient. The Chinese did not seem to have any at all.

Driving at suicidal speed was a given, but it was not compensated for by having all cars going in the same direction. It was not unusual to see a car or tractor turn in from a side road to come straight toward our taxi. Evasion techniques were often complicated. The choice was limited to either running down a group of pedestrians crossing on one side or an old man with a lifetime's worth of furniture stacked on his bicycle on the other.

What we couldn't understand was why people would drive like lunatics when numerous crash sites provided first-hand evidence of the downside. All we could think was that, like so much Chinese development, what the rest of the industrialised world had gone through over the course of a century had been foisted upon China in a decade.

Villagers who until recently had cycled down small roads and tracks were now presented with large highways. As the emergence of these had been sudden, there was not a readjustment period where the local population could learn the new rules. Instead, they saw the roads as a nicely surfaced alternative to the dirt track, and they were used in the same way, a means to get from A to B in the most direct way possible.

We were pleased with our theory, its comfort in its simplicity. But faced with a twenty-ton lorry thundering towards us with no room for escape, it became rapidly less assuring.

After a few near-death experiences and a couple of face-saving situations, we came to Sugong's house. There we were treated to a feast. As would continue to be the case for the duration of our stay we had no say in the type of food, the time of eating or the quantity consumed. An iron-hard stubby finger would point at the food, and then at us, followed by the order 'chia'. Knowing the damage the finger could do when put to more aggressive purposes we ate.

At the end of dinner on the first night Sugong spoke to Mr Tan.

'Sugong wants us to go to his niece's karaoke bar,' he translated. 'It's still new and it's not doing that well. If we turn up it will help support business, especially if there are a couple of gwei lo there.'

As two enthusiastic, if not particularly talented, singers, Michael and I readily agreed.

A change of clothes later we all hopped on the back of motorbike taxis outside the hotel and headed off.

The karaoke bar was quite basic – essentially just a large rectangular room. In the corner was the bar. This was followed by a couple of booths, flanking knee-high tables. And in the middle of the room on the opposite side was a low stage topped with a large TV in front of some decorative panels on the wall. It had not been done on a high budget, but the enthusiasm employed more than made up for it. We would match the energy levels over worryingly long periods in the coming week.

During our stay we realised that the Chinese have quite a macho approach to the idea of manhood. This was most immediately apparent in attitudes to smoking and drinking. Metrosexual Man had definitely not made his way out this far. The extended Quek family were true to form. As soon as we arrived beers were hauled out and cigarettes thrust at us from all directions. Both ex-smokers, both with a weakness for the odd relapse, we looked at each other, shrugged and lit up. Integrating with social customs and all that. Besides, Sugong wasn't due for an hour.

Five hours later, Sugong still hadn't shown up. We had more than made up for his absence. The high-ceilinged room looked as though someone had blown in the smoke from a forest fire. The sixth case of beer lay empty at the side. Mr Tan was serenading imaginary beauties of the world, mic in hand; Michael was dancing on stage; Master Wong was demonstrating some aerobics moves from days gone by; and I was on an incredible losing streak at the drinking game *dice*.

It was not the most complicated of games but this hadn't stopped us from playing for the majority of the night. It involved putting two dice in a cup, shaking then slamming it down and checking the numbers. The person with the lower total had to down what was in their glass. Despite the vast range of methods used – blowing on the dice, whispering to them, or shaking the cup with special pizzazz – it remained a game of luck and should have evened out to ensure equal, if heavy, drinking. I was on my tenth straight loss when the beer finally ran out.

'Ai-yah, it's half one,' said Master Wong. 'We should get going.'

Half one wouldn't have been so late if we had not been told we would start training at half five the next morning. Invincible in our drunken stupor we were unconcerned but finally we were ushered outside. Once there our drinking partners mounted their bikes and waved us on pillion.

'You think they're OK to drive?' I asked.

My driver answered by accelerating straight into a wall. After the imposed stop he righted himself and we set off again. The others had already screeched off. We soon caught up as the five-minute ride turned into a two-minute race, with the pillions shouting and gesticulating as the bikes criss-crossed. A minute in and I had to check to see whether we had gone over a steep hill. We hadn't. Rollercoaster stomach. I started to have my first doubts about getting up.

Knock knock.

'Hi Master Wong. What's up?' said Michael sleepily, once again the one to get to the door.

'Get dressed quickly. Sugong's been waiting downstairs for half an hour and he's upset.'

'I didn't know we were meant to be meeting him,' responded Michael, confused.

'Nor did I. But anyway, move quickly.'

Sugong shared the view of the British justice system when it came to pleading ignorance. It was not a valid defence. We had had another night at the karaoke bar, again at his suggestion, and despite the post-training nap, we were feeling it. We dressed clumsily, staggered out of the room and made our way downstairs.

Sugong was there with Quek Junior, not looking best pleased. We were fortunate not to be able to fully understand his gesticulated complaints and just followed meekly to the van outside, hiding behind our sunglasses.

'Where are we going?' I asked.

'I don't know,' said Master Wong.

'Mr Tan?'

'I don't know.'

In many ways Sugong was an excellent host, but as with all aspects of his life he did things in his own unique way. He wasn't really one for democracy or even an element of choice, and he certainly wasn't a great believer in the necessity of information. Every day we clambered into a van and were taken off to see the sights of Fujian. And on each day we were left wondering where we were going until we got there. Sometimes we were not much the wiser even then.

The most important of these trips were to the Shaolin temples dotted around the area. While there is controversy about the existence of *the* South Shaolin Temple, it is widely accepted that there was Shaolin kung fu activity in the area. Relics found suggest that certain temples were martial arts practising, and we went to two: Quanzhou and Putian, although it would probably be fairer to say one-and-a-half. Because, despite his obvious love of Shaolin, and the long journeys on bumpy roads that were required to reach our destinations, Sugong was a restless tourist.

Once we arrived we would all pile out, enter the temple grounds, and start looking around and snapping away. But we would be working under a time limit. Sometimes this extended to our looking at the whole temple in a leisurely manner and escaping without reprimand. Other times we could look around but were then scolded for our tardiness. But on the occasion of the Putian temple things were cut a bit short.

'Come on, we have to go,' said Mr Tan.

'But we're only halfway through, Mr Tan. We haven't even seen the buildings over there,' Michael said.

'I know, but he's had enough and he wants to go.'

So we went.

To be fair, I think Sugong had done all of the spots numerous times before and was just playing the good host. But after a two-hour drive, turning around for home just as the blood had begun to circulate in our legs was a different approach to pilgrimage than I had imagined. I wondered if there were Muslims who turned back a couple of laps into their seven circuits of the Hajj.

So a routine was established. We would get woken for early morning training, eat breakfast, try to grab a little more sleep, get woken, drive for a couple of hours, quickly view a temple, and then move on to the next. After that we would make the long journey home, get changed in the hotel, be force-fed at Sugong's, and then plied with alcohol and cigarettes at the karaoke bar. Before it started all over again.

If I had become slightly obsessive about sleep in KL, it was nothing compared to my endless daydreams about undisturbed rest now. But before I knew it the week was up and we were off on our separate ways. Sugong to stay on another week in his hometown, Master Wong and Mr Tan back to KL, Michael and I on to Shanghai, and then a zigzag tour across China. And maybe even some sleep.

29

Beyond the codes of conduct

Sun Ah Hock was a student at Siow Hua San. He would later forge a reputation as a formidable fighter, but in 1959 he was still just sixteen: a hot-tempered sixteen.

One afternoon he was cycling in the area of Siong Kheng and rode past the temple. Koh Chun and Sugong's differences were now behind them and Sugong happened to be inside. Any problems that had existed had been kept purely between the two. But the students of the schools had noticed some tension and, confusing loyalty with rivalry, a degree of edginess had emerged. There were those among the students who remained who had reservations about others who had left.

Sun was among the number who had changed school. And as he cycled past the temple some of his former sihengs were standing by the gates.

'Sun, what are you doing here?' they taunted him. 'There's no one who wants to see you anymore.'

Sun displayed customary reservation in the face of provocation.

'Go fuck yourself. You think you're something special, but you're no better than me.'

They were the kind of comments that would have drawn a reaction whoever made them. But abuse from a sixteen-year-old was not something the Siong Kheng students could accept. They chased after Sun, who escaped on his bike. His advantage was quickly neutralised when he flew straight into a trishaw, ending in a heap on the floor.

Sun had managed to raise quite a commotion and people rushed from the temple to see what was going on. Sugong heard the noise and made his way out as well. When he reached Sun there was a crowd surrounding him. Still unconvinced, or incapable of seeing the need for diplomacy, Sun continued to point out the deficiencies of his siheng. For his efforts he was pushed between them in the centre of the makeshift circle that had formed. Just as Sugong reached it, Sun went sprawling on the end of a slap.

'Don't hit him again,' warned Sugong, announcing his arrival.

Some of the students had been taught by Sugong; the others knew him by reputation. All stopped still. Except for Sun, who staggered up, rubbed the swelling on the side of his face and spat out another curse.

'Shut up, Sun.'

Sugong turned to the others.

'I don't know what's going on here but you're all hengdai and you know not to fight your brothers,' he said. 'I'm not going to let one of my students be beaten whatever the reason. If he's done something wrong let me know what and I promise I'll deal with it.'

Still nobody moved. Sun had ruffled more than a few feathers and the students were more inclined toward dispensing the punishment themselves. Yet none of them wanted to tell Sugong.

'Come on, Sun, let's go,' said Sugong, motioning for Sun to join him.

Sun started toward Sugong but someone grabbed at his shirt. His arm flailed out as he was drawn back and it struck another student on the head. Incensed, the student hit back and a scuffle started. Sugong waded into the group to grab Sun and chaos ensued.

Whether the intent was to hit Sun or himself, Sugong found himself under siege. He struck back, and as his punches connected students went to ground. With a number of his attackers lying prone, Sugong found himself with a bit of room. He shouted for Sun to make his escape. Sun scrambled to his bike and took flight.

Sugong knew he had been lucky to escape so lightly to this point. He also knew that good fortune would not see him through much longer. He looked for the point his opponents were at their thinnest, threw a punch and darted through the space left by his sprawling foe.

Siong Kheng Temple was situated on Waterfall Road. At its end were the Botanical Gardens. Sugong sprinted through the entrance with angry students in pursuit. A short distance in he ran into a gardener chopping wood. Sugong grabbed his axe.

Through numbers the chasing students had gained the confidence to pursue Sugong. When they saw him turn and bear down on them with an axe they became less bold. They scrabbled back into one another and fled.

As they did the blood drained from Sugong's head. He knew that walking down the street with an axe in his hand was not the best way to remain a free man in Penang. He returned it to its owner and made his way back across town to Siow Hua San. It was a troubled journey. He knew there would be repercussions from the afternoon's events.

Later the same day, Sugong stood on the pavement in front of the shophouse that was home to his school. He had time to kill before his next class. Looking down the street he saw a trishaw come round the corner and make its way toward him. It was moving quite fast and as it approached he recognised a familiar figure in the front.

'Don't even try to run,' Koh Chun bellowed, rising up in his seat as the trishaw closed in.

Sugong didn't. He was frozen to the spot. Koh Chun's thick eyebrows were drawn in and downward, the skin between them contracted in rage. His eyes were black and bored through Sugong, unblinking. They drew Sugong in, mesmerising him so that he could see nothing else. And as the trishaw pulled in to the kerb, Koh Chun leapt.

It was this sudden movement that broke the spell. His black robes billowed as he flew toward Sugong, the momentum of the trishaw accelerating his leap. At the last moment he thrust out his arm, single finger extended and aimed at Sugong's chest.

Fortunately his tutelage had not been in vain. Sugong snapped from his paralysis and twisted sharply to his left. His reaction was enough to deflect the main thrust of his master's blow. Yet there remained enough power in the strike to rip through his shirt and rake his chest.

The monk's momentum took him past Sugong, giving Sugong a split second to look down at the tatters of his shirt. It hung in two pieces, and the space between them revealed a swelling welt. He turned to Koh Chun and briefly caught his eye. Black fury.

Now Sugong ran.

There are various codes of conduct in martial arts. Some are spoken, others not. Of the unspoken, some are not voiced because they are subtle, like the giving of ang paos. Others because they are so clear they need not be said. Fighting a group of students taught directly by your master would number among them. It was definitely not good form.

All of which left Sugong in a very difficult position.

185

One thing was certain: he would not be welcomed by his sifu for some time. If Koh Chun had really intended to hurt him, Sugong would have been powerless to prevent it. But he knew his master would never really harm him, even in the darkest of moods. Koh Chun was not beyond handing out a short-term lesson, however, and the consequences of his strike would not have been fun. It was not an incident that would blow over quickly.

Sugong needed to determine the best way to accelerate the healing process.

A month or so earlier he had been contacted by a relative on behalf of the extended Leongs. They were a husband-and-wife team, assisted by their son, who worked as contractors and supervisors at a port near Kuala Lumpur. They had some trouble and needed help. Sugong had not been interested. He took pride in the schools he had established and the students he taught. Furthermore his bond with Koh Chun had been growing stronger once again. At the time there was no reason he would want to exchange his situation.

But that had been then and this was now. And for Sugong there was a world of difference between the two. As he assessed his options he came to the conclusion that excluding himself from Koh Chun's vicinity might allow conditions to cool. He could do a favour for his cousins while allowing Koh Chun's hackles to subside. Once done he could return and make good with his master.

30

OPPOSITE SIDES OF A
DIFFERENT COIN

Sugong arrived in Port Swettenham with a light bag and a heavy heart. He had reasoned the move to himself repeatedly and was convinced the decision was right. But for eleven years he had only been apart from his master for weeks at a time. Now he was committed to a separation that had no fixed end date in sight.

There was a positive and it was a considerable one. Sugong may not have had much to bring with him, and he no longer had a master from whom to learn, but he did have a young wife.

It had been Sugong who put an end to relations with Pek Lian and Su Ching but he was still left feeling melancholy after the event. As a healthy young man, having the freedom to sample the delights of Penang should not have been a great distress. But the obligations of society weighed heavy and according to their rules his time for marriage was overdue. Having been through a stream of relationships and engagements he found himself abruptly reduced from a choice of two to options of none.

A relative and her friend noticed Sugong in sombre mood.

'Ah Chong, what's up?' his aunt asked. 'You're kicking your heels and moping around.'

'It's nothing, I'm fine,' he lied.

'Don't try to pull the wool over my eyes, I can see right through you,' came his aunt's retort. 'You've got no one to make you lunch, no one to fuss over you, and nobody to use up your energy on.'

She and her friend cackled with laughter, clearly enjoying themselves.

'But don't you worry, Ah Chong,' his aunt continued gleefully. 'You can trust your auntie to help you out.'

It turned out that the friend had a daughter. The friend knew Sugong through his aunt and with her offspring of marriageable age she felt she had found the right man. Arrangements were made for an introduction.

On meeting the daughter Sugong's emotions were mixed. Beautiful, quick-witted and good-natured, she was everything he could hope for in a future Madame Quek. But with vastly contrasting backgrounds Sugong had reservations whether a relationship could last.

He was a native Chinese raised in the fields of his homeland. Buddhist by religion, his education had been as limited in quality as it had been in time. She was Chinese–Malaysian, born in Penang. A Christian to his Buddhist, her education had been in English provided at one of Penang's better schools.

Significant enough for reflection, they were problems that could be overcome. Of more concern to Sugong was the fact that her education was still to be relegated to the past. At just eighteen, she was in the last year of school. He was about to hit thirty.

When he met with her mother again he made clear his admiration but he was adamant a marriage could not take place.

Good luck and bad were to combine. The future Madame Quek's father was a customs officer. A couple of months after Sugong met his daughter he was inspecting a package when it exploded. Out of respect to his aunt's friend Sugong visited the father in hospital and the two struck up a mutual regard. The older man asked Sugong to meet his daughter again to give her another chance.

'It's not that there's anything wrong with your daughter,' said Sugong. 'But she's so much younger than me – I just don't see how it could work.'

Her father would not take no for an answer.

'What's the difference?' he asked. 'Ten years or so. Meet her again. If your characters aren't suited then look elsewhere. But don't turn down a good marriage because you think a few years might create problems that aren't even there.'

Sugong consented to the request. Within two years the couple were married.

With a new bride in tow and work to be done, there wasn't much time for rumination when Sugong reached the port. And the work was challenging. When he received the invitation from the Leongs, the impression he had been given was of routine security. He turned up to a more complex situation.

Good money could be made handling shipments at ports and there were plenty of parties interested in making it. One of them was a family operation run by the Tngs. They were trying to muscle in on the Leongs' business. The difficulties were compounded by a mutinous atmosphere among the coolies, who felt their supervisors were getting an undue cut of rewards. Combined, the problems were explosive.

There was no chance of Sugong single-handedly seeing off an established gang. The prospects of his quelling worker unrest alone were just as unlikely. The plan was for him to ease the situation by working on the docks, mediating where possible, and acting as the eyes and ears of the Leongs.

For the first couple of weeks it went surprisingly well with only some minor scuffles to resolve. They were in fact more help than hindrance, as they allowed Sugong's presence become known. The third week brought greater drama. One afternoon a fight broke out between a Leong and a Tng.

Both were armed with makeshift weapons, and both had the backing of a powerful clan. For the other workers there was no incentive to intervene; there was much to lose and little to gain. Sugong was not a great deal more enthusiastic to put himself in danger but he had less choice – it was his job to get involved. Taking advantage of a wild lunge he steamed in. Shoving the unbalanced attacker, he saw the man fall to the ground. As the other fighter moved in to seize this opportunity, Sugong turned and dropped him with a punch. Fight over.

Sugong's position at the docks was precarious. While he worked alongside the other men, it was no secret that he was there to assist the Leongs. Shows of strength had their use but docks housed secluded corners where grudges could easily and unexpectedly be settled. They were not happy places for those mistrusted or disliked.

Sugong had thrown himself into the work, anxious to prove his worth to his workmates and eager to share in their banter. His efforts had lessened the suspicion with which he was viewed, but this was not quite the same as winning trust. Now he had a chance. When the supervisor came to investigate the disturbance Sugong lied to cover the fighters' backs. With employment flexible, docked wages, suspension or redundancy were punishments easily meted out. Sugong managed to prevent any, winning favour from the fighters and increasing his standing with those who had watched.

Which wasn't to say that he immediately became well liked. It also did not bring an abrupt stop to the docks' troubles, or put an end to all future fights. But slowly, as he proved himself worthy of respect and deserving of confidence, Sugong's standing with the other men grew, and the Leongs' troubles began to decline. As they did, Sugong turned his attention to matters more important.

It was more than a year since he had left Penang, enough time he thought for waters to settle. With circumstances improved at the port, Sugong decided to broach the situation he had left in the place he considered home.

31

THE SADDEST RECONCILIATION

In the late spring of 1960, just before his intended return to Penang, Sugong received an unwelcome call. The caller himself was not offensive; he was one of the Siong Lim disciples. It was his message that turned Sugong's world upside down.

Koh Chun was dying.

Sugong didn't know his master as a young man. Koh Chun was already in his sixties when Sugong started training and he had passed seventy by the time Sugong left Penang. But despite his advancing age, Koh Chun had always exuded health and vitality. He may have grown a little frailer as the years passed but the force of his presence had remained.

Evidently his health had deteriorated rapidly. Aware he was approaching his end, Koh Chun instructed one of the students to contact his estranged disciple, anxious for a reconciliation before it was too late. Sugong left for Singapore at once.

Arriving at Siong Lim, he went straight to the abbot's chambers. He was shocked by what he saw. Koh Chun lay on his bed, weak and thin. To see his once formidable master a shadow of the man he had been was too much for Sugong and he burst into tears.

When he was able to regain some composure he went to his master and sat at his side. He had spent the last year running through the things he wanted to tell Koh Chun: explanations, apologies and expressions of appreciation. Now he was finally in a place to do so he found his words consumed by sobs.

But they were not needed. Koh Chun had made his feelings clear when he sent for Sugong. Now, as Koh Chun took Sugong's hand in his own, words were unnecessary. Both understood what the other didn't say.

There was not an obvious cause of Koh Chun's impending death. Supremacy in medicine and martial arts might be able to prolong life but they do not equate to immortality. Old age had caught up with him as anyone else. During the time Sugong had known him he had at times suffered complaints he put down to internal injuries from his fight with Tai Hor. His internal energy and knowledge of medicine had enabled him to counter these. But at seventy-three, it was possible he no longer had the strength.

Sugong was not one for idle moments at the best of times. Now he was desperate for diversions as he fretted for his master. His reaction was as much relief as honour when Koh Chun asked him to make his casket. Sugong threw himself into the task, determined his sifu's final resting place would be worthy of the man. Any time not dedicated to this duty he spent with Koh Chun, comforting him and reminiscing, in an attempt to make his last days as pleasant as they could.

Less than a week after arriving he was sent for by his master. He trudged to the abbot's room with a sense of foreboding. When he entered he saw that Koh Chun had weakened noticeably from the day before. Only the faintest grasp on life remained. As on his return, Koh Chun took Sugong's hand in his own. He spoke quietly, the words requiring obvious effort.

'Ah Chong, while you are around Shaolin will shine.'

At this point he started to cough and Sugong brought up a handkerchief. When he removed it he saw blood. Koh Chun had almost reached the end.

'Ah Chong, take me to my casket.'

Sugong helped ease his master from the bed and carried his frail body to his final place of rest. Propped up and seated within it, Koh Chun went into meditation. Sugong sat at the foot of the casket and wept.

Two hours later Koh Chun died.

(In the world of martial arts it is not uncommon for there to be contention in the wake of a great master's passing. Sek Koh Chun's superlative knowledge and ability negated debates as to his successor; there was nobody able to justify the claim and it is widely agreed none was named.

This didn't stop debate on which disciple was best in ability or who had been closest to Koh Chun. The above tells the account of his death as recalled by Sugong. Two other students, Tay Eng Guan and Ong Tiong Ann, also claim to have been the ones to take Koh Chun's hands and comfort him at the end.)

Sek Koh Chun passed away on 16 May 1960. At his death his casket was displayed publicly for viewing. It was during this time, in the days prior to his cremation, that problems started to emerge. The first centred on a disagreement between two factions of followers over where the ceremony should take place.

The situation seemed to have been resolved when an eminent Singaporean monk sought direction from the deceased's spirit through a *bei jiao* ceremony. Thousands lined the streets leading to Quan Ming San, where the cremation was held and a fitting conclusion to Koh Chun's life appeared to have been reached.

But there was a final drama to be played out. Prior to his death, Koh Chun had let it be known that he wanted his ashes to be scattered in the Singaporean Sea. But before his wish could be fulfilled the ashes disappeared. There was shock and consternation in the temple and the monk responsible for carrying out Koh Chun's request could not be consoled. An investigation was launched but without success. Koh Chun's remains could not be found. For almost three months their whereabouts remained a mystery and it appeared he would be denied the dignified send-off he deserved. Then one day, as suddenly as his ashes had vanished they reappeared in the ancestors' hall.

The mystery of their return equalled that of their departure. Speculation suggested that the thief might have been a well-wisher rather than someone intending harm. With some Chinese believing the dispersal of a person's remains prevents the onward journey of their spirit, it was suspected that guilt overcame traditional thought and compelled Koh Chun's vestiges to be returned.

A definitive answer at his death would remain as elusive as the details of his life. But with the ashes returned, Koh Chun could be put to rest, his cycle could be concluded and his spirit be free to move to wherever fate held.

32

A FAMILY AFFAIR

Sugong had already left Singapore by the time Koh Chun's ashes reappeared, making his way back to Port Swettenham shortly after the cremation. His welcome was not warm. Unfortunately Mr Leong was not there on Sugong's arrival. Instead Sugong found his son.

'What are you doing back? There's no work for you here,' said Leong Jr. Sugong was taken aback by his aggressive tone. 'What do you want? A handout?'

Before he had left for Singapore, Sugong had passed on word of his emergency leave. It had not reached Leong Jr, who assumed Sugong had gone AWOL. Leong Jr's anger was immediately matched by Sugong's, who believed his past efforts worthy of a more gracious welcome. Blood rushed to his head and before the thought reached his mind, he had already thrown a slap at Leong Jr's face.

Knowing his parents had hired Sugong because of his fighting ability, Leong Jr's response was not the most shrewd. Grabbing a hoe resting against the wall, he swung it at Sugong. Sugong blocked and grabbed the hoe's end. As he yanked it, Leong Jr stumbled forward, doubling the force of the blow when Sugong thrust the hoe back. It caught Leong Jr flush in the chest and he fell to his knees, retched once and then vomited. The omens for a long stay in Port Swettenham did not look good for Sugong.

When Sugong returned to work the next day he was denied entry; his pass had been revoked. He had no job, which would mean no money. Which in turn would give him no reason to stay. Fortunately, he did have a circle of workmates he could now call friends. And one had a relative who worked in a rubber processing plant in Kuala Lumpur. He would be able to put in a word for Sugong. What Sugong had to pack was soon bundled in a bag.

KL did not prove an immediate haven of peace and goodwill. Within days of arriving Sugong was hauled to the police station, the local constabulary responding to a complaint by the Leongs. There he had an overdue stroke of good fortune. At the station in Circular Road (now Jalan Pekeliling) he found himself in front of an interviewer who shared the same surname. Delighted to come upon a 'relative', Inspector Quek was immediately better disposed toward Sugong. He accepted his plea of self-defence and released him on condition he did not return to Port Swettenham.

This was less simple than it might have been. Sugong had started giving kung fu classes while living at the port. The money he charged had been inconsequential beside the rewards he received from the Leongs. But pay in the rubber factory was considerably lower and Sugong now needed the supplement to his income. Interpreting the police warning as returning to live, he started to make the four-hour round trip three times a week.

Hard graft in a factory was physically taxing and a couple of hours' teaching wearing on body and mind. The journey between locations pushed things still further and Sugong was soon exhausted, hard-up and in need of a change. It came courtesy of the Quek Kongsi.

Sugong

A kongsi is a clan organisation usually formed through shared geographical roots or the same name. The people of a kongsi provide a support network, particularly when overseas. The Queks, mostly hailing from coastal Fujian, had many seafarers in their numbers and a base had emerged at a port in Penang. Members of the kongsi did their best to ensure sea-based business in Penang was conducted at this port and in return they benefited from a discounted fee.

Some local gangsters failed to appreciate the fraternal spirit, and goods from Quek shipments had started to go missing. It was not easy to catch the thieves, and once caught there was a good possibility that catcher, rather than the miscreant, would be punished. The Quek Kongsi needed someone for whom this would not be the case.

Sugong had retained his affection for Penang, and he was happy to help his kongsi. But there were further reasons the chance to return was welcome. A couple of months before Koh Chun passed on, a new potential Shaolin torch-bearer had entered the world. Recent events had made for a turbulent time for baby and parents and the support of a family network would be well received.

While he wanted to assist his kongsi, Sugong needed a source of income. They responded by giving him a coffee shop to run at the entrance to the port. It was ideal. He could earn for his family, while providing a visible deterrent to thieves for the kongsi.

Sugong had not been absent from Penang long enough for his reputation to have been forgotten. When word got out of the new watchman, enthusiasm for pilfering quickly decreased. To consolidate his early success, Sugong sat down with local triads and spelled out the situation. Security was now in his charge, and it would be vigorously enforced. They too decided to do their business elsewhere.

It seemed a perfect solution; Sugong was back earning

in Penang and crime levels at the dock were down. But as time passed, the attention of some in the kongsi averted from the amount they were saving to what more they could gain. The coffee shop had become a much sought-after asset. Aside from the site's excellence as a watch-post, it was a prime piece of business estate. Its position meant it enjoyed a stream of customers, the till rang often and the money rolled in.

The first hint of the trouble this might cause came in the form of a local gangster who believed himself a more suitable proprietor than Sugong. He did not find Sugong in agreement, and after an unsuccessful attempt at usurpation a second endeavour was not made.

Repelling a thug was one thing but when difficulties arose with his kongsi, Sugong could not find as easy a resolution. Regretting his unwittingly generous compensation, the kongsi head began to retract his support. Whether aware of the plight of the gangster, or uncomfortable trying to withdraw a reward it had been his idea to give, he did not broach the situation head-on. Instead, Sugong began to find life less easy. Deliveries were delayed, he found himself at the centre of rumours, and a once convivial atmosphere now seemed to have soured.

The turning tide hit Sugong at a bad time. Six months into his return, his first born was taken down by illness. Despite all efforts, mother and father were left childless once more. When festival fireworks led by the kongsi left the facade of the shop blackened, Sugong interpreted it as an intentional gesture of disregard. He was not in combative mode and the thought of battling his own clan was not one he would have contemplated at any time. With Penang no longer appearing to offer happiness, Sugong and his young wife decided to make another fresh start.

33

UNDER THE BRANCH OF A PEACH BLOSSOM TREE

The association between China's most famous criminal export and a Buddhist sect is not a likely one to make. Yet there is a link between the triads and Shaolin, even if it is one based on mythology the former are anxious to advance and the latter disinclined to accept.

By definition, tracing the history of secret societies is a difficult task and a precise outcome unlikely. Their origins may lie in undefined acts from centuries past, and many die out with their members. The triads are a relatively recent and better-known incarnation, having more distinct, albeit contentious, roots. The unlikely affiliation is claimed to go back to the burning of a Shaolin temple, said to have taken place in the early years of the Ching (1644–1911).

The story goes that when faced by an invading force from a neighbouring state, the emperor appealed for assistance, a cry for help taken up by the Shaolin monks. One hundred and twenty-eight of them went into battle and heroically defeated the barbarians, for which they were lauded and offered rewards. Conscientious monks that they were, they declined the offerings and returned to their monastic way of life.

But instead of concluding another gallant episode in their history it was to prove the start of a long struggle. A conniving official with a grudge against Shaolin turned the emperor against them, suggesting the emphatic nature of their victory was proof of collusion with the invading force.

Wary of the monks' fighting prowess, the court employed underhand tactics when the decision was made to destroy them. They first uncovered a treacherous ex-monk named Ma. Expelled from Shaolin for immoral behaviour, he had been thirsting for revenge and was eager to assist. Once he had provided a guide to the temple, they took a further precaution, presenting a gift of poisoned liquor to the unsuspecting monks. Compromised by treachery and poison, they were helpless against the forthcoming attack and only eighteen escaped the conflagration that ensued.

In the escape, their moral rectitude was repeatedly affirmed by assistance from heaven. Trapped at the side of a river by the pursuing Ching army, they were sent a bridge of clouds to enable a getaway. At another juncture they came across the wife and daughter of a fallen comrade worshipping at his grave. Ambushed by their pursuers, a sword materalised out of the branches of an overhanging peach blossom tree. With it, the monks defeated the soldiers.

(Peach trees frequently appear in triad lore, most likely as a result of their symbolism of long life in Chinese culture. Plums also have a similar significance, which may explain their appearance in Chinese martial arts and religion.)

Despite the help from on high, the monks' numbers gradually depleted and only five made it to the sanctuary of a mountain in southern China. Fortunately the Five Ancestors, as they came to be known, were exceptional. Just how extraordinary depends on the limits of one's personal beliefs. They certainly displayed more than average abilities as they fled the pursuing Ching army, attaining semi-divine stature as they went. As martial artists they were also deemed beyond the ordinary, with southern Shaolin kung fu styles, including Hung Gar and Wing Chun, credited, if not to their origination, then to their influence at least. (Different versions of their story place the destroyed Shaolin temple in various provinces but it is most popularly cited as the South Shaolin temple. Whether mythical in influence or not, the Ancestors had a significant impact on the development of a south Shaolin specific art.)

Once they reached their mountain sanctuary they met a wise monk and, after receiving auspicious signals from heaven, they pledged with their blood to restore the Ming. With that they became the first triads. Drawing together other followers, their combined numbers totalling an auspicious one hundred and eight, they launched an attack against the Ching. Despite initial success they were defeated and the Five Ancestors withdrew, separated and spread across China to gather forces for a future uprising.

As historical accounts go, it is not exactly iron-clad. The few existing written versions contradict one another, as does the triads' narrative lore. The first hard evidence of the society's existence came in a rebellion against the authorities in Taiwan in 1787. Confiscated written oaths and confessions combined to announce this new 'force' and initiate Ching suppression.

The intent of the group on a larger scale was debatable. While the Taiwan experience revealed the desire of some to rebel, the coming centuries showed the triads to be anything but united. While they undoubtedly included an anti-Ching element as time progressed, their members had wildly disparate aims.

Among the most common were the financial gains that resulted from initiation fees collected when a chapter began. These served as a catalyst for growth but the spread of small groups that resulted was not conducive to a strong centralised creed: some focused on self-protection, others on extortion or rebellion. But many members were hardly aware of any objectives beyond the common pledges of mutual aid.

Rather than the image of organised crime their name conjures today, the triads were disorganised and not uniformly focused on crime.

Just as triad interests differed, so did the view of the authorities. In China, the Ching overestimated their political ideals and strength. As they tried in vain to extinguish the triads, they probably enhanced their appeal. Outside the mainland, triads appeared among Chinese emigrants eager for, or unable to decline, their social support.

In Hong Kong, the British authorities were as hostile as the Chinese but for different reasons. Here it was the triad groups' foothold in smuggling that led to a clampdown. It was less a matter of illegality than unwanted competition as the British were importing great amounts of opium themselves.

British pragmatism was evident in their welcoming of triads elsewhere. The Malay Peninsula needed Chinese workers, and the organisational abilities of the triads were well received. They brought in immigrants, assimilated them, and kept order in their areas (although justice was at times administered harshly and extortion was not unknown). Triad activities were practised quite openly, and they were viewed much as guilds, such as freemasons, more familiar to the colonialists. It was only toward the end of the 19th century, after rioting between rival societies, that their legitimate functions were taken over. They were outlawed in 1890, leaving them only criminal ventures to pursue.

The British also had a role in naming the triads. On joining, new members undergo a ritual journey that mirrors that of the Five Ancestors and culminates in their rebirth to a new family with the surname *Hong*.

The Taiwan uprising was launched by a society named *Tiandihui* (Heaven and Earth Gathering), but alternatives – such as the Three Unions, Three Rivers or Three Dots – became commonly used as new chapters sought names not yet banned by the authorities. All had an emphasis on the number three. While this may have represented heaven, earth and man, it was more likely a derivative of three dots in the character for Hong. The British authorities picked up on it and coined a new term. They were thereafter referred to as *triads* (although in Chinese, they are most commonly referred to as the Hong Society – *Hongmen* in Mandarin).

(It has been said the surname Hong was based upon the first Ming emperor Hongwu, but evidence suggests it resulted from the monk name of the Tiandihui's mythical founder.)

Back in China, the nationalist movement was attracted to the increasingly vocal anti-Ching message and heroic 'history' of the triads and saw its potential for their cause. The triads were not wholeheartedly reciprocal; for all the rhetoric, self-interest lay at the heart of many groups. A system of growth that encouraged financial gain had led quite naturally to robbery and extortion in the triads' early days. This increasingly extended to gambling, smuggling and prostitution in the 19th century. When they were involved with rebellions, they more often focused on feuds and local disputes rather than a battle to depose the Ching.

In the colonies, the bans on triads had robbed them of their legitimate functions. When the Ching were overthrown in China the triads' claimed political relevance was also lost. By the middle of the 20th century there was not much room left for ideals of righteousness. The focus was almost solely on making money now, mainly through criminal means.

But their self-proclaimed link to Shaolin remained and the triads weren't anxious to let it slip; in addition to bestowing a grand heritage, martial arts had practical benefits for a gang. But the advantages were one-sided. The attitudes and activities of the modern triads were anathema to *wude*, the moral code of martial arts.

Yet it was one thing to disapprove of the triads. Staying beyond their reach was another matter.

34

FLESH, SAND AND STONE

With charmed timing, Sugong was contacted by some of his old students. They were members of the Youth Association of Malaya who wanted him to return to KL to teach. It was a welcome invitation.

The year was 1963 and KL was at the height of the P Ramlee era. P Ramlee was Malaysia's superstar. Singer, songwriter, actor and director, his fame extended throughout Asia. His star was as bright as a one-man combination of Frank Sinatra, James Stewart and Billy Wilder's would have been in the west and his life no less colourful. Rising from a humble background to superstardom, he had numerous lovers and managed three wives before his untimely death.

His appeal transcended race and his popularity was such that the 1950s and 60s were referred to as his epoch, instead of a politician's or king's. Malaysian society seemed not only to fall in love with his flamboyance, it also reflected it with liberalism and a sense of fun. KL wasn't a bad place to be.

On his return Sugong found the Youth Association's martial arts programme had still to begin so he opened a school of his own. Numbers grew, but the reputation he had fought for in Penang had yet to be won in KL. The best way to build a name was to demonstrate, but he wasn't the only one to offer kung fu in KL and he needed something to stand out from the crowd. In his case it was literally in his hands.

Not long after he began training at Siong Lim, Sugong came to the conclusion that, if he was going to practise an art that focused on the fist, he should have hard hands. Incredible skills and great power were all very well but if you broke your bones when you punched someone they weren't going to be much good. He was far from the first to come to the conclusion, and many others have reached it since. But he did differ from the vast majority in his dedication.

Conditioning is a neutral term for an unpleasant activity. It involves battering parts of the body that need toughening until bone and flesh become hard. Sugong started by hitting a sandbag filled with dried beans. He would hit it about a thousand times a day, not only with his knuckles but with the back, sides and base of the hand as well. At the end of each day his hands would be bruised and swollen but gradually they became resistant to the contents of the bag. This was the signal to up the ante. The beans were emptied out to be replaced by a fine gravel. When this had no discernible effect, larger stones were used and so on. Throughout, the constants were pain and repetition.

Slowly Sugong's hands hardened. He had initiated this aspect of his training himself, but when Koh Chun noticed his disciple's interest it was encouraged and enhanced. He honed Sugong's technique to incorporate breathing so it became a form of hard chi gung. He also provided medicinal ointments to help strengthen his hands and ensure they weren't harmed. And, when no filling in the sandbags could impact on Sugong's hands, it was he who introduced hot sand and gravel. This saw Sugong thrusting his hands into a bowl of sand and stone suspended above a flame.

After a couple of years, Sugong was the only student able to break in one strike the bricks and tiles piled up during the temple's renovation. With hands and arms the nearest equivalent to sledgehammers that flesh and bone can provide, Sugong's training helped in more practical situations as well.

He now applied them to another end, building up his school. The sight of someone hammering six-inch nails into a thick plank of wood with his hands was not a familiar sight for the population of KL. In case that failed to capture an audience's attention, Sugong would demolish with a punch a wooden chair held up in his non-striking hand. To add local flavour, he would finish by smashing one of the colonial marble-topped tables common to the coffee shops of Malaysia and Singapore. It was quite a spectacle and student numbers rose.

By the end of 1963, Sugong's school was established and he was also chief instructor at a Salesman Association and teaching in the Youth Association. Typically, there was more.

When he arrived at the start of the year, the money earned from his start-up school had not been enough to live on and he had kept his eye open for other jobs. With the help of friends and old colleagues he found himself able to choose between two, a supervisor in a marble quarry and one in a tinmine. He took both.

They were industries not unlike their counterparts in other corners of the world. With a large labouring workforce, law and illegality pushed at one another's doors, providing an irresistible lure to factions and gangs. As supervisor, Sugong's role wasn't to oversee the practicalities of work. He didn't ensure diggers followed geological plans, and it wasn't him who was turned to if there was debate over a new tin seam to mine. He was there as a peacekeeper and mediator, to prevent rivalries and disagreements exploding into violence and to ensure interests and squabbles did not impact on the mines.

As at the port, it wasn't a risk-free job, and again he couldn't swagger in and expect everything to be fine. The factions he had to control included labourers whose everyday living was based on physical toil. Not pushovers in themselves, they were in turn led by serious men. Yet the position required a physical presence. Even if they knew they could collectively out-muscle him, respect was earned in the knowledge they would be defeated alone. But in order for that respect to be maintained they also needed to know that there would be others behind him if the situation required.

Koh Chun had always viewed gangsters in a dim light and he shunned all but those he felt could be redeemed. Sugong's circumstances were more complex. The influence of triads in Chinese urban societies was strong in the 60s, particularly in less affluent areas. As these were the places in which Sugong tended to live, total disassociation was impossible as it would require an end to relationships with neighbours, family and friends.

Sugong was not so naïve as to believe that teaching members would end their associations. But he felt that by learning a martial art, and being guided by its rules and regulations, the bad could be restrained even if it wasn't necessarily turned to good. So it was that Sugong had students or ex-students who were involved in triad activities. Some were even triad heads. And if their boss was to defer to Sugong by calling him Sifu, lesser members were not in a position to disagree.

From these workers he received automatic respect. Others, he tried to win over with reason. But for those reticent to arbitration, it was essential he had back-up in physical strength.

For the most part force was not needed. Sit-downs could be arranged and negotiated ends agreed. Sugong, in fact, gained most credibility at the tin mine when he identified the thief of an electrical transformer. Examining the tracks that led to the building that housed it, he concluded there should have been two sets of tyre tracks if anyone but the installer was involved. The police visited the said contractor and the transformer was recovered and returned to its home.

At other times negotiations needed to be more forceful. On one occasion, Sugong was called by the management at the marble quarry. A strike, organised by the workers, had started to turn hostile when picket lines were crossed. Sugong decided a greater presence would be useful and called up some disciples to join him.

When they got out of their cars at the quarry, they were immediately surrounded. Jostling and shoves soon turned into fists and a fight. At its conclusion, the workers sprawled prone around Sugong and his disciples became more amenable to negotiation. Sugong was able to talk to their leaders, and then the management, and bring about an agreement between the two sides.

Yet factions and gangs, whether Chinese or Malay, were not Sugong's biggest problem. With them he knew where he stood, and how to work. The biggest gangsters could be the most deceptive. In this case they were the police.

Paid to protect and obey, there are always policemen who do the opposite, becoming the people they are supposed to prevent. KL had its share, and among them was one notorious for his backhander-happy ways. Ignorant of the change in security, he came to the mine looking for a boost to his official pay. It was a quiet day, and Sugong was in the canteen listening to records with some of his men. The policeman's entrance was flamboyant. He strode in, marched to the table and swept everything, including the prized gramophone, to the floor.

Despite the authority the officer's job bestowed, Sugong struggled to contain himself. He leapt to his feet, bristling. Accustomed to the restraint his uniform usually encouraged, the officer's hand moved toward his gun. His anger yet to subside, Sugong rashly challenged him to make the move, with a promise to take the weapon from his hands.

It was not something he would have done in calmer mind. It certainly wasn't the response the officer expected. He was used to his badge ensuring his will. He was not used to being forced to reach for his gun and he definitely didn't expect to be confronted once he had.

Despite the unexpected turn of events, he retained the confidence that came with the uniform and a firearm and he reached down. Immediately Sugong kicked at his hand. Having just clasped hold of the gun's butt, the officer's grip was still weak and the pistol flew out of his hand. Shocked, he stood still. Sugong, on the other hand, darted after the gun and before it stopped sliding had it at his side.

'Don't come back again,' he told the dumbstruck policeman. 'I'm heading up security now and if you can't take me on when you're armed you'd do best not take me on at all.'

Sugong then signalled to his disciples. One by one they smashed the wooden benches pulled up by the tables with their bare hands. As a display of force it seemed effective; the lawman left and he didn't return.

35

SHAOLIN™

Up at 5.30 for a run, then a snatched spell of sleep. Training for a couple of hours, before a brief return to bed. An hour for lunch, followed by a few more in training. It was déjà vu all over again. Except this time we really were meant to be on holiday. And we were hating it.

Like Koh Chun, Michael and I decided to travel around China. Unlike Koh Chun we were doing it for selfish reasons. We just wanted to see the country and have some fun. If that meant undoing the last few months' good work with copious eating and drinking, we were willing to take the risk. We definitely didn't want to train.

While we didn't travel to the four corners of the country like our great-grandmaster, we had made a pretty good zigzag of it. And with almost two weeks to go all that stood between us, Beijing, and our plane home, was Song Shan mountain and the Shaolin Temple. On the one hand there was no decision to make. It was the birthplace of the martial art that had invaded our lives. But word in many circles put it down as a commercialised shell of its former glory and we weren't sure if we were better off sticking with our idealised images of yesteryear.

We decided to go.

While it was kind of on the way, getting there wasn't without inconvenience. Which meant that it wasn't worth going for a day trip. So we might as well stay for a few days and check out the training while we were there. After some cursory research we decided to stay at Tagou. It was one of the few surviving schools of a recent government crackdown. In the aftermath of Jet Li's 1980s film *Shaolin Temple*, a number of schools and tourist traps had opened. At the prompting of Shaolin's abbot, the Communist Party, belatedly deciding Shaolin was an asset to China and its tourism, shut down most of them.

Tagou was the biggest of those that remained. It housed about six thousand students in its base a kilometre or so from the temple. A dizzying twelve thousand more apparently resided at its second branch, in the nearby town of Dengfeng.

As statistics, the figures were impressive. As a spectacle the scenes even more so. Walking down the road to the temple, the fields and car parks at either side were packed with formations of shaven-headed youths. Some were as young as four or five, and all were in unison, punching, kicking and shouting with blood-curdling vigour.

And we were here to join them. To have every tendon stretched to its limit, every muscle worked to its extreme, and tiredness and sleep deprivation taken to American military interrogation standards.

We decided to stay five days, a) to tick off another pilgrimage box, b) because it would be interesting to compare styles and training methods, and c) because we were sure that looking back our memories would convert the experience to an enjoyable one. Despite that we were hating every minute.

Considering its history, it is perhaps appropriate that the Shaolin Temple was at the centre of controversy once again. For the first thousand years of its existence, Shaolin played its political cards adroitly. Their assistance to the future Tang emperor in 618 won them favour, land, and an imperial letter that effectively sanctioned martial activities from then on. When the Ming later came to power, they developed such close relations that some observers questioned whether the resultant temple splendour was compatible with Buddhist faith.

It was the highpoint of their history. Toward the end of their reign the Ming dynasty weakened. As their army declined they looked outward for militia recruits. The Shaolin temple housed prime candidates and the final years of the Ming saw the monks' numbers depleted in doomed battles.

The Ching dynasty that succeeded the Ming in 1644 would later be vilified as Shaolinophobes. Yet the worst damage to Shaolin was inflicted in 1641 by a powerful bandit, who destroyed the temple prior to the Ching's rule. (The Ching's infamous South Shaolin temple destruction may be a liberally embellished misunderstanding based on this act.)

Nonetheless, they were suspicious of a monastery so closely associated with the vanquished Ming and their relationship with Shaolin was testy at times.

After the demise of the Ching, Shaolin again found itself caught between feuding rivals, this time warlords. Again they erred, siding with a general who had trained in the monastery. As a result it was destroyed in 1928 by his victorious opponent.

A decade or so on, and the Japanese were too busy with their invasion to appreciate the birthplace of Zen. The Communists when they came to power proved no more sympathetic. Further to their suspicion of rebel-associated martial artists, more compelling priorities and a distrust of religion meant the temple was left to rot. This passivity was not shared by the Cultural Revolution Red Guards.

They inflicted yet more suffering, not only to the temple but also to the remaining monks. Not many survived to witness a new incarnation of Communists' change of heart.

But renewed state approval in the 1980s led to a new set of problems. The strained relations Shaolin had at times endured with the Ching, who harboured suspicions of martial art associates of the temple if not the monks themselves, were inverted under the modern Communists. Instead of government fears of agitation from within the monastery, there were concerns of government infiltration from without. Close relations between temple and party were viewed with particular suspicion, as some monks held theological and political positions concurrently, and others made the transition from Shaolin to CCP (Chinese Communist Party).

Aside from the politics, there were fears for the art. While the 20th-century sacking brutalised the temple physically, most damaging was its loss of monks. Some were killed, others fled and more passed on without replacement. After the Cultural Revolution apparently only twelve remained. Shaolin's 1980s rebirth saw efforts to retrace the lost arts and the authorities tracked down past masters and monks. It must be remembered that Shaolin had recovered from similar decimation in its past, but all the same a great deal of martial knowledge must have been lost.

In its place, it has been claimed, came *wushu*. The characters for wushu translate literally to 'martial arts', and the term is used by Chinese as kung fu is used in the West. But in the last half-century they assumed further meaning. In the late 1950s the Chinese government, acknowledging the historical role of martial arts, devised a unified version. With the arts considered a national treasure, they wanted to create a cohesive body, and forms and rules of combat were standardised to this end. In reflection of its broad scope it became known as wushu.

From one perspective their actions were positive. They took an anarchic art form and created one of unity, popularising and spreading the influence of all Chinese martial arts. But it was not a move free from criticism. There was suspicion it was aimed partly at taking control from masters considered subversive in the past. More importantly, there was contention over the art.

By focusing on a unified style comparable through competition, wushu moved from its foundation as a martial art toward sport. Its techniques all had foundation in the traditional arts but over time the forms became increasingly spectacular. Although impressive to watch, they could no longer be termed as traditional kung fu, lying somewhere between this and gymnastics. Noted for their athleticism and aesthetics, their practicality, one of the defining characteristics of a martial art, was generally not held in as high regard.

(Wushu also contains a *sanda* element, where competitors engage in actual combat. If the martial aspect of the forms has been questioned, the ferocity of wushu sparring is not in doubt.)

Shaolin's detractors claim modern wushu muscled in on the gaps in the curriculum left by the exodus of martial monks. It is hard to believe Shaolin's home hasn't retained significant martial treasures, but the fact remains that wushu was incorporated, something openly admitted by the monks. As a way to enhance the dynamism of performances, it has certainly had success. But with explanations generally not offered, the public perception of Shaolin kung fu has been skewed. And one is left to wonder what has changed since the time monks proudly showed off a more practically-focused art.

It would be naïve to think that a major Chinese institution can thrive, or even survive, without a good relationship with government. And only a rose-tinted idealist would argue that Shaolin didn't strive for one in the past. With recent history showing the dire consequences of official disapproval, failing to negotiate peaceful co-existence would be a dereliction of duty for senior Shaolin figures (although the extent of their political involvement is certainly open to debate).

There are defences to Shaolin's other controversies. Un-monk-like tales of chauffeur-driven clerics are countered with the necessity of reliable transport in an international age. Trade-marking 'Shaolin' as a brand may be cynical to some, but others see an attempt to prevent misuse of the name. And the relentless promotion of Shaolin, far from indicating subordination of faith to tourism, could be an effort to safeguard Shaolin, and spread its kung fu and beliefs across the world.

Its importance to both faith and martial arts emotionally charges the debates and leaves them prone to exaggeration and false claims. But, for all the reasoned justifications, nagging suspicions remain of a subversive temple subverted.

But to be honest, the philosophising came later. At the time, we were mainly trying to catch a moment's sleep any time a lean-muscled, doing-splits-from-the-age-of-three instructor wasn't trying to rips our legs off. We were also trying to eat. Because, despite our foreign dollar gaining us access to the school's premier dining room, this didn't amount to much. Josh and Nikolaj, two long-term foreign students, assured us food poisoning was a weekly reality. Despite this I remained more intimidated by the taste.

The excitement displayed by Josh and Nikolaj at the mention of their weekly trip to province capital Zhen Zhou revealed the depths of their despair. For despite the

Colonel's apparent refusal to share with Asia all of his secret herbs and spices, a visit to KFC was the highlight of their week. That and the fact that Zhen Zhou was a city of about seven million, of which about ten seemed to hail from the west. While their province may have housed thousands of exceptionally talented martial artists, to many locals nothing could compare to an aptitude for blue eyes and blond hair.

Mine wasn't a beauty by any standard. I had my doubts even after my share of a crate of beer, shots of every kind and a five glass-storey drink set on fire. China is home to some of the most beautiful women in the world. But a country of well over a billion is bound to contain a number of more earthy types. Somehow I found myself walking with one while my friend, in a steady relationship, wastefully chatted to a princess behind.

As we made our way to the next club mine burped loudly. She followed this by hocking up a lump of phlegm and spitting the goo to the ground. Then she grabbed my hand. Had I been feeling more generous I might have appreciated her efforts at femininity; a rasping fart was never released. But I couldn't help feeling that love would have to wait for another night.

We had been surprised by the quality of clubs and bars in China. They weren't necessarily for the minimalist, but the enthusiasm for light displays, and the money spent on décor, dazzled and blinded all complaints. The one we had just come out of did not number among the more restrained. Its music may not have been cutting edge but it was among the lightsiest places I had ever been. Now our new friends wanted to take us to one of their favourites.

The plain metal door part way down a side-alley was the kind I would have had serious reservations entering in London. The combination of alcohol and the blind faith of tourism meant there were no questions asked. But as we descended the dark stairwell I started to harbour doubts. With each step, I could hear the unmistakable beats of gabba banging a notch louder. Never a big fan of techno, I hated its speed-fuelled brother, its thumping bass beating aside mid-range, treble and any attempt at melodic effect. Michael and I turned to each other and winced.

A wave of smoke from dry ice washed over us as we reached the foot of the stairs. Walking through it, our eyes slowly adjusted to the gloomy light. They were met by a room making an apparent attempt to compensate for the exuberance of all of China's other clubs. The floor was concrete and had a small dance area in its centre with podiums at either side. At the left of the room were some worn booths to sit in, to the right a rudimentary bar. Having been exposed to some of the country's more basic toilets I vowed to focus any chi I had accumulated toward the control of my bladder.

We settled in a booth. If the music hadn't been so deafening we might have made an attempt to fail in conversation with our non-English-speaking friends. The brother of the pretty one emerged out of the crowd to protect her virtue from Michael, unaware it should really have been me. But her friend continued to blight my pre-destined romance.

There was only one thing for it. Drinking games.

A lot of drinks and a few tortuous visits to the toilet later I found myself intercepted on my return. I turned in panicked desperation to the person I considered my friend. Michael smirked through some bottles as I was dragged to the dance floor. What she lacked in feminine charm, my chosen one seemed to have compensated with a stunning capacity for alcohol. I was at her mercy and she took full control.

Twenty minutes of podium dancing later I was frantic. Somehow I managed to persuade my sweetheart to head back to our booth.

'Michael, we've got to get out of here,' I slurred, with the strength of conviction only possible five drinks beyond your limit.

'Mmnhah.'

Michael's head shot away from the wall. He bolted upright with impressive alacrity for someone just woken. 'Le'sgo.'

We mumbled to our Chinese friends in incoherent English that couldn't be heard and wouldn't have been understood. We pretended to take their numbers, then staggered and tripped up the stairs. Outside we hopped straight in a taxi. I looked out of the back window to see my lost love crouch to her knees and throw up.

Despite the fact that the Order was supposedly granted dispensation to consume alcohol I did not feel very Shaolin. The next day, thumping hangover in tow, even less so.

36

CHILDREN, MISTRESSES AND WIVES

Sugong's return to KL was an initial success. His schools were in their infancy but student numbers were growing and he had four branches to his name. His mediation services were also proving successful as he won the trust of his employers and their workforce. But the end of 1963 saw a hiccup in Sugong's fortunes, and it was not a well-timed blip.

Work at the marble quarry dried up and he was soon a job down. It was unfortunate but not disastrous, as an increase in student numbers combined with the tin mine wages to compensate the loss. Then the price of tin dropped. Mines had to make sacrifices and Sugong's position was one of the easier to detach from the payroll.

The loss of a substantial part of his income meant economies had to be made to an already frugal lifestyle. It would not normally have been something to worry Sugong, but his wife was pregnant again, and he was very aware his responsibilities extended beyond himself.

As a respite from the stress of their circumstances, Sugong decided to take his wife on a trip to the seaside town of Morib. Madame Quek was now seven months pregnant and easy opportunities for weekend breaks would soon end.

Out of the main cities, roads in Malaysia were not of universal excellence. The journey to Morib was true to type, and negotiating the dips, dents and bumps was a challenging task. An hour into the journey the front tyre of the car caught the edge of a pothole, tripped on its lip and burst.

The sudden lurch of the car jolted driver and passenger, and Madame Quek felt a sharp pain. Panicked and unsure of their location, Sugong swung the car around and headed to the most recent town they had passed. They were directed to its clinic and the sight of the frightened couple saw them waved to the front of the queue. The doctor quickly saw that Madame Quek needed more specialised care and gave a sedating injection before re-directing them to Port Swettenham (now known as Klang).

Immediately on arrival, Madame Quek gave birth to a tiny son. But their delight was tempered with concern. Premature births were hazardous and, weak from the two months' development stolen from his mother's womb, their baby faced a fight. It was little easier for his parents. Coming after the death of their firstborn, they were beside themselves with worry that they would lose a second child. To make matters worse, Sugong was not in employment that offered sick pay and he had to continue to earn in KL. Every morning he would remain at the hospital as long as possible and every night he would return as quickly as he could to the side of his wife and son.

After three long weeks, their baby boy's battle for survival was won and he was discharged. On this final journey home Sugong was at last accompanied by his son and his wife. Their child still needed to be nursed to full health, but as his strength grew the family's prospects also appeared to ascend.

But again Sugong's fortunes yo-yoed. The relief at his son's recovery was followed by another pregnancy and delight when Madame Quek delivered another baby boy. Then despair struck as again the child succumbed to sickness within a year. But just as his personal life hit a trough with the death of his young son, Sugong's financial fortunes began to climb toward a peak. They continued to rise throughout the latter half of the decade, and by its end his schools and a burgeoning construction business he had started were enjoying great success. With it came popularity.

One of the larger construction jobs he was supervising was the development of a drainage system behind a hotel. A member of his sometime team lived en route to the job, and the man's daughter worked nearby. As her father wasn't working on this assignment, Sugong would stop by their home as a favour and drop her at work. She was pretty, young and fun. Soon Sugong was seeing her more often than just on the trips to work. Within two years she bore him a son.

Concubinage persisted longer in China than in many other parts of the world. This may have influenced the attitudes of some corners of Chinese society, where success continued to be seen as something to be reflected and rewarded with a mistress or additional wife. It was a perspective from which Sugong was happy to view life. Madame Quek did not observe the world in quite the same light.

The difference in opinion meant that Sugong's extra-marital relationship was the cause of tension in their home. But, with the norms of society against her, there were limits to what Madame Quek could do. A resourceful woman, she decided that what she could, she would. Not having seen success from voicing her dissatisfaction to Sugong, she resolved to take her complaint direct to his mistress. It was a resolution that was easier to make than achieve; Sugong had no intention of telling Madame Quek how to locate her.

His wife was not prepared to give up and her persistence won her a break. Finally managing to persuade one of his disciples to give away the mistress's whereabouts, Madame Quek travelled to her home. A discussion of sorts took place in which Madame Quek made her feelings on the relationship and its future known. After the confrontation it didn't last long.

Sugong was an impetuous character in areas far less prone to emotion than love and romance. So despite the problems his esteem for female company brought, it was almost inevitable he would fail to act with restraint. On his drive home from work there was a grocery store he used to drop in on. He had often come by with his mistress and was on friendly terms with the girl behind the till.

'Hey, I don't see you around with your friend any more,' she commented after a few months of solo visits.

'We broke up,' replied Sugong, new emotion dancing across his eyes.

Before long the company they provided each other began to extend beyond the boundaries of the shop. Rumours filtered through to Madame Quek that the ejection of one pretender had only led to another. She was no happier about the second than she had been the first. Things came to a head when she spotted Sugong taking his mistress to the cinema. She delayed the confrontation until he returned home but its conclusion saw Sugong spend the next few days away.

The balance of their marriage was left precarious by the affair. Rather than taking direct action, on this occasion Madame Quek called in a lawyer and the three of them sat down to thrash out what could be done.

The family of Sugong's first mistress had been happy for her to have an unofficial relationship with him. The family of his second were not. A marriage to an unmarried man would have been more welcome. But if this wasn't to be, a union with a married one was better than being mistress to the same man. Faced with the option of losing his mistress or marrying her, Sugong decided on the latter. His problem was in winning acceptance from his wife.

With the lawyer they went through the various possibilities. Divorce was not something that either wanted. Its social stigma remained strong, and despite their difficulties they were still in love. But Sugong was almost as opposed to separation with his mistress. Which left a second marriage, something that did not appeal to Madame Quek. Whether for the good of their family or out of her love for Sugong, Madame Quek finally relented and Sugong married for the second time in 1969.

37

MELTING POTS AND SIMMERING CAULDRONS

When the opposition made striking gains in the May 1969 elections in the Malaysian peninsula, they were jubilant and the incumbents shocked. This turned to resentment when some of the celebration rallies descended into gloating and name-calling. And this, in turn, either led to spontaneous revolt or a cynical conspiracy.

The official line for the 'May 13th Incident' – named for the date the riots started, even though they continued for a number of days – has been weakened by inconsistency. Communists, terrorists, saboteurs and secret societies were variously blamed in the aftermath of the violence. One of the final versions suggested that two busloads of Chinese provoked a group of the governing party's supporters, gathered to demonstrate their support. Spontaneous violence then erupted.

The counter-argument suggests planned riots that were part of a political coup. These enabled emerging leaders in the governing party to force out the old guard and overturn the election results. Racial issues were, they suggest, a camouflage thereafter used to divide and rule. Their telling of the story had Malay demonstrators bussed in from afar, many already armed, who benefited from the connivance of Malay-dominated security forces, who pitched in rather than placated.

The aftermath lent some credence to these claims. The ruling party's leadership changed, parliament was suspended and emergency rule allowed the incumbents to continue, unaffected by the election results. Longer term, the constitution was amended guaranteeing Malay dominance, Malay-centric policies were introduced, and the government never changed (many of its number became conspicuously rich). Today the spectre of another May 13th is raised in threat when the ruling party's power is challenged. Emergency powers remain in use and the media is heavily censored. Not factors to support the 'spontaneous eruption' case.

The riots resulted in one hundred and ninety-six official deaths. Every unofficial count reads far higher, but all agreed the majority were Chinese.

Manchester United manager Alex Ferguson once said of the footballer Dennis Wise that he could start a fight in an empty house. Sugong had a similar predilection toward trouble. And if he could find it in an unoccupied dwelling, the chances of him avoiding mishap in the riots that swept Kuala Lumpur weren't high.

He was at one of his schools in Old Klang Road when they began. The trouble hadn't yet reached that corner of town, but his phone started ringing with requests for help from the areas it had. When he arrived in the Chinese-dominated area of Tiong Nam, he found the road blocked with hastily hacked down trees and oil drums. He parked his car and followed the crowds. They led to a group, numbered in the hundreds, setting off, its purpose unclear.

Whether it was a protest, a demonstration of force, or a defence group, the atmosphere was in marked contrast to the victory parade Sugong had joined two days before.

They made their way toward the Federal Theatre. There the procession stopped. Again the situation was mired in confusion. There were whispers that a Malay militia was gathered within but it could just as well have been a halt initiated by vengeance seekers who had found an outlet for their intent. Whichever was the case, there were Malays inside and when they realised a group of Chinese had surrounded them they came out fighting.

Outnumbered, they did not initially do well. But their paucity in numbers was soon compensated. On high alert, the security forces were not slow in responding to disturbances where Malays were victims. They did not waste time on niceties when they arrived.

Sugong instinctively ducked at the first burst of gunfire. He saw rioters drop with the next. As the army drove into the throng, soldiers lashing out with batons, he ran, scrambling to get off the main road and escape down side streets. His desperation was shared by many others and there was pandemonium as they fled, pushing and jostling in their panicked escape. But numbers thinned as the distance from the theatre increased, and by the time he reached home Sugong was alone.

Sugong had been determined to stand alongside friends as they found themselves attacked. But he had never had an issue with Malays and had no inclination to hurt them. He was even less keen to be shot. He resolved to stand back from the situation, to only defend his friends or himself when under direct attack. He was aided by a restrictive curfew imposed upon the city. It allowed residents out only for very short periods, and on some days confined them entirely to their houses and flats. It was not prohibitive enough.

Two days after the troubles began, Sugong was upstairs at his home when he heard cries from outside. He rushed to his window and saw a Malay lady, babe in arms, hurrying from three Chinese youths.

There were limited reasons to defy the curfew. A delay to a journey might explain brief transgression; an outsider getting lost could also be an excuse. Beyond that there was cause to at least question the motives of those left on the streets. That a distressed young Malay mother was in the heart of a Chinese zone suggested she was lost. The youths had a less vulnerable look.

Sugong rushed downstairs, flung open the door and called to the woman. She turned, but hesitated, unsure the risk posed by her apparent saviour was any less than that of the approaching men. At his continued urging she took the chance, and at the last moment bolted through the door.

After settling the young mother, he called the police and hung a white sheet from a window to identify the location. With more urgent calls to attend it was some time before the constabulary arrived to rescue his unintended captive. She left relieved and grateful; Sugong's emotions were much the same. His involvement in the Federal Theatre affair had been playing on his mind. Now that he had engaged in more positive action, he felt he had at least partially atoned for the unintentional sin.

38

The long arm of the Lord

Sugong may have felt he had made amends for his earlier indiscretions but there were others less disposed to the view. Unfortunately they were the police and their opinion held some sway. There were a number of reasons Sugong found himself on their radar. He ran a successful kung fu school. Rightly or wrongly these were associated with secret societies and treated with suspicion at the best of times.

The aftermath of race riots was not the best of times. In addition it was no secret that Sugong's abilities extended beyond the theoretical. On occasion his mediation work went beyond the verbal and he was not known to step down when a situation became physical, work-related or not.

Sugong had also joined one of the opposition parties on their election victory parade. They, or at least some of their members, were accused of involvement in the troubles, so the connection was not ideal. And if that were not enough, the aftermath of May 13th had provided opportunities for vengeance-seekers. A finger pointed at a person held in disregard could cause trouble. Sugong was evidently not in favour with someone more influential, and his name entered the frame. All of which meant that he was not in a very good position come the summer of 1969.

In normal circumstances there would have been limits to what the authorities could do. While questions had been raised, there was no compelling evidence. Outside his attendance at the peripheries of the Federal Theatre riot his only involvement had seen him save a Malay mother and child. But the emergency rule imposed in May 13th's aftermath meant that suspicion had replaced evidence as a requirement for imprisonment and possibly more. Sugong decided to lie low.

At the time he officially lived in Chow Kit. It was also where he had operated one of his schools. But from the time of the riots onward he tried to return home infrequently. There were rumours Special Branch was looking for him and he wasn't keen to be found.

Sugong was fortunate at the time to have a student whose family owned a building in Tengkat Tong Shin in Bukit Bintang. There was a room upstairs in which he could teach and a coffee shop below where he could earn. The student's name was Christopher Lai Khee Choong, although I would later address him as Sifu.

It was not the first time Sugong had needed to maintain a low profile. At various times he had had one gang or another seeking him out, looking to avenge the outcome of his own administration of justice. On other occasions it had been the police, often in connection with the same thing. But rarely had the cause of his discomfort been so persistent and by the start of 1970 it was becoming a bane.

If the police suspicions had centred on anything major it is unlikely they would not have tracked him down. As it was they wanted to keep him under surveillance while he attempted to stay beyond their gaze. Evidently the police became frustrated and decided it was time he was brought in. It was then that Siong Lim's tentacles sought him out.

After the incident with Officer Yew increasing numbers of policemen had trained under Koh Chun. As a senior student, Sugong had got to know many of them. One was now a high-ranking policeman in one of KL's police stations. Through intermediaries he passed on a message to Sugong. The authorities had had enough cat-and-mouse. They wanted to question Sugong and he could either come along voluntarily or make a doomed attempt to resist. His questioning would be altogether less pleasant if he chose the latter option.

Sugong trusted his sidai but he was less convinced by his colleagues. He made a call and was given reassurances. His actions saving the Malay mother had been noted, and for that at least he would not be subjected to ill-treatment. The next morning Sugong made his way to the station. Despite the promises it was not a journey made in the brightest of moods. But his sidai proved true to his word; while Sugong was received with suspicion he was not mistreated in any way.

It was nonetheless a long day. He first had to make a statement detailing his activities during the riots. Imprisoned at home by the curfews, he had done very little and accordingly his account was not long. Rebutting the allegations levied against him was more onerous, each needing refuting with explanations and alibis. He provided all the information asked of him, and even restrained his temper at the more far-fetched contentions. But by the end of the day his patience was starting to wear thin.

'If I was really spending half my time looking for Malays to hurt, why would I spend the other half defending them?' he demanded.

The question was treated as rhetorical and the interrogation went on. It took the best part of twelve hours before it came to an end. The Malay officer questioning him looked as exhausted as Sugong.

'Do you need me to come in again tomorrow?' Sugong asked, hoping for a negative response.

He found he had misjudged the other's stamina and Sugong was told to return the next day.

He arrived the following morning to find small but significant changes. The previous day the interrogation room had been bare except for a pen and paper laid on the table. Now coffee and bread buns were in their place. The officer motioned for Sugong to sit and then began to recount the allegations against him. Sugong shuffled uncomfortably as he listened to charges that could keep him detained for a long time. The officer then came to a 'but'.

'But, you've provided solid alibis and I don't think you were involved,' he said. 'I'll process your files and unless anything new comes in you'll be free to get on with your business again.'

It was a huge weight lifted from Sugong. But as he made to leave the officer shifted awkwardly. When he spoke again his tone was less assured.

'Um, I've heard that Ting Feng does kung fu with you,' he began.

Ting Feng was a junior member of the station who had trained sporadically with Sugong before the riots.

'That's right,' Sugong replied. 'I can't say he's good, but he trained once or twice.'

The officer then continued, enquiring whether Sugong taught Malays. Even in calmer times it was a question that had pertinence; in the current climate particularly so.

Kung fu traditionally was not taught to outsiders. At the more extreme end of the scale it was passed down only to family members. But for centuries it had been an important tool of war, and even the least possessive of masters were not keen to give away their weapons. For this reason teaching non-Chinese had sometimes been frowned upon. The 19th and 20th centuries saw the relevance of martial arts recede in their importance to warfare, but the line of thought had not been totally lost. In the aftermath of race riots the idea of a Malay policeman starting kung fu lessons from a Chinese master was one at which many would baulk.

Sugong had no qualms.

'I teach Indians, I teach Chinese and I teach Malays,' he said. 'And if you're willing to work hard I'll even teach you.'

So his next class saw a new enthusiastic Malay in attendance. And as word spread through the station, Sugong was again hunted by the force. But now it was for tuition, and he was more happy to be found. A modern Shaolin tradition of sorts, started by his master, would continue another generation through Sugong.

39

A GOLDEN HARVEST

Freed from the binds of police suspicion, Sugong was able to return to normal life. He was happily married, albeit with one more wife than the definition would normally include, and prior to the riots both his construction business and teaching had been going full steam. He was keen to pick up where he had left off.

His first move was to register a new school, the impressively named Quek Heng Choon Institute of Physical Culture. Under suspicion, martial arts schools had been banned from the time of the riots, leaving Sugong's classes sporadic and unofficial.

The hidden benefit of the ban lay in the restricted possibilities there were for students to drift elsewhere in the absence of regular lessons. With a new stream of police recruits, Sugong picked up ahead of where he had left off.

Perhaps anxious to work off the excess energy accumulated during the previous year's lull, Sugong was not idle outside of his schools. His construction activities benefited from his renewed vigour and he continued to manage the coffee shop as well.

His roaming instinct also persisted. For the past decade he had maintained his connections with friends and disciples in Penang through frequent, sometimes prolonged, visits. He now decided to cement the ties further and pay homage to his sifu at the same time. The Seow Chu Sang (Shaolin Merciful Mountain) Physical Culture Association was opened in 1972 with Sugong as chief instructor and supervisor to the disciples who taught in his absence.

Just as he was paying homage to his master, the martial arts world began to show its appreciation of Sugong. He was invited to be a judge of the third South-East Asian Martial Arts Tournament in 1972. And in a separate acknowledgement, equal in honour but more generous in remuneration, he was hired as fight-scene choreographer on a British film the following year.

Again, a young Lai Khee Choong was instrumental in his good fortune. Among the people Sifu had in his contacts book was a casting director. She had been approached by British producers preparing a shoot in Malaysia, with a request for martial artists to act in the fight scenes. She contacted Sifu, who in turn went to Sugong, and a meeting was arranged in his school.

In the early 1970s martial arts made inroads in the west with the TV series *Kung Fu*, and other shows followed the trend with cameo roles for martial arts henchmen. The first large-scale Hollywood kung fu success had only just been released that summer (1973), however, as Bruce Lee's *Enter The Dragon* gripped the imagination of East and West.

For Europeans, displays of martial arts feats were not yet common on screen, and they certainly weren't frequent in real life. So when Sugong started to annihilate bricks and granite slabs he quickly gained the casting crew's attention. It did not take long for contract details to be agreed.

Despite his best efforts, David Niven couldn't raise *Paper Tiger* to classic status and in the UK the film was not a success. For Sugong in Malaysia it was a different story altogether. His wages were generous in the extreme and, to sweeten the deal, the money was the easiest he had ever made. Jetted around the scenic spots of the country, his task was to offer advice on how to make combat look real.

As taxing to his imagination as asking a barman how to pull a pint, it was less dangerous than being in real fights and beat labouring as a way to earn. After around forty days of over-paid under-exertion he had accumulated enough money to buy a house.

While tills may not have been ringing out of control in the film's home country, it did decent business in Malaysia. Its distributor, Cathay, was one of the biggest in Malaysia and Singapore and had connections to Hong Kong. Among these was a young, upcoming company called Golden Harvest. Established in 1970, they had not taken long to upset the existing order. Luring stars like Bruce Lee, and later Jackie Chan, their impact had been immediate in Hong Kong, where they would dominate for the next twenty years. Looming large over the empire was co-founder Raymond Chow.

Through his contacts in Cathay, Chow became aware of an international production's local hit. He had made a success of Golden Harvest by luring the best and newest names from competitors and it was his business to identify new upcoming 'stars'. On his next visit to Malaysia a meeting with Sugong was arranged. Chow arrived with an offer. He wanted Sugong to choreograph fight scenes for Golden Harvest in Hong Kong. Financially generous, it was also work in which Sugong knew he would excel, and would enjoy. And while less directly than through teaching, it would still allow him to honour his pledge to spread Shaolin.

Yet there was much to hold him back. His schools were thriving, providing direct fulfilment of his promise to his master. Their income, when combined with his other businesses, meant financial worries were a thing of the past. Last, but far from least, he had two wives and a handful of children; relocation would not be easy.

Normally not one to hesitate, a fretting Sugong took an unusually long time to decide. Had it come ten years earlier it was a chance he would have jumped at. But for all the excitement on offer, it was an opportunity he could no longer take. Sparring with Bruce Lee would have to wait until another day.

40

THREE BITTER YEARS AND THE TEN-YEAR CATASTROPHE

Flush with the money from *Paper Tiger*, there were other avenues suddenly opened to Sugong. After buying a new home his thoughts returned to his first. It was more than twenty-five years since he had left China and in that time he had not gone back. Restrictions on travel made it a complicated journey and limitations in his finances meant it was an expensive one too. Freed from the second burden he resolved to tackle the first, and after battling bureaucracy for his permits he set off on a laboriously slow ship from Singapore. It was not a quick hop across the ocean but in the late summer of 1973 it was a crossing Sugong finally made.

He had little time for reflection when he first arrived. A quarter-century away left a lot of times to catch up on and endless tales to be reminisced. But when he got a chance to look around him what struck Sugong most was what didn't strike him. In the years since he had left, his personal circumstances had fluctuated and his fortunes ebbed and flowed, but overall his living conditions had inched up. Singapore and Malaysia had seen as much change as he as they relentlessly strove forward. Back in Chai Lien Bu village his family seemed to be living as they had when he left. But reality contradicted the stagnant impression that lay on the surface.

After he left, it took just a year for Sugong's resistance to the KMT army to be vindicated. Undone as much by the unravelling of his party within as its dismantling without, Chiang Kai-shek led its remnants in hasty retreat to Taiwan.

Wholesale Communist change in China was not immediate, but by 1956 a transition had largely been made. Agriculture and industry lay in the hands of the state, and more even distribution of their benefits improved peasants' lives. But Mao was restless. He believed Party officials had become arrogant and aloof and he opened them to criticism. He was shocked when intellectuals turned their ire on the party itself. His response was the 'anti-Rightist' campaign, destroying many for the criticisms they had been invited to make.

Continuing to exercise his idealist zeal, Mao launched the Great Leap Forward, its aim to increase production with people power. His faith in the masses appeared justified when the first year saw huge gains. Buoyed by success, outrageous demands were made. In the wave of euphoria, wildly exaggerated claims of success were believed even by their makers, food was distributed excessively and targets went sky-high. Planners believed the country, so often wracked by shortfall, was now producing too much food.

The return to reality was jolting. Famine in the following 'three bitter years' claimed at least fifteen million lives. As architect of the madness Mao was sidelined while Party pragmatists tried to restore control. The views of the educated were heeded once more, and as the standing of intellectuals rose the peasants were again an underclass. Again Mao seethed.

His opportunity to re-impose his will came in 1966. Failing to have a play critical of him condemned, Mao launched the Cultural Revolution, attacking intellectuals and bourgeois influence in the arts. Mobilised by his call, students at Beijing University began to rebel. Sensing a chance to manipulate power, Mao leant his support to these 'Red Guards' and others quickly emerged.

The Red Guards attacked the 'Four Olds' – ideas, culture, customs and habit. They ransacked temples, destroyed western goods and beat intellectuals to affect their end. Within weeks deaths had resulted from their beatings but the police and military were under orders not to intervene.

Chaos ensued. With few grounds needed and no evidence required, anyone could be condemned for following the 'capitalist road'. Vengeance seekers implicated their enemies and let the Red Guards enact retribution. Even Red Guards were not safe. Different factions diverged into militias and, backed with military hardware, disagreements became armed battles with numerous deaths.

By 1968 the system was on the verge of total collapse. Even Mao realised the situation could not continue and he allowed the military to re-assert itself. But anarchy was not so easily quelled and only the enforced migration of millions of urban students, supposedly to help the rural masses, allowed order to be restored.

While cause was controlled, effect was not so easily remedied. The aftermath saw politics reduced to slogans and Mao achieve a near-divine state. Cultural treasures were lost and education set back a generation. Crime rose and corruption soared. And the period from 1966 to 76 became known as the Ten-Year Catastrophe.

It was seven years into the ten that Sugong found himself back in the country. Fortunately his remaining family were not politically orientated and, although they suffered during the Great Leap Forward, they escaped the worst of the famine. With the more severe excesses of the Cultural Revolution in the cities, they emerged relatively unscathed from its clutches as well.

The monks at Kai Wan Temple were less lucky. To complete his homecoming Sugong had decided to track down his old masters. In the case of Lao Ping Sun it was not possible. Where he had gone was anybody's guess; he may have found his higher mountain. Kai Wan Temple was easier to locate but it presented problems of a different kind.

Having heard of the austerity of China pre-Cultural Revolution, Sugong was surprised to find how easily rules could be bent in its wake. Now a 'foreign' Chinese, he was seen as a walking dollar sign, receiving offers of all kinds of services as a result. Although Kai Wan was designated as a restricted site, nothing was impossible, and in reality nowhere out of bounds.

Kai Wan's fortunes had been mixed during the Cultural Revolution. The local authority had retained enough control to prevent irreversible damage, and despite a cursory ransacking it had not been destroyed. But this was the extent of its good luck. Sugong's return was accordingly a bittersweet affair. Although the temple was undamaged structurally, Sugong was shocked to see once resplendent deities without their heads. He was delighted to recognise the monks, and charmed when they insisted on teaching him. Yet he was equally dismayed by their plight.

Their number had dwindled to just seven, and with the youngest nearing eighty their ranks would only decrease. At a time when they would normally have enjoyed support and respect, theirs was a struggle to survive. They lived alone in a temple stripped of its glory and robbed of its congregation.

Sugong returned regularly. But each time he left he could not be sure if he felt warmed by the monks' kindness or distraught at their unfortunate state.

It wasn't only at Kai Wan that Sugong struggled with his emotions. Familiar surroundings took him on a journey through forgotten memories almost everywhere he went.

On a trip to the beach he was taken back to a time he went oyster picking as a boy. The returning tide had stranded him and his rescuers had only heard his frantic screams when the water reached his neck. Wandering through the fields he remembered the love–hate relationship of the villagers and local tigers; the fear that had seized him when he came across a peasant's half-eaten remains; and his awe at a tigress's dash into the village to reclaim the cub they had saved from a pit.

He was forced to confront difficult recollections. The makeshift shelters by the river that served as temporary homes when family relations were tense; his brother knocking him out with a blow to the back of his head when he was caught slacking at a time he was supposed to work. But for the bad memories there were others that were good. For every escape or beating there was a smile at the mischief that lay at their cause. Even when it came to his brother there were fond recollections to balance those less friendly.

This didn't mean the bad were forgotten. Sugong had left when still a child and he returned not only a man but a master. The significance of this was not something he wanted overlooked. He suggested to his brother that they do some sparring, for old time's sake. As it had often been the pindar stick that had been used against him, he proposed that they fight with it again.

To give his brother a chance he invited two others to face him at the same time. Also trained from childhood, his brothers were not unskilled, but the stick was Sugong's favourite weapon and it did not take long for theirs to be dispatched to the floor. The days of bullying were a thing of the past.

As on his original departure, Sugong's emotions were strong when the date of his return to Malaysia arrived. His thoughts as a young man had all looked forward, filled with anticipation and excitement. Now concern for his family preoccupied him, combined with a guilty relief to escape their ongoing past.

41

FRIENDS, FAMILY AND A FALL

Sugong's relief at his return was short-lived. His nomadic inclinations meant flexibility was needed in the powers of attorney he granted at his schools. In the case of the one in KL's Tong Shin they were abused. With some students hailing from the rougher sides of society, Sugong had to be strong to maintain order and ensure his rules were adhered to. While they may have been the more obvious candidates, students with triad associations were only a part of the problem. The police could be relied on for the other share.

Kuala Lumpur's police force was no more immune than most in its elasticity about the law. Some officers were thoroughly corrupt, another link in the chain of organised crime. Others lay in a greyer area, not evil, but far from pure. One of these was a student at Sugong's school and his weakness was the love of gambling his father had bequeathed.

Sugong made it clear he expected members of his schools to avoid the vices but he was not so innocent as to believe they would all maintain a righteous line. KL laid bare a tantalising array of options to young men, and of these Sugong felt that gambling was one of the lesser sins. Having an eye for a game of cards was one matter; converting his school into a betting den was something else. When he found Shao Wen had done exactly this while he was away, gaming moved rapidly up the list.

If hell hath no fury like a woman scorned, Sugong came a close second. Raging like a demon, he destroyed the gambling hall and threw out the guilty student. Yet a problem remained. Starting from an oft-questioned base, the reputation of martial arts schools had been further (unfairly) tarnished by May 13th. An association with illegal gambling added fuel to an already raging fire and Sugong temporarily closed the now-blemished school.

But he still had two others and he continued to teach. For his students it was a fortunate time to learn. Many sportsmen reach a high in their late twenties or early thirties, but for Sugong it was during his forties that he reached his peak.

The blessing for his students was mixed. Never uncompromising, his own heightened standards led to raised expectations of those who learned. As with his own master the combination of high demand and hot temper was a challenge for his pupils. As at Siong Lim this led to a fluctuation in numbers. It also meant that those who remained usually excelled, helping Sugong's schools garner the cream of KL's martial arts crop.

Sugong's friends also found benefits, but those who crossed them found a less sympathetic man. When he had taught, Koh Chun repeatedly emphasised the good fortune Sugong and his hengdai had in learning the art. His expectation that it was used to help others was made just as clear.

Protection rackets were still common in parts of Kuala Lumpur. Small businesses, from hawker stalls to grocery shops, paid out to avert a threat that existed only in the supposed saviours themselves. It was a well-established system that Sugong would not change alone, but he could ensure his friends gained immunity.

With reputation riding high, he rarely had to rely on physical persuasion. His preferred approach was to simply make his presence known. If there were a store or coffee shop whose patron felt threatened, Sugong would turn up regularly and share a pot of tea. His presence would indicate the premises had his support and that an approach would likely offend. Presented with this scenario the gangster would usually move on elsewhere.

A newcomer to the area, or someone looking to make his name, could prove less amenable to insinuation. On these occasions subtlety had to be subjected before Sugong could ensure his friends were left unharmed.

Although it proved a more mundane decade than those that preceded it, the 1970s ended with a bang. In 1978, Campbell Komplex, a shopping centre Sugong had helped build, was gutted by fire. Its owner, Tan Sri Lin – the honorific title of Tan Sri is equivalent in stature to that of a Lord in Britain – had maintained contact with Sugong since he had supervised the shopping centre's original construction. He now came to Sugong to request he return for its renovation. The respect between the two was mutual, and Sugong closed the bak kut teh shop he was running and came back to help. (Bak kut teh is a meal of pork, marinated and boiled in herbal broth. All cuts, from the leaner, such as ribs, to artery-blocking inductions, such as the tail or hoof, are offered.)

The arrangement ended abruptly. Late in the year, Sugong joined some of his workers on the eighteenth floor of the offices being built atop the shops. They were pouring concrete from the edge to the floor below. Safety regulations were still lacking in application, and Sugong had neglected to wear his hard hat. He straightened just as some metal piping was being hoisted. It swung around as Sugong's head rose, and skull and pipe met with a jarring crack.

The impact stunned Sugong. He staggered precariously to the edge of the scaffolding and then plummeted over its side. The rush of air brought back his senses and he flailed out wildly with his arms. Miraculously, after two floors, his lifetime of grabbing and grasping helped find a life line and his hands caught a section of pipe. The sudden halt to his descent almost ripped his arms from their sockets but he was able to hook his arm over the metal bars and hang on for dear life.

Two floors above, the abrupt depletion of their number had not gone unnoticed and the shouts of the men carried the commotion to the levels below. Seeing their supervisor appear from the skies, the men on the sixteenth floor bounded into action and hauled in Sugong. Battle for survival over, he saw black.

His injuries were not life-threatening, but they were more than minor. Sugong had damaged his skull and the ligaments in his wrists and arms were injured from the arrest of his fall. But his hospital stay should not have been unduly onerous. Tan Sri Lin did not neglect his employee in sickness and ensured Sugong had the best doctors and even a Hokkien-speaking nurse. But hospitals and Sugong didn't make easy bedfellows, and when he was finally discharged it was a relief to both patient and rapidly tiring staff.

He decided to recuperate in Penang. As well as recovering from his injuries, he had another problem in his hands. Having proved they were demonstrably harder than rock, in recent times he had found them little more malleable. He could smash a marble coffee table without a thought but picking up a tea cup required far greater effort.

While Sugong had always acknowledged the importance of chi gung in theory, he had perhaps not paid full service in practice. Now he devoted it more significant time. His move to balance external art with internal was rewarded and slowly his limbs began to soften again.

Although his recuperation did not demand it, the temptations of Penang meant Sugong remained for a year. There were frequent trips back to KL, but it was only in 1979 that he made a permanent return. As always his permanence was temporary.

42

TOO MUCH SEX

Training was hard with Sugong, and this placed demands on life in general. Often in action seven days a week, I was usually exhausted and unsurprisingly submitted to the odd bug and cold. I saw the illness as a result of being run-down. Sugong disagreed.

'The rascal. Too much sex!' he roared in my absence, disapproving yet delighted. (Literally the words *luan kun* that he used translate as 'chaotic tumbling', but in this case the intended meaning was quite specific.)

This was not an idiosyncratic invention of his own; concurrence is to be found in Chinese medicine and martial arts. While chi forms the body's intrinsic energy, there is a belief that *shen* comprises the spirit, and *jing*, the physical essence of man, regulates the body's functions. Together they make up *sanbao*, or the Three Treasures.

It was jing, or rather my supposed wasting of it, that lay at the root of my problems. Although something we are born with, jing remains in a constant state of flux. It can be increased through exercise and meditation but declines with improper living and stress. Improper living can take many forms, one of which is sex. Furthermore sex, or specifically the production and release of semen, is considered the worst offender, consuming the greatest amounts of jing. This is what apparently lay at the root of my self-inflicted ills.

By following a monk's life, Koh Chun's jing had not been threatened and this was said to have contributed to his power. I was less convinced that similar restraint had lain at the foundation of Sugong's prolonged good health.

But in any case, instead of an excess of sexual relations, Sugong's imposed lifestyle placed obstacles to a regular supply. I was more inclined to the view that increased indulgence might be my elixir. For while many claim abstinence as a boon to martial arts, others suggest vigour as a route to success. With neither offering conclusive proof, my sympathies lay with the latter view.

Whichever was correct, it had no bearing on Sugong's level of patience with sickness, which was limited. After three days' absence I received a text from CG.

'Sugong asked if u hv gotten better. He wants u 2come even if not able 2train. No need 2hit ur stomach.'

The stomach part related to the *nei gong* practice we were doing to develop an iron stomach. In addition to breathing techniques, this involved us pounding our bellies. As to attending class, Sugong was a long-time medicinal self-prescriber and he treated his own illness and injury with chi gung. I knew I should feel relieved at his leniency – not only would I not have to hit my ailing stomach, I was even excused from training. But I just couldn't muster the energy.

His attitude on this occasion was indicative of a gradual softening of character over the years. He had been a man to avoid trifling with when younger and I wasn't keen to tangle with him even in more benevolent days. When he was in a dark mood and sniping at all before him, I would duck for my linguistic cover. But apparently the scoldings

I received were just a fraction of what had once been. At many times, with a conscious effort to block more ferocious memories, he could even have been described as sweet.

His charisma automatically placed him at the centre of proceedings. He exuded such an abundance of natural energy it was difficult to turn from its glow. He had a boyish enthusiasm, with the smallest of details delighting him so easily repetition was encouraged. The reward would be to see his face light up with a beaming smile and his gestures become even more animated in excitement.

Eating particularly 'Chinese' food such as pig's tail or chicken's feet, was one way. A great cackle of laughter:

'Ah, he eats just like a Chinese.'

Remembering some steps he expected me to have forgotten was another. A wide smile, accompanied by a finger repeatedly stabbed in my direction:

'Ah Lek's so smart, he can remember anything.'

(On occasion he was as prone to positive hyperbole as he was, more commonly, to negative.)

All in, despite the fact that I cowered like a timid cat in the face of his rage, over time he became like a surrogate Chinese grandfather. Just a slightly scary one.

We formed an odd couple. A barrel-chested 80-year-old Chinese man and a leisurely Englishman just over 30 walking through the areas of KL tourists don't visit, a foot in height and a continent in culture between us.

A few basic pidgin Mandarin and English words and a lot of hand gestures would confirm that yes, I would be there at six sharp tomorrow morning and no, CG wasn't able to make it. A flat palm high in the air reassured that I would be fine getting home on the monorail; the rotation of an imaginary steering wheel indicated the bus.

I slowly learned a few Hokkien terms and phrases. Unfortunately, most were among the more colourful, picked up as they often were from the comments Sugong made to drivers who'd incensed him. Whatever the appropriateness he would indicate his delight with raucous laughter, complimenting me to anyone in sight.

For his part, Sugong would catch me out with random efforts, surprising me with an early morning bark, 'MOR-NING', or admonishing me, 'ku-mon, ku-mon' when locking up.

One area he had shown less enthusiasm toward was our names. It took a long time before communication reached beyond 'Oi' and 'Ay', either of which was a cue to spring to attention. While I had heard of westerners receiving poetic Chinese alternatives, Michael and I accepted these less melodic offerings.

It still came as a surprise when, a few months after arriving, we heard Dr Yong trying to teach our names to Sugong. I had assumed he had found them too difficult to pronounce and had decided not to use them. It turned out that he had been so convinced of their impossibility, he had not asked what they were.

So there was some delight when he realised Michael was called Michael. Courtesy of his Christian wife, it was a name shared with one of his sons. Great roars of laughter and the novelty was tried out.

'Mai-kle, Mai-kle.'

I have no idea why, but Nick remained a more challenging proposition. Laughter, a turn of the head, and a shake of the hand. It was too ridiculous to even try.

'Oi.'

Oi it was then.

When I returned to Malaysia to write a book on his life, I think Sugong decided I was worthy of a name with more substance.

'He's decided to call you Ah Lek,' said Tien Chai when I got back.

'Why?' I asked, failing to see the similarity to my name.
'I don't know.'

It seemed appropriate.

Two possibilities were later suggested by some of the other students. Depending on the Chinese character used, *Lek* (the 'Ah' being an addition of familiarity) could be translated as Younger Brother, or Intelligent. I was the youngest of the present crop of students and Sugong had questioned my intelligence on numerous occasions. So the former seemed the more likely. I asked to be scribed as Intelligent.

43

To mug an uncle

Sugong was no longer a young man in 1984. But at fifty-seven he didn't see himself as old and his restless nature still drew him to new opportunity and adventure. So when an ageing uncle in Taiwan asked him to come over for support, Sugong's thoughts were not on the if, but went instead to the when.

The invitation was based on a business proposition. The niece of Sugong's uncle (a half-cousin of Sugong) knew he had trained in Chinese medicine during his time in Siong Lim. She was keen to set up a clinic with him as consultant. All of the schools he had established to this point had been martial arts based. The idea of doing something with his other Shaolin training appealed to Sugong, and an agreement was reached.

Preparations for the clinic began before Sugong made his move, so he arrived to a rolling start. The premises had already been found. All that was outstanding was for refurbishments to be made and medicines and equipment ordered in. But before they could open up shop, he found himself in a familiar scenario in an alien town.

Three days after arriving, Sugong made his way to the bank. He needed to make a large withdrawal to pay for the clinic's refurbishments. He took out the cash and stored it in the place he knew to be safest; clasped in an iron hand in his pocket. He then walked out of the bank in the Lai Lai Building and made his way down Bu Cheong Street.

The early 1980s had been financially kind. While Sugong ensured the cash he was holding was secreted away, a not inexpensive watch and a jade ring glittered tantalisingly in the late morning sun. Neither was a bad day's take for a thief or gangster. And there was no shortage; he was in the middle of the Ang Boon Huay – Hong Sect Society – triad territory.

Most people turn to look for an explanation if they feel their arm grasped. In Sugong's life he had found unnecessary hesitation could lead to harm. The moment he felt a hand make contact with his arm he slammed his elbow back. He followed with a sharp snapping backfist to the face of the falling man. It was only then that he turned and only at this point did he see his would-be assailant was not alone.

He knew the five others were associated with the fallen man because they reacted as one, reaching for the knives they had concealed. As their weapons flashed open from hiding places at their ankles or in their belts, Sugong knew he was in trouble.

Less than a decade from his peak, he wasn't far into physical decline. But surrounded by six young men, all of them armed, he knew this was a time for concern. The chances of escaping injury in a knife fight were low even if he did emerge victorious. He tried to even the odds.

'Look at me – I'm just an old man,' he reasoned. 'You don't need knives. There are six of you – what am I going to do?'

Sugong was not the only one with doubts. Surprised by the speed and strength of his reaction, there was not a rush to be the first man in. In Taiwan, knowledge of martial arts could also carry with it possible triad associations, and hurting a connected man could lead to repercussions.

As a rule of thumb, Asian culture is disinclined to tackle awkward issues too directly. Ascertaining whether someone is a member of a secret society is not low on the list of sensitive subjects and the question is not usually asked without some delicacy being shown. Sugong's attacker tried to explain away the situation, claiming he was a businessman and the situation a misunderstanding. Sugong was not convinced.

'If you're a businessman, what are you doing trying to grab me?' he demanded.

'No, no, no,' said the triad, unsettled. 'I thought you dropped something – I just wanted to get your attention.'

'I'm pretty sure I didn't drop anything,' replied Sugong. 'But if we've got crossed wires please accept my apologies for hitting out at you and I'll be on my way.'

But he knew it would not necessarily be so simple. An unresolved situation could lead to a loss of face, which in turn might have ramifications. If there were to be any, he wanted them dealt with there and then. In the country less than a week, he didn't want to look over his shoulder wherever he went.

'So it's settled then?' he asked.

'There's nothing to settle,' said the triad, the situation manifestly not resolved. 'I hope you accept my apology for the misunderstanding.'

He finally got to the point in hand.

'May I ask you your name, Uncle?'

The purpose of the question wasn't to allow him to hail Sugong properly next time they met. Suspecting his involvement with triads, the question indirectly being asked was which one he was with.

Despite their 'secrecy', the codes and signals of different triads were not completely unknown. Apparently created when the Five Ancestors fanned out to create five 'houses', of which the Hong House was one, their signs enabled them to identify one another discreetly.

Heading downtown in a Chinese-dominated Asian city in the 1950s and 60s was a pretty sure-fire way to run across a gangster. This would often just mean recognising a likely member from their strutting confidence, but it could also involve paying a levy of sorts to enter a particular place. Knowing relevant signs and signals could provide a boost to one's own safety (although the benefits would move into drastic decline if the wrong sign were used).

Taiwan had a reputation for being more society-dominated than most other places. Now Sugong relayed codes he knew as he told the triads his name. The modern Ang Boon Huay had moved far from their supposed ancestors. Nonetheless, they claimed their heritage traced back to the same line. If Sugong had an association, and was older, it made him their senior, an 'uncle' toward whom respect should be shown. Trying to mug him wasn't the most obvious way.

They apologised profusely and asked for his contact details with an offer of help should it ever be needed. Sugong had no desire to escalate the situation but he didn't want to let them escape altogether.

'I don't need any help,' he said. 'But if you want to buy me tea you can do so tomorrow and I'll accept your apology then.'

With that he gave them a phone number and went on his way.

When he returned home later, he was given a message to call an uncle who was an inspector with the local police. Sugong had given this uncle's number as his own. When they found Mr Quek to be Inspector Quek they had been nonplussed and then nervous. After some hasty apologies they had made their excuses and hung up.

'Ah Chong, you've been here less than a week and you're already getting into fights,' his uncle said, wary of the trouble he feared his nephew might bring.

'Uncle, it wasn't my fault,' said Sugong before giving a more detailed explanation. 'I was just making a bit of mischief and teaching them a lesson. But it's all settled – there's no need to worry.'

'OK,' said his uncle, not completely reassured. 'But it's only been a few days. God help us if you keep on this way.'

44

THE HUNDRED-CATTY ARM

Now that he had been entangled and disentangled from the local triads, Sugong's focus returned to the clinic. Its home was the front room of his uncle's house in the Taiper district. Within weeks of his arrival the modifications to the building were completed, the equipment and medicinal herbs were delivered, and they were ready to begin.

Sugong quickly established a routine. The clinic opened at 9am, but his early rising habits meant his training was long finished by then. He would leave the house at 5am, jog to the park, and by 8am he would be done. Breakfast, a leisurely walk back home, and surgery could begin.

His activities attracted a group of early-rising pensioners who gathered at the park. They approached him, asked for lessons and soon he had an early morning chi gung class. They offered little more than pocket money and their ability was in no greater abundance. But they were enthusiastic and Sugong was happy to teach.

Good value was also to be found in his clinic. Used to Malaysia's lower costs, Sugong was satisfied with his prices. But compared to others in the capital, they under-charged.

Combined with word-of-mouth recommendation, this keen pricing encouraged a fast-growing business and the clinic started to boom. With a growing centre, enthusiastic students and a public training routine, Sugong's profile began to rise. It was a sure-fire way to stir things up in Taiwan.

Like China, Taiwan has a proud heritage in martial arts. Unlike China its fighters aren't dispersed across a vast sprawling nation but are packed into the confines of a couple of islands. Its fighters were, to a degree, China's fighters. Prior to the 17th century Taiwan had been populated by Polynesians. Ethnic Chinese had since migrated, and many that arrived before 1949 considered themselves Taiwanese. But their roots and their arts lay in the mainland, which had regularly bolstered their numbers.

At the tailend of the Ching dynasty and the chaos that followed, the activities of mainland martial artists made the authorities distrust them. On occasion, suspicion ceded to persecution, and when it did it was wise to get out. In other periods it was poverty and famine that had encouraged a new start. For whatever reason, South-East Asia benefited from the misfortunes of Chinese martial artists and the proximity of Taiwan meant there were disproportionately high numbers found there.

After Chiang's retreat, travel to and from the mainland was banned and the influx ended. With new numbers down, fresh arrivals aroused interest. This was often accompanied by a belief that their skills should undergo a test.

A couple of months into his stay Sugong was in his clinic when the owner of a neighbouring shop came by.

'Sifu, a man came to my shop this morning asking about you. He said he'd heard about a master from Malaysia and wanted to know more.'

Sugong had a fair idea of what was coming next.

'He says he's an expert in pushing hands and he'd like to see how you'd do against him,' the shop owner continued. 'He was very confident – he said he would take you out.'

Tai chi is best known for its slow-moving forms, but they are only one aspect, teaching technique and providing a foundation to generate chi. Pushing hands is a kind of non-violent combat which tests how successful the endeavour has been.

When pushing hands two opponents will face one another and extend bent arms until they rest against the other's. They then circle their arms, feeling for one another's energy flow. If they sense their opponent letting down his guard or over-extending himself they will take advantage of this loss of 'centre' and push or pull their adversary down.

Centre refers to the store of chi in the tantien at the centre of the body. A skilled tai chi master is supposed to use minimal force of muscle to fell his opponent. Their chi should so root them to the ground it is near impossible to move them. And they should be able to use their energy to displace their attacker, no matter how powerful. While many masters claim the accomplishment, far fewer have the ability. The rest use a combination of chi, a good stance, balance and brute force. Which was the very same combination Sugong used in his kung fu.

'Tell this guy, whoever he is, to come here tomorrow,' he said, more than a little displeased about the manner of the challenge. 'Please let me know when he arrives.'

The following afternoon the shop owner returned to the clinic. When Sugong had finished his appointment he followed him back across the road.

'I hear you're a master in tai chi,' he said to the man, after their introductions had been made. 'Who did you learn from?'

'I learnt from Cheng Man Ch'ing,' the man said. 'I'll be interested to see how your skills compare.'

Cheng Man Ch'ing had been one of the most famous tai chi masters in Taiwan. His renown extended west when he emigrated to America in the 1970s, making him one of the best-known tai chi practitioners in the world. This fuelled claims and rebuttals to his place in the list of outstanding masters but, wherever he stood exactly in the pantheon of greats, there was no doubt that he was very skilled.

Sugong was still not intimidated. While his opponent may have learned from Cheng, he had learned from Koh Chun, and he believed his master a match for anyone.

'So how exactly would you like to test my skills?' Sugong asked.

'Why don't we push hands a little?' the master replied.

Cheng's disciple reached out his arm to push hands, and waited for Sugong to do the same. Sugong did not doubt his own martial arts ability but he knew he was at a disadvantage playing someone else's game. Stepping away from your own art brings different techniques and a divergent set of rules. He had no intention of letting his opponent get in the swing of things.

He reached out, but on making contact immediately grabbed the man's wrist. He snapped down and jerked back sharply. The tai chi fighter went sprawling in the dust.

Sugong looked down at him.

'So this is what you learnt from Cheng?' he asked. 'I haven't even broken sweat and you're already crawling around on the floor.'

At that point he saw a piece of brick lying just outside the shop. He leant down to pick it up.

'You say you're an expert in martial arts? I can't say I think much of your push hands but as a great master I'm sure you'll have no trouble breaking this brick,' he said.

Not yet ready to back down, his opponent tried to talk up his game. He took the brick from Sugong's hand and laid it on the edge of the kerb so that it stuck out halfway. Holding it in place with his left hand, he used his right to smash down. But he was so incompetent that instead of hitting the flat of the brick, he hit the stronger, sharp-edged corner. It didn't break. Twice more he struck down but the only damage done was to his hand.

'Are you quite finished?' Sugong asked, as he eyed the man's swelling appendage.

Taking the silence as an affirmative, he called the owner of the shop over and had him fetch another brick. When it arrived, Sugong laid it on top of the first and broke them in one.

His opponent started to gush praise, and asked Sugong to take him on as a disciple, as traditionally a vanquished fighter might ask his victor to teach him, the supremacy of the latter's art apparently established. But Sugong had had enough.

'You know nothing about me, but you come here full of boasts, making threats. I do some simple things and suddenly I'm a god,' he berated the man. 'Don't bullshit me. There's no way you learned them from Cheng. Who taught you?'

The man withered and admitted to his lies. He had learned from a third-generation minor disciple of Cheng, and had received no direct tuition from the master at all. Sugong gave a final disgusted look, and turned on his heels.

He wasn't safe from challengers even within the confines of his clinic. One morning a regular client brought along her husband. She was fond of a drink and it looked as though her hubby was also the worse for wear. When he claimed to be suffering aches and pains Sugong had his suspicions, but he led him to the treatment room all the same. After checking the supposed ailments, Sugong started to massage him. As he did he relayed his diagnosis to the man.

'There's nothing wrong with you,' he said. 'I'd just say you're having a bit of a rough day. You've got no problems you need to worry about.'

In search of sympathy the man was not amenable to being told he was fine.

'What do you mean there's nothing wrong with me?' he said. 'I just told you I'm hurting. I know my body, and I know when something's not right.'

Sugong bit his tongue and instead intensified the massage. It seemed to lift his client's mood and loosen his tongue.

'I'm sure you can tell by now you've got a kung fu expert in your hands,' he boasted. 'I've been learning peh hok since I was seven.'

Sugong maintained his composure.

'I'm sure you're very good.'

'Maybe I am. But I'm not just about technique,' the man continued. 'Feel my bicep. That's a hundred-catty arm.'

A catty is a Chinese weight measurement, equal to just over half a kilo. Lifting a hundred with one arm was quite a claim.

'Now come on, massage me harder,' he demanded. 'What's wrong – not got the strength to deal with a man like me?'

Wrong from the moment he had first opened his mouth, the customer was definitely no longer right. Sugong's patience had reached its end.

'I'm trained in traditional medicine. I treat you and give you good news. I put up with your boasts, and give you the treatment you need,' Sugong reprimanded. 'You want to know what's wrong with you? You drank too much last night and you've got a hangover. Now pay up and go home.'

The white crane 'expert' struggled off the treatment table, and after dressing went to the till. Yet he was not ready to give up while behind. When he saw the price he expressed astonishment at its value and questioned whether Sugong's competence was similarly low.

'Your hundred-catty arm,' said Sugong. 'I've never come across something so powerful. I'd like to try it out.'

He held out one of his hands.

The man took up the challenge with confidence and locked fingers with Sugong. Sugong jerked downward and twisted to the side. The man dropped to his knees and rolled across the floor. Once righted, his attitude changed as suddenly as his fall.

'I submit,' he said, as he looked up at Sugong from the floor. 'Take me as your student.'

His arrogance evaporated, he looked so pitiful Sugong could not maintain his anger.

'I would have to be a very sorry master to have a student like you,' he said, the reprimand half-hearted. 'There's no way I'll take you on. Now go home and sleep it off.'

The man now did as he was told. But later the same day he returned with an apology and ang pao. Again he asked to become a student, and again he was refused. But he continued to return and made a point of regularly taking Sugong for tea.

So while a master–disciple relationship did not emerge from the morning, Sugong did make a friend. With a new business, in a sometimes hostile environment, allies were definitely preferable to enemies. And as the number of allies increased, the challenges went down.

45

THE GRANDSON OF A DICTATOR

Taiwan is not a nation without historical trauma. Once populated by indigenous Polynesians, past centuries saw it colonised by the Chinese and battling with the Spanish and Dutch. Adapting by necessity to a Japanese style of life would have appeared a wholly expedient move following half a century of sometimes brutal colonial rule. But when Chinese mainlanders deposed their usurping rivals in 1945 it meant the Taiwanese were viewed with distrust.

When Chiang Kai-chek was expelled from the mainland by the Communists it was to Taiwan that he beat a hasty retreat. Erring on the side of caution, he was even more robust in repression as he imposed his rule on the potentially disloyal 'foreigners' with might. While there were periods when his rule was less brutal, Chiang's leadership could never have been said to be light; martial law was not lifted until 1987, more than ten years after his death. But while US dollars never seemed to reach their target in Chiang's China, in Taiwan they more often found their goal, bringing in foreign expertise and helping develop the nation. Rumours of institutionalised gangsterism remained, but enough money reached its target to ensure the 'economic miracle' of the following years.

A dominant figure in 20th-century China, Chiang unsurprisingly received mixed reviews. Quasi-warlord origins, corrupt leadership, and the loss of the mainland could be added to triad affiliation and repressive rule. But his forceful leadership did bring some unity to post-dynastic China when the country might otherwise have broken up. And while his ideas on social freedom would not be championed by progressives, under his rule Taiwan's finances at least dramatically improved.

But none of this had much to do with Sugong. He arrived almost ten years after Chiang died. The struggle for democracy was at its most intense but as a fresh immigrant it was a fight Sugong was happy to sit out. He did have a connection to the situation, however, and it came through his uncle and Chiang Kai-shek's grandson.

Chiang's grandson was a distant cousin of another uncle's wife; not the most immediate link to Sugong. But when Chiang Jr suffered complications with his health it was enough to ensure Sugong's name came up. With numerous western and Chinese physicians on hand to treat him, Chiang Jr was not looking for a new doctor. But he, or his family, did want a chi gung master to complement the other treatments being advanced.

With a flourishing clinic and enthusiastic students, there was not much missing from Sugong's life. But an illustrious patient wouldn't do any damage and he agreed to take on the young Chiang. With life in Taiwan looking prosperous, it gave Sugong cause for thought when it was suggested he apply for citizenship. It began to look as though his life on the move might come to a settled stop. Then things started to change.

Chiang Jr died before Sugong could begin treatment. Having not met the man, it was not news to devastate Sugong but he was disappointed at an opportunity lost. It was his first setback since he had arrived in Taiwan. Of greater significance was his uncle's decision to return to the mainland. Having held a reasonably senior post in the KMT, a sharp retreat had been advisable at the end of the civil war. Distanced from his wife at the time of the escape, he'd made increasingly desperate attempts to extract her, each without success. In his absence she was condemned to forced labour and succumbed to early death, a wound from which her husband never recovered. He had yearned for his homeland, and a reunion with his son and unseen grandchildren, ever since.

Travel between the rival Chinese government-run lands had been banned in the aftermath of 1949 but, as relations improved, limited visits were allowed. Sugong's uncle had repeatedly applied for a visa but had just as regularly been denied. Desperate for a return, he had been on the point of giving up when the Communist Party suddenly relented to his wish. Sugong was delighted for his uncle but he was also saddened by the good news. Following the death of Chiang Jr he began to wonder if it was a sign of fortune's tides turning and his stay in a country again became unclear.

Still undecided, a letter from the Singapore Shaolin Association made the difference. Within was an invitation to become chief instructor with responsibility for training its teachers. The opportunity to head the association his sifu had started was not one he could easily refuse. It appeared that fate had ruled his Taiwanese adventure at an end.

46

CAUGHT IN THE
WORLD OF WILLOWS

Sugong took up his position as chief instructor and served for a year. Having spent the past four teaching students of limited ability, coaching highly qualified instructors was a welcome change. At the end of the year, he decided to remain in Singapore to set up a school. Feeling the island an appropriate place to pay homage, Sugong named it Shaolin Koh Chun. Numbers grew steadily and Sugong capitalised with a second branch in the neighbouring Malaysian city of Johor Bahru. All of which would have seemed good reason for the return to Singapore to be lengthy.

The studio Sugong taught in was located above a coffee shop. It was a typical shophouse in a convenient area and ideal for a school. It was similarly well suited for the coffee shop, and within months Sugong was displaced by their expanding operations. Deprived of their training hall, Sugong and his students also moved upwards, requisitioning the roof. It wasn't perfect but it was a workable space and lessons continued.

Yet before long change came again. The building's owners received a new offer with better financial terms. The coffee shop's operations were scaled back to one floor and more renovations began. When the rooms were partitioned and beds brought in it seemed as though a small hotel was being established. When the renovations were complete and the new employees arrived the assumption was exposed as naïve. All female, under-dressed and over-made-up, they catered solely to a male clientele. It was a hotel of short stays and extravagant service.

There were times in Sugong's life he had been successful in following Koh Chun's tenets. At other times he had strayed. But he had always tried to let them guide him. Teaching his master's art in a school named in his honour above a brothel was not the homage he intended to pay.

An inconvenient relocation would not necessarily have ended his stay in Singapore had he been in a different phase in his life. But since turning sixty, Sugong had started to turn his eye toward the next stage – death.

He had a desire to pass on from life in the place he had entered it, and although he had no plans to do so imminently he wanted to be prepared for the time this was no longer the case. Filial duty to his ancestors also played its part. His grandparents and parents had been buried in different locations. He wanted to buy a plot of land to bring them together and prepare the place where he and they would eventually be united.

So instead of searching for new school premises, in 1992 Sugong packed up and headed to China again.

Having been underwhelmed by the change to the country when he returned in 1974, he was surprised by the speed with which it had progressed since. It was Mao's death, in 1976, that acted as catalyst. After a power struggle between Madame Mao and other leading figures, the pragmatists, led by Deng Xiaoping, had emerged victorious by 1979.

Gradually, market principles began to replace Mao's less-considered policies, and living conditions started to rise. While reforms were tentative at first, by the early 1990s the economy began to shoot up. For all the benefits, this rapid development had an unwanted effect on Sugong. Having purchased land and begun construction of the family tomb he was compelled to sell the plot when the authorities decided to build a road on its site.

His Chinese tenure now extended, Sugong fell into old habits. He started to teach and he continued to get into trouble. If build, reputation and demeanour had deterred aggressors in his youth, opportunists confused advanced age with weakness as he grew old. Whether faced with gangsters or muggers the outcome remained the same – bruises and bloodshed for the attackers, outraged indignation from the 'old' man.

For despite his age, Sugong still began practise in the small hours and he had continued to train his iron palm. For more than sixty years he had refused to allow others dictate his actions and at seventy years old he still considered himself too young to start.

Sugong stayed in China for five years; except as always it was a shared home. He would return for considerable periods to KL and in 1998 he ran into an old student. Mr Ang invited Sugong to his office to catch up on old times. Sugong was saddened to see the effects of a stroke on his old disciple. So when Mr Ang asked him to start teaching he agreed, confident he could help Ang's condition. Classes began with just two, Mr Ang and a friend, Mr Khoo. But student numbers grew and the time Sugong spent in China shrank. Within a year his trips back home were just visits.

As before, not all of his students continued in the face of his scoldings. But some of them did remain. And they were the ones present when a visiting gwei lo turned a corner and came face-to-face with his sugong.

47

A THOUSAND WAYS OF THE FIST

There are a thousand ways of the fist but at the end of the day they're all the same. It's just the way of the fist. You can know all the advanced forms, stand in all the fancy stances but, when it comes down to it you do what you have to. And you make sure you win.'

Sugong had never received much of a formal education and his manner of speech could at times reveal a youth spent on the docks. But when it came to discussing martial arts he would always have some words of wisdom. He could even be quite poetic when in the mood.

There are hundreds of different martial arts practised throughout the world. And in all there are those that excel in skill and strength. This inevitably leads curious minds to question which is the best. Sugong's thoughts were typically straightforward. His experiences came from a time and place when mixed martial arts fights were common and likely to happen in the street. Art was incidental, as argument rather than intrigue was usually the catalyst for action. Holds weren't barred and weapons would often turn up as well.

'Unless you fight with people from other schools, how are you going to know who's good and who isn't? It comes back to the same thing: a thousand paths lead to the same road – if you learn and you can apply what you learn, it's good. If you know the best form but you don't know how to use it, it's not. You're sitting here and someone attacks you from behind. What form are you going to use? You're not. You just react.'

He didn't have much time either for disputes between north and south Shaolin or any of the numerous styles.

'You want to know what's better? Go and fight them and then let me know.'

(This was not a suggestion to get into fights [I think], it was intended instead as an observation that opinion and theory are of limited use in this debate.)

To be able to apply what you know in the chaotic, charged atmosphere of a fight is far more difficult in practice than in theory. It might be that a martial artist trained for years will use just one technique from thousands. Or he may swing the kind of haymaker any untrained hopeful could do. Despite his skills it could even be that he freezes for that important split second and gets knocked out.

Fully battle-tested, for Sugong being able to apply what he had learned was just a starting point. There was a necessity to improvise as well. He didn't have much time for the 'mine's better than yours' debate (although he had no doubts that the kung fu he had learned was better than all others). Martial arts were there for protection, not to be shown off or boasted about. If your life was in danger there was little point in artistic merit. You did what you needed to do, and you applied the most effective strike. If a weapon was available then that should be used as well. A set of keys, a pair of chopsticks, a mobile phone; anything sharp, handy, heavy or pointed when the need came to fight.

His disregard for preoccupations of style was reflected in his view of fighting skills and mentality. He considered only thirty per cent of a fight to be won by technique. The more important factor in deciding the outcome was attitude; having the courage to fight without fear, and the confidence to see only success.

Sugong may have believed that combat was the only way to test the skills of another but that did not mean he felt it desirable or necessary. There is a tradition among martial artists, perhaps less common now, to challenge others to test their skills. While he may have strayed on occasion, Sugong held strong views on what martial arts should be about: righteousness, discipline and proper conduct. To his eyes a challenge was none of these things, instead it showed disrespect.

He had his own ways of sizing up a fellow martial artist. Shaking their hand he would assess their grip and get a feel for their chi. Someone who claimed extensive internal powers would find the friendly slap on the back or pat on the stomach harder than expected as Sugong sized up their strength.

He was involved in countless fights in his life, most valid, some avoidable, and a few he regretted. But he never went to another school to challenge its sifu. And not many came to his. There were some straightforward reasons. He was trained by a monk of great renown, one other fighters would not dare challenge. And when Sugong started teaching, his schools gained a reputation as the fiercest in town. Only the brave or foolhardy would come to request a likely beating.

His attitude also played a part. Martial arts had been his passion to learn and became his pride and joy to teach. And they were his livelihood. Someone challenging him questioned the security of all of these things, while disrespecting him and his lineage. Most times a challenge would not be a challenge but more of a test. The other fighter would visit the studio to size up the style and check him out. They might go in extra hard when working on pads, conditioning or sparring, and such situations would need like to be met with like. Sugong's conditioning training was not limited solely to his hands. So if a new student wanted to test him by kicking harder than necessary, an iron-hard block would serve as a reminder of their limits and prevent them from doing so again.

But if a direct challenge was made, it was imperative not to lose.

'You've got to be brave, you've got to be strong, and you've got to be ruthless. Don't hold back.'

Most commonly a senior student would be dispatched to spar with the newcomer and send him away with something to ponder. On a few occasions when a newly established school precluded such a student or a direct challenge was made to Sugong he might step forward himself. Those who presented little threat would leave with their pride hurt but their injuries minor. Those who presented a threat found their treatment more robust.

While in Penang, a well-known Thai boxer decided to boost his reputation by taking on Sugong. He was knocked out and carried from the studio. Koh Chun's thoughts on losing had not been forgotten by Sugong.

His teaching style was also influenced by Koh Chun. Martial arts have traditionally been taught in a disciplined manner. Sugong claimed that Koh Chun's approach – stern in teaching, temperate in life – was a template he tried to replicate, although it might be argued he got only half of it right. The cause of Sugong's strictness – whether conscious decision or an extension of quick temper – could also be debated. But he could not be faulted in application.

'I used to give three chances. "One, two, three, out!" Everyone can get things wrong, but if you're doing the same mistake after three explanations, you're either incapable or stupid.'

He also followed the example of Koh Chun in the amount of tuition provided. Those who worked harder would be granted more teaching; others would receive less. But even for the more dedicated, much of their understanding would have to be found in themselves.

'I'll teach you thirty per cent, the rest is up to you. You have to practise hard, look at what you're doing and work it out for yourself. Otherwise you'll never progress.'

Sugong had concerns about the direction martial arts are heading. Believing modern life to place wealth-generation above culture and health, he feared kung fu's decline. His unease was greatest when it comes to the ethnic Chinese population (westerners in general were viewed favourably for their apparent dedication), in a case of familiarity breeding contempt.

Having trained for nearly seventy-five years, it was an attitude that baffled Sugong. To say that he was obsessed or fanatical was to misunderstand him in the assumption of conscious choice. To Sugong kung fu was as much a part of his life as eating, drinking and sleeping, as integral to him as breathing to others.

Aside from the fact that they had been at the centre of his life for more than seven decades, he viewed martial arts as a necessity not a luxurious pursuit. On occasion forced to use the martial part of the art, over the years it became as much about health.

'At 80 I can still walk, still run, still touch my toes. I can do things people half my age can't. That's the testimony of martial arts.'

EPILOGUE

BASHING ROAD-RAGERS

I entered the darkened doorway, and my eyes adjusted to the gloom. I was confronted by a wall and forced to the left. My ears, alert to the high-toned chings of a chopper fight, heard nothing.

I made my way down the short corridor, increasingly unsure of my surroundings. There was no scent of food or drink, nothing to suggest a coffee shop. My stomach felt like it was in the grasp of Sugong's vice-like grip.

I turned right into a back room and a vague sense of recognition emerged. But bright sunlight glared from the open storefront, making it impossible to identify the store or the silhouettes at its front.

As I moved forward my eyes readjusted to the light. Suddenly it all clicked into place. Sugong was laughing with a hand on the shoulders of a disciple, Ah Hock (this was not Sun Ah Hock from the fight outside the Siong Kheng Temple).

Subec's scope of expression on any day ranged from inexpressive to impassive, but there was a hint of good humour in his eyes. We were back in Ah Hock's bike repair garage, from where we had picked him up for lunch the day before. Although he hailed from a batch of students renowned for their ferocity, Ah Hock was as friendly and unaggressive as the others I had met.

'Hello, hello,' he greeted me, grabbing my hand with a hard shake and a welcoming smile.

Before long we were joined by Mr Tan, possibly the only addition to the group less well equipped to beating off triads than me. With him came an explanation of what was going on.

Ah Hock's wife had been driving past on the other side of the road when she saw him handing money over to some shady-looking characters. The garage was on the outskirts of a triad stronghold and she was worried something untoward was going on. When she couldn't get through to Ah Hock's phone her concern intensified. Knowing Malaysia's premier triad-bashers were in town, she had called Subec.

As it happened, Ah Hock had just been passing change to a customer. Unfortunately for his wife's nerves (and mine), he had the look of a hard man. Now with no situation to settle we headed back out of the now unimposing rear exit.

There was poignancy in the outcome. While there are still numerous unruly parts of the world, I wasn't from one of them. And for all of the dangerous places, there are more where levels of safety have increased. Malaysia is one of them. Times have changed and the need for fighting has declined.

While Sugong had been forced to rely on his skills in a more rough-and-ready environment, Mr Tan, I, and others of our generation, were more representative of the people now training in martial arts. While it was good to believe our efforts would provide options if we were in trouble, the main incentive was enjoyment and a passion for the art.

But old habits die hard. Sugong had also moved on from a more precarious world, but on occasions he was still dragged back. In an incident of road-rage (the other driver's, surprisingly), an angry, shoving aggressor was flattened with one punch. The twenty-something had jumped back in his car, probably pondering how to change his story to an act of heroism, a beating from an eighty-year-old unlikely to impress colleagues and friends.

Sugong's rings continued to prove popular too. Twice in the time I was in KL, there were unsuccessful attempts made to relieve him of them. The second occasion was particularly notable for its timing as Sugong was beginning to show signs of the heart failure that would have him hospitalised. The call to battle outweighed scientific law as he turned back the years, breaking a walking stick on one of the muggers as he beat him back.

As for me, I started kung fu because I loved the movies and I thought it would be fun. I continued because I was bitten by a bug from the first minute of my maiden class. I hadn't come to KL a weakling, but I wasn't going to leave a battle-hardened iron man. I pretty much left as I came: a run-of-the-mill Londoner, but with an uncommon couple of years and an impressive vocabulary of Hokkien curses.

Sugong didn't seem to have changed much either. The scoldings continued coming but they were increasingly edged with a smile. His emotions still changed more in a sentence than mine did in a week but they too were more positive than negative. And he still retained a bullishness toward future plans that would have been impressive in a twenty-year-old.

His body was as unwilling to accept the ravages of time as his mind. A chill caught on a trip to an unseasonably cold China developed into pneumonia, and we took him to hospital for checks. The illness put stress on his organs, and culminated in heart failure. Test results revealed readings multiple times higher than a normal person suffering cardiac arrest.

It was very worrying on the one hand. But on the other it was not. Sugong was Sugong. According to his results he should have been long dead. But he had remained living, teaching, scolding and fighting throughout. We couldn't be sure what would eventually lead him to test himself against his Shaolin ancestors, but it didn't look as though science would be given much of a say.

It wasn't. Sugong recovered, and as far as I could make out his only concern was whether he would be back in China for his centenary year.

'If you come back in five years' time I'll still be here, I'll still behave the same way, and I'll still be just as healthy.'

I didn't doubt it.

CODA

Having bounced back from major heart problems on two occasions, Sugong's bullish outlook was not completely unjustified. Anyone losing a couple of stone in muscle should face a struggle rebuilding their strength, particularly when more than eighty years old. But within a couple of months Sugong was back to his brawny best. Mid-July 2009 saw him visit England to teach Master Lai's Nam Pai Chuan school, break concrete blocks, confuse waiters and hotel staff and generally blaze a cyclonic trail of energy across London.

But there were warning signs. The small successes we'd had in restraining some of his less healthy eating habits were already well and truly over. The suggestion he shouldn't add a knob of butter into his coffee to 'soften his heart' was greeted with an impressive burst of invective that concluded:

'Tell this idiot that when he gets to my age and can still do what I can, he can start to lecture me about how I live my life.'

Aside from the fact I had clearly pushed things as far as they could go, it was a pretty decisive end to the debate; while unconventional, his methods had undeniably proved effective so far.

Yet it was just six months later that I received a call from CG. Sugong had always talked about returning to home soil to pass from life in the place that he entered it and he had returned early that winter. All reports suggested he was healthy and happy to be back in China, and one could only assume he was creating customary havoc around him. Then on 17 February 2010 he complained of a pain in his leg and was taken to hospital to have it checked out. Within half a day he was dead.

There was something surreal in receiving a call in the middle of a busy working day in London telling me of a Shaolin grandmaster's passing in China. Furthermore the uplifting emotions I felt sat uneasily alongside my inevitable and more understandable sadness. But while Sugong had absolutely no desire to move on from his present life, he was more intimidated by the possibility of remaining in it incapacitated. In that context a life of eighty-two years that ended with half a day's discomfort after he had been practising his beloved kung fu just the day before seemed a pretty good deal bartered out of life.

I'd returned to London more than half a year earlier and already escaped the frenetic energy that surrounded Sugong and lured those around him into its web. So after his passing I missed him as I already had; a smile when a situation caused me to picture his response; a burst of energy in the midst of laziness as imagined hectoring invaded my brain. But the images were tinged with sadness now. There would be no future occasion when he could apply himself in person.

There is no doubt that life without Sugong is quieter, that it is easier, less controversial, less chaotic and lesser in strife. But for all that, it is undoubtedly poorer, with an empty gap an outsized character once overfilled; without the humour, energy and kindness that, wanted or not, he thrust into our lives.

In memory of Sugong, 1927–2010.

LIST OF CHARACTERS

Quek Chong Tze – Sugong's original name

Leong Heng Choon – The name Sugong assumed to gain entry into Singapore

Quek Heng Choon – Sugong's name once he settled in Singapore

Ah Chong – Sugong's nickname when younger

The Queks – Sugong's family clan

The Leongs – The Queks' neighbouring clan in Fujian

Lao Ping Sun – Sugong's first master

Quek Wei Leng – Sugong's father's elder brother, and a local wielder of power

Quek Mei Li – Sugong's cousin, at whose wedding he was kidnapped

Leong Tat Keng – Mei Li's original fiancé

Sek Koh Chun – Sugong's sifu. Chinese characters are pronounced differently in various Chinese dialects, and there can even be regional variations in the same dialect. For this reason Koh Chun is also known as Gao Can, Koh Sum and Koh San, among others. Koh Chun is a standard Hokkien pronunciation

Chow Piao – Sek Koh Chun's first martial arts master

Huay Jin – Sek Koh Chun's defining martial arts master

Tai Hor – The 'lei tai tiger' Sek Koh Chun defeated to end a village dispute

Bodhidharma – The patriarch of Chan/Zen Buddhism and Shaolin kung fu

Vajrapani (Narayana) – A warrior deity which apparently served as the inspiration for Shaolin martial arts before Bodhidharma supplanted him in the role

Red-Faced Auntie – The 'aunt' responsible for arranging Sugong's passage to Singapore, and his first employer in the country

Quay Kim – Red-Faced Auntie's daughter, and Sugong's first fiancée

Ah Peng – A girl Sugong courted in Singapore

Ah Koo Kiah – A workmate of Ah Peng, and Sugong's second fiancée

Ng Ser Kow – One of Siong Lim's senior disciples, and a firm friend of Sugong since their journey from Fujian to Singapore

Officer Yew – The first of Siong Lim's policeman students

Lang Soh – An initial benefactor in Penang with a dark underbelly

Pek Lian – Lang Soh's daughter, and an unwanted seeker of Sugong's affections

Su Ching – Pek Lian's workmate and rival for Sugong's heart

Batai – One of Sugong's hengdai from Indonesia

Diong Hor – One of Siong Lim's senior disciples, and an early instructor at the Penang Shaolin Association

Sun Ah Hock – One of Sugong's sidai

The Tngs – The Leong family's rivals on the Port Swettenham docks

Sifu/Master Lai (Christopher Lai Khee Choong) – One of Sugong's earliest disciples and my sifu. Named as Suong's successor on his 2010 trip to London

List of Characters

Michael – A friend who joined me in Malaysia

CG – One of Sugong's senior disciples, and my translator and diplomatic advisor

Mr Tan – One of Sugong's senior disciples, my Malaysian /Chinese facilitator, and a co-conspirator in Chinese drinking games

Master Wong – A senior disciple, and a martial arts master in his own right

Tien Chai – A senior disciple, and Sugong's successor in Malaysia

Mr Goh – One of Sugong's senior disciples, and head of one of Malaysia's nicest families

Ji Hang – Mr Goh's son. A questionable navigator

Quek Junior – Sugong's nephew, and uncle to Junior Quek

Junior Quek – Sugong's great-nephew

While there are many variant Shaolin styles in existence, Sek Koh Chun referred to the art he taught only as Siow Lim Kun (Siow Lim is the Hokkien for Shaolin; Kun literally means fist, but in a martial arts sense it is used to represent 'style' or 'school').

Acknowledgements

I received a great deal of kindness and assistance during the writing of this book – favours I will probably never be able to repay fully. In particular I owe my parents for financial, emotional, and pretty much every other kind of support. I hope you enjoy the book. I cannot express enough gratitude to CG (Chong Guan) Tan. Without his patience and repeated willingness to be shot down as messenger, there is no way enough material could have been eked out of Sugong. Equal thanks go to Mr Tan for information seeking, Chinese fact checking, translating and facilitating, alongside endless lifts and all sorts of other help. Master Wong served as a constant source of referral for martial arts in general, from the different styles of kung fu to the boundaries of master–student etiquette. Thanks also to Michael, for the idea of the book, the good times in KL and China, and quite a bit more.

And Sifu, without whom none of it would have happened.

I also want to thank Robert Twigger for being so generous with help and advice.

My debt list would not be complete without expressing gratitude to the martial arts instructors who have taught or advised me. In particular: Sifu Lai Khee Choong and

Acknowledgements

Sifu Jerome De Silva from Nam Pai Chuan in London; Sifu Jeff Guishard from Shaolin Sung Chuan in London; Sifu Wong Seng Choong from Chang Choy Wong's Physical Training in Kuala Lumpur; and of course Sugong.

Further thanks to all those I have trained with, and especially my Malaysian suchecs and subecs, not only for their help in training, but for levels of warmth, kindness and hospitality I could never have expected. I doubt I can properly repay you but I hope you know how much I appreciate it all.

I am also indebted to the other masters and students of Sek Koh Chun's lineage for their information. Suchec-gongs Tay Eng Guan and Ong Tiong Ann of the Singapore Siau Lim National Art Association; Quek Dong Chik; Ong Kim Chwee of the Penang Seow Seet San Health Culture Association; Goh Chuan Seng and Tan Beng Chong. Thanks also to Subec Tee Ah Lam of the Singapore Sao Hua San Athletic Association, and Suchec Ah Hock from Penang.

Professor Tim Wright and Dr Jeremy Taylor from the School of East Asian Studies, University of Sheffield, and Professor Victor King from Leeds University were kind enough to offer valuable suggestions and advice. I hope my extensive historical deficiencies don't make the association a burden. Thanks also to Mr Leung from Cheras and Woon Wee Teng for their contributions.

Finding the copyright holders of some of the images featured has been complicated. I have done my best to identify the appropriate people for approval, but I will be happy to acknowledge anyone I have missed in future editions if you get in touch.

My thanks to Chew Kien Lee, Leng Tieng Chai and Mr Tan for your help tracking down the images, and Chan from Cultural Compass for the information on Siong Lim.

BIBLIOGRAPHY

Chapters 4, 40 and 46: Edwin E Moise, *Modern China: A History*

Chapters 7 and 23: C Mary Turnbull, *A Short History of Malaysia, Singapore and Brunei*

Chapters 8 and 35: Meir Shahar, *The Shaolin Monastery – History, Religion and the Chinese Martial Arts*

Chapters 9 to 11: Liang Jun Yi, Article on Sek Koh Chun, title unspecified

Chapter 33: Martin Booth, *The Dragon Syndicates – The Global Phenomenon of the Triads.* Dian H Murray, in collaboration with Qin Baoqi, *The Origin of the Tiandihui: The Chinese Triads in Legend and History* and Barend J ter Haar, *Ritual & Mythology of the Chinese Triads – Creating an Identity*

Chapter 37: Kua Kia Soong, *May 13 – Declassified Documents on the Malaysian Riots of 1969*, and C Mary Turnbull, *A Short History of Malaysia, Singapore and Brunei*

Chapter 45: Murray A Rubinstein (editor), *Taiwan: A New History*

Selected further reading
Booth, Martin. *The Dragon Syndicates – The Global Phenomenon of the Triads*. Carroll and Graf, 2001